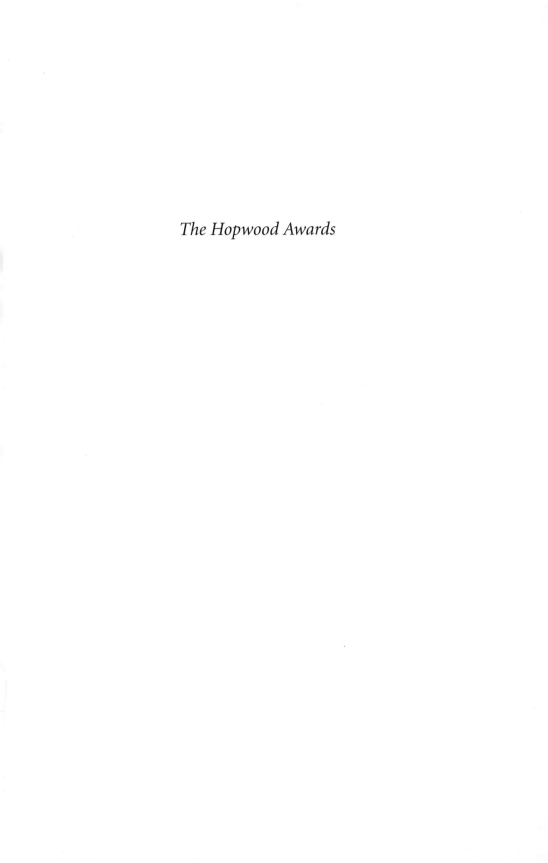

The Hopwood Awards

75 YEARS OF PRIZED WRITING

The Hopwood Awards

Edited by
Nicholas Delbanco,
Andrea Beauchamp, and
Michael Barrett

THE UNIVERSITY OF MICHIGAN PRESS | ANN ARBOR

Copyright © by the University of Michigan 2006
All rights reserved
Published in the United States of America by
The University of Michigan Press
Manufactured in the United States of America
♾ Printed on acid-free paper

2009   2008   2007   2006   4   3   2   1

A CIP catalog record for this book is available from the British Library.

Library of Congress Cataloging-in-Publication Data

The Hopwood awards : 75 years of prized writing /
edited by Nicholas Delbanco, Andrea Beauchamp,
and Michael Barrett.
    p.   cm
  ISBN-13: 978-0-472-09926-9 (alk. paper)
  ISBN-13: 978-0-472-06926-2 (pbk. : alk. paper)
  ISBN-10: 0-472-09926-4 (alk. paper)
  ISBN-10: 0-472-06926-8 (pbk. : alk. paper)
  1. American literature—20th century.
I. Delbanco, Nicholas.   II. Beauchamp, Andrea,
1946–   III. Barrett, Michael, 1953–

PS535.5.H67   2006
810.8'005–dc22   2005046662

Contents

75, and Counting

This is the sixth in a series of books celebrating the tradition of the Avery and Jule Hopwood Writing Awards for students at the University of Michigan; it is, however, the first of its kind. Each of the previous volumes collected the lectures delivered at the annual awards ceremony, where, under the general rubric of "Advice to the Young Writer," an accomplished author talks about his or her trade. Often the Hopwood Awards have functioned as an imprimatur, a signal to the world beyond that the recipient is someone now to watch. The prize offers cachet as well as cash, and the former continues long after the latter is spent.

Avery Hopwood graduated from the University of Michigan in 1905. He became a successful Broadway playwright, by most accounts the "richest" of his era, and at his death endowed the prize that bears his name and that of his mother. This year the Hopwood Awards Program observes its seventy-fifth anniversary. The first awards were offered—and the inaugural lecture delivered—in the academic year 1931–32. No other program in the nation equals it; no other system of institutional reward has recognized so many with so much and for so long.

That may sound like hyperbole, but it is researched fact. In the world of higher learning, the Hopwood Awards reign supreme. As of this present moment, we have awarded more than twenty-three hundred separate young writers more than three thousand prizes; half of those writers, approximately—a percentage maintained in this volume—have therefore received more than one. In aggregate, the program has dispersed well over two million dollars, and though it may happen in the future that some other university decides to challenge or surpass our record of institutional generosity, that day has not yet come.

I served as editor for the last two volumes in the series, *Speaking of Writing* and *The Writing Life*, published by the University of Michigan Press in 1990 and 2000, respectively; I have served as the program's director since 1987. Always before we have published the talks, and we will do so again. Yet as a way of recognizing the deeper purpose of the Hopwood Lecture Series, we decided to reproduce here the work of those to whom the speakers speak: young artists in the room. This anthology, therefore, celebrates the achievement of Hopwood Award winners over the decades of the contest—a representative sampling of their poetry and prose.

My colleagues Andrea Beauchamp and Michael Barrett and I shared the unenviable task of dealing with an embarrassment of riches. We could well have published a series of books; the authors represented are at best the iceberg's tip. So we here acknowledge that our choice has been constrained by space; in a program with more than two thousand honored writers, exclusion is the rule. We have weighted the selection slightly in favor of the past, since many of our more recent winners have a long future ahead. Next year, the *Michigan Quarterly Review* will publish a special issue of the work of recent Hopwood winners, and that issue can and should be read as a supplement to this volume. To those authors not included here, we offer our apologies; to those who are, our thanks.

Some editorial decisions may bear some explaining. First, we chose not to represent the categories of drama, screenplay, and essay writing, since the book's focus would have then become irredeemably diffuse. For the same reason, we selected short poems and stories, not excerpts from novels (with the single, self-contained exception of the extract entitled "Nelson in Nighttown" by James Hynes). Many important playwrights, screenwriters, and journalists have won these contests; you will not find their work here.

Second, we decided not to reprint the Hopwood Award-winning entries themselves; these authors have traveled much writerly distance from their achievements while enrolled at the University of Michigan, and it seemed simply dutiful to reprint apprentice work. Early promise is everywhere attested by the receipt of a Hopwood Award, but we wished this book to document more than mere potential; it's the rare author indeed who hopes to be remembered by the pages of his or her youth. *The Hopwood Awards: 75 Years of Prized Writing* is not intended as a historical curiosity but as an engrossing read.

Third, we did ask the contributors to select their less-than-routinely anthologized poetry and prose. We wanted this volume—or else it would have been only a grab bag of much-printed work—to represent, where possible, personal preference; when we asked for permission and reprint rights, we urged those writers still alive to send us something that not everybody knew. So this collection is idiosyncratic and, to a degree, original: women and men who earned their first important public recognition through a Hopwood Award here recognize the work of which they are privately fond.

A writer who makes a career as poet does not always win in poetry, or a writer of fiction in short fiction; the adjectives *major* and *minor* represent not the level of achievement but the level of enrollment and can be roughly translated as "graduate" or "undergraduate" awards. Our arrangement is chronological, and we provide a listing of the prizes won. The book concludes with both a full listing of Hopwood Award winners down through the years and a complete list of the lecturers in the Hopwood Lecture Series.

The inaugural lecture of the series was given by Robert Morss Lovett in 1932. The writers referred to therein are all dead, and many long-forgotten—as has been, indeed, the speaker. But for three-quarters of a century established authors have talked to those who hope to emulate and perhaps surpass them, and there's something timeless in the occasion itself.

It has to do with the instructed awareness of tradition, and one's relation thereto. My model is that of the medieval guild, with its ordained sequential progression from apprentice to "master." These last must teach the first. They do so from the page when they have quit the stage. Their voices speak with undiminished resonance to a private reading audience, as well as to the public one gathered each April to hear . . .

The previous lines comes from my Introduction to the omnibus volume, *Speaking of Writing,* and it feels worth restating. This tradition of passing *down*, of handing *on*, of urging *along* a younger artist is one of the ways we can honor our art, and does include repetition. So I want to repeat some paragraphs of what I wrote.

Among the writers mentioned in that inaugural lecture, by Robert Morss Lovett, is the author of the second, in 1933. And this man, to my glad surprise, was someone I had known. The sense of colleagueship as "handing-on"—of membership in a community—became therefore immediate. What follows is a private account that may suggest in its public accounting what one writer owed to another and each of us to all.

Max Eastman was in his eighties when I was in my twenties. We met on Martha's Vineyard and grew close. He welcomed me, whether in Gay Head, New York, or Barbados; he was tolerance incarnate, with an amused abiding sense of how youth preens. I postured; I was working on a book (*Grasse, 3/23/66*) that was recondite in the extreme. I'd labor in an ecstasy of self-congratulation, producing perhaps a hundred words a day, intoning the sibilant syllables until they appeared to make sense. One such passage, I remember, contained a quotation from Villon; a description of Hopi burial rites; an anagram of the name of my fifth-grade teacher; an irrefutable refutation of Kant; glancing reference to Paracelsus; suggestive ditto to my agent's raven-haired assistant; paraphrase of Cymbeline's dirge; and an analysis of the orthographic and conceptual disjunction between Pope and Poe. I took my time; I let it extend to ten lines. That night I brought my morning's triumph to Max and permitted him to read. He did so in silence. He tried it aloud; so did I. When he said it made no sense and I explained the sense it made, he looked at me with generous exasperation. "Sure," he said. "That's interesting. Why don't you write it down?"

I remember staying with him on Martha's Vineyard one October. His wife, Yvette, was off to New York for a shopping trip, and she asked me to stay in their house—a favor to me, really, since my own hut was unheated. I was full of beans and bravado then, and would get to work by six—waking up and clacking at the keys in my upstairs bedroom. In the first pause, however, I could hear his steady hunt-and-peck in the study underneath; he'd been at work well before. So we'd share a cup of coffee and a comment on the news, then I'd fuss at my novel again. At nine o'clock I'd take a break—tear off my clothes and run down the hill to the pond. The morning would be glorious: that crystalline light, those sizeable skies, the pine trees somehow greener against the sere scrub oak. And always, out there from the still warm water, Max would lift his hand to me, his white mane on the wavelets like some snowy egret's, grinning.

Time passed. He died at eighty-six, in 1969. But it takes no effort to see this again, see it always as tradition's emblem: an old man waving from the water at the youth on the near shore. They are naked, both of them; the sun slants over Lobsterville. A few day sailors might be on the pond, or someone in a kayak, or musseling or digging clams. The sea-birds settle, incurious; the beach smells of sea-wrack and tide. There's a busy imitation of silence: the man in the water, bobbing, flutters heels and hands.

The young one runs to meet him and it's all a perfect clarity until he does a surface dive and, splashing, shuts his eyes.

Young writers are both brash and abashed; we will none of us displace our masters but all of us must try to, and the distance between aspiration and achievement narrows, with luck, over time. So, to read a collection of published work by those who began their careers with a Hopwood Award is to chart the distance traveled in the course of a career. This conjunction of the finished work with the trace of its old origin is, for me at least, inspiriting; it's why we study, after all, and teach and try to learn. *One Writer's Beginnings,* as Eudora Welty phrased it, necessarily entail a sense of continuity: whatever's worth preserving began with a first word.

The Hopwood contests are entered pseudonymously, and the national judges are strangers; they have neither taught nor previously read those students who enter their work. So the system of judgment is double-blind, as close to objective as such contests can be, and there's a special pleasure in the allocation of prizes and prize money. When the members of the Hopwood Committee sit to assess the verdict of the judges, there's the sense of a succession and distant laying on of hands: A chooses B, Y favors Z, and says of a career begun that it may plausibly enlarge. This volume demonstrates that.

The Hopwood Awards: 75 Years of Prized Writing represents, therefore, both creative potential realized and early promise delivered; it signals both what these artists have done and what others still may do. In and of themselves, these stories and poems are each and all rewarding; the whole is, however, more than the sum of the parts. And this is the comfort the editors took in our difficult task of selection; we chose examples of a lasting process and not a procedure now lost. The Hopwood Awards will continue when Max Eastman's young friend is as long gone as he, and the language of art will continue when no present practitioner writes. Carrion comfort, possibly, but real.

One Michigan alumnus and author has been most famously associated with the Hopwood Awards Program and the receipt of Hopwood Awards. The late great Arthur Miller was, all his life, a devoted proponent of the program; he delivered two of our lectures and never returned to Ann Arbor without supportive words. In his autobiography, *Timebends,* he re-created luminously the experience of winning a Hopwood—both as recognition of work done before and as a kind of prior ratification for the work yet to come. The following passage is emblematic of what such encouragement means.

> On the day my name was called out before the assembled contestants and their guests as a Hopwood winner, in the spring of 1936, I felt pleasure, of course, but also something close to embarrassment, praying that everybody would soon forget my poor play in favor of my next one, which would surely be better.
>
> I immediately called my mother, who screamed and left the phone and rushed outside to arouse relatives and neighbors to the new day dawning while my new wealth trickled away into the phone company's vault. On Third Street I was now famous and no longer in danger of watching my life shrivel up in touch football games on the streets all day, and there is no fame more gratifying.

Here, unforgettably, is the paragraph in which the fledgling playwright learns the effect of his language and dreams of taking wing. This happened seventy years ago and happens every year.

> Outside, Ann Arbor was empty, still in the spell of spring vacation. I wanted to walk in the night, but it was impossible to keep from trotting. My thighs were as hard and strong as iron bars. I ran uphill to the deserted center of town, across the Law Quadrangle and down North University, my head in the stars. . . . The magical force of making marks on a piece of paper and reaching into another human being, making him see what I had seen and feel my feelings—I had made a new shadow on the earth.

So wrote Arthur Miller. It is to his memory we dedicate this book.

Where Does Your Music Come From?

When I was sixteen and a junior in high school, my whole life changed. Until then I had led a very ordinary existence, growing up in the postwar years with my younger sister on an elm-lined street in the house in which my mother had been born. I had a Rudge bicycle, a chemistry set and a crewcut, and the only thing that marked me out from the rest of the kids on the block, apart from my height, was that I really liked my piano lessons and shone at the annual recitals of Miss Wakefield's students. Indeed, I used to daydream of going to New York City and playing the Grieg Piano Concerto under the stars at Lewisohn Stadium, with thousands cheering me as they did Artur Rubinstein.

My father, an uneasy real-estate broker, regretted an enthusiasm fostered mainly by my mother, and tried to steer me from music toward medicine, starting with the chemistry set and later taking me on long Sunday-morning walks in the course of which he tried to convince me, man to man, that there was nothing like being your own boss. He ran his business from a wooden cottage attached to the back of our house, so he was home a lot, between phone calls, and he probably exercised more of an influence on me than most of the fathers on the block did on their kids.

It was only after I finished junior high and began to flounder around with swarms of strangers in Franklin Pierce High that I discovered how many different worlds lay beyond the placid, comfortable one of Buchanan Street. There were boys who smoked marijuana and girls who got pregnant; longhairs who did math problems in the caf while the others fiddled with their jalopies and hot rods; Negroes who disappeared after school as though they had been swallowed up; jocks who stayed until it got dark, playing soccer or jogging around the track as if they had no homes to go to and no pianos to practice. I didn't settle into any of the cliques, because I wasn't ready to limit myself. Belonging to almost any of them would only have confirmed me as being what I already was on Buchanan Street, and I was getting a little tired of that.

So, with the seamless illogic of the sixteen-year-old, I limited myself almost exclusively to one boy's company for so long that people used

7

to kid us about going steady, as if we had been of different sexes, or about being twins, as if we had been brothers.

In fact Yuri was a twin himself, and he walked to school every day with his sister Yeti (born Yetta), the ballet dancer. Yeti's beauty was so immediate that it was frightening. She had long, straight, shimmering blond hair that hung uninterruptedly down her back to her waist, eyes the color of delphiniums in July, set shallow and slantwise above her Slavic cheekbones, and skin smooth as eggshell. She walked with the characteristic half mince, half prance of her craft, toeing out as she advanced, she was as slim and flat-chested as a boy, and because of her self-absorption she was—besides being my best friend's sister and therefore inviolable—as close to being absolutely uninteresting as any girl I had ever known.

Yuri was something else. He was bowlegged, his tough and kinky brown hair barely grew above my shoulder (after a while they called us Mutt and Jeff), and his thick, passionate lips were usually twisted in a cynical grin. He played the fiddle—which he carried with him nonchalantly in its weathered case wherever he went, even into the john— with dazzling fervor and dexterity. He had been the concertmaster of our school orchestra since his freshman year, but I hesitated to approach him not only because he was so good but because of that grin. The other members of the string section said he was decent enough, if somewhat condescending, like a big kid playing for an afternoon with little ones. They said too that his mother awoke him at dawn so he could practice for two hours every morning before school—later I found that this was true.

One day after ninth period I was in the music room practicing on the Mozart A-Major Concerto, the K. 414, the first movement of which the conductor, Mr. Fiorino, had promised me I could play with the orchestra for the spring festival, when Yuri Cvetic sauntered in and leaned his elbows on the tail of the piano.

He listened for a while, his fiddle case wedged between his torn sneakers, that grin showing the spaces between his front teeth. Finally he said, "Ever do any accompanying? I got a Brahms thing here we could try."

Within days we had exchanged confidences never before revealed to anyone else. Everyone took it for granted that we two would eat together in the cafeteria; and when, because of homework or music lessons, we couldn't see each other after school, we would talk on the phone, more quietly than our sisters but just as lengthily.

Yuri never came to my house more than once or twice. My father complained that he couldn't bear the squeal of Yuri's fiddle being tuned up to the piano. It was no more legitimate than his shouting, after we were in tune, "I can't hear myself talk on the telephone when you guys are playing." I knew I was losing respect for my father when he came out and said that he mistrusted Yuri not only because he encouraged me to have musical ambitions but because he came from the other side of Pierce High, from Cotter Street, a noisy neighborhood of teenagers tuning up go-karts, women arguing loudly in foreign tongues and drunks too shameless to go on indoors.

Yuri shrugged it off with the grin that I suspect bothered my father more than anything else, for it bespoke that wise invulnerability that can unsettle an adult more than any adolescent surliness. After that we hung out together at the park in fair weather, at his house in foul. His family never objected; they were always delighted to see me whenever I turned up at their second-floor flat.

In addition to his twin sister, who, when she was around, was usually polite enough, in her self-centered way, there was a younger sister, Helen, a freshman when I first met her. Not only had her parents used up their inventiveness on the twins' names, but they also seemed to have taken one look at their last-born and decided that a ballerina and a violinist would be enough and that this time they would settle simply for a daughter. Helen was a nice enough girl, with a sweet, even smile and dark, gentle eyes unlike Yuri's and Yeti's in that they were always shadowed, as if she didn't get enough sleep, but she had no interest in music or dance and she never opened a book. She appeared content just to get by in school and to keep the household going while her parents were off working and the twins were off practicing. And besides, she was buxom; she gave you the feeling that if she didn't watch herself, she'd wind up looking like her mother.

I think that was what put Mrs. Cvetic off her youngest and convinced her that it would be profitless to push Helen into the arts as she had done with the twins. Mrs. Cvetic, a practical nurse, was a heavy-breasted, shapeless woman who breathed through her open mouth and waddled so alarmingly that you could practically feel the friction of her thighs. She always wore a wrinkled and stained uniform, not quite white, its pockets bulging with Pall Malls, wooden kitchen matches and professional samples of Anacin and Bufferin, which she chewed as other people do gum or candy.

"Hiya, boy," she would greet me on those occasions when she

happened to be home of an afternoon. "You gonna play some music with Yuri today? Okay, stay for supper."

If I declined, she would wave aside my hesitations, the long cigarette bobbing from her lips, ashes sprinkling the bosom of her uniform, while she growled at Helen, "Move away the goddam ironing board so the boys can practice. And let's see how much goulash we got for supper."

The ironing board had no legs. Sometimes Helen would balance one end of it on a kitchen step stool, the other on the edge of the upright piano, and press away at her mother's uniforms (I never could understand why, since Helen was always ironing them, the uniforms were never clean). When I wanted to lift the keyboard lid, she would take the ironing board and lay it on the round oak dining-room table. When she had to set the table for dinner for the six of us, she'd set the plank against the wall. But Mr. Cvetic had bolted a full-length mirror and a long section of three-inch galvanized pipe to the wall for Yeti, and when Yeti hung onto the pipe with one hand, doing her ballet exercises, Helen had to drag the plank, heavy as a painter's scaffold, out to the front hall, where it teetered at the head of the stairs, announcing to you as you mounted the worn rubber runners to the Cvetic flat that Helen must be busy doing something else.

Often it was the meals which, while her mother tended the afflicted and her sister flexed her back, Helen prepared by herself and served as well, eating off in a corner like a European mama, only after she had made certain that the rest of us were taken care of. More than once Mr. Cvetic, having worked overtime, came in when we were already on our dessert and had to be served separately. But Helen never lost her composure, even if her father complained that the meat balls were no longer piping hot. It confused me that a girl so downtrodden should look so contented.

In our house the dinner-table conversation was predictable. If mother had the floor, it would be cultural, with quotations from the day's speaker at her club, John Mason Brown perhaps, or Gilbert Highet. If father was in a talkative mood, and nothing of note had happened in his business during the day, he would inform my sister and me of George Sokolsky's opinion in the afternoon paper, or of what Galen Drake had philosophized about on the auto radio.

At the Cvetics, you never knew. They ate noisily and greedily, as though each meal was to be their last, and they talked fast and loud— all except Helen, who rarely spoke—about whatever popped into their

heads. Slender Yeti put away enormous quantities of everything—
three slabs of seven-layer cake were nothing for that girl, whose bare
arms, when she reached for more, were like match sticks—and she rat-
tled on, in a voice as thin as her arms, about Madame Tatiana's yelling
fight with the accompanist at ballet school. Yuri, chewing fiercely,
mocked Mr. Fiorino's efforts to conduct Von Suppe ("You'd never
catch me doing that, teaching fifth-raters to play fourth-rate music"),
and simultaneously, in counterpoint, his mother gave us free professional samples of the folk wisdom she had picked up from her years of
nursing chores.

"Gertie blew up like a balloon, poor thing," she would say, spoon-
ing up her soup with a loud trill, "and when the doctor stuck the drain
in her belly the smell was like the stockyards. But sometimes you got
to do that, you got to let out the poison, Helen, bring in the rest of the
cauliflower."

Her husband was small, wiry, wizened, and good-humored. I never
saw him (but once) in anything other than working clothes—a brown
leather jacket over khaki shirt and trousers—just as I never saw Mrs.
Cvetic (but once) in anything but that wrinkled white uniform, size
forty-six. Mr. Cvetic worked as a journeyman plumber—actually as a
plumber's helper, I think—on the new housing projects that were
going up; he drove a clanking old Ford with a busted muffler, and you
wouldn't have thought that he would be mad for theosophy.

I hadn't been in his company more than ten minutes when he asked
me what I knew about Rudolf Steiner, and when I said, Wasn't he the
man who wrote the operettas? I was in for it. Yuri groaned rudely and
Yeti wandered off to do her bar exercises before the mirror, but Mr.
Cvetic ignored the twins and plunged ahead into a basic description of
the anthroposophical life view. It was all very confusing—it seemed to
take in everything from organic farming to better kindergartens—but
after a while I took some comfort in observing that it was confusing to
the rest of the family too and that even Mr. Cvetic himself grew hazy
when it came to details.

"But I learn," he would say to me, snapping the calloused fingers of
one hand while he picked his teeth with the other. "That's the big
thing, to learn from the great minds of the ages. You'll see some day
how beauty comes from unity."

"From unity?"

"And unity comes from variety. The flower comes from the seed, the
seed comes from the flower. Where does your music come from?"

"I don't know. From the composer?"

"The mind comes from the body, the body comes from the mind. You get me?"

Mr. Cvetic took magazines I had never heard of. In our house we got *Reader's Digest* (my father would still be reading the February issue when the March one arrived) and *Harper's* and *Book of the Month Club News*. But Mr. Cvetic read *Tomorrow* and *Manas* and a magazine the name of which escapes me, published in some town in Pennsylvania and dealing with compost gardening, even though he didn't have so much as a potted plant. He liked to read, moving his lips as he did, about subjects that he didn't agree with or even understand, which startled me, and what was more he was always grinning with happiness over the wonderful variety of material for argument. He stayed up late making notes (for what purpose I never found out), while his wife shuffled about in house slippers the heels of which had long since been crushed to death under her bulk, dropping ashes on the bare floors and opening windows so the kids wouldn't have tired blood and sluggish bowels.

Yuri was fed up with all this, just as I was growing tired of the atmosphere in my house, but at least his folks didn't quarrel with what he was doing; they were proud of it and encouraged him in fulfilling their jumbled-up expectations. Besides, they accepted me practically as a member of the family and were frankly proud that Yuri's best friend was from Buchanan Street and a musician to boot.

"Man, when the day comes," Yuri said to me one afternoon in his quick slurred way, running the words together between tongue and full lips much as his father did, "I'm going to have an apartment with Oriental rugs so thick you can drop a golf ball on them and never find it again. I'm *sick* of bare floors just because they're supposed to be closer to nature or better for Yeti's posture."

I tried to sympathize, when actually I envied him. But what did he mean about when the day came? We both had our dreams of glory and were bound together by the discovery that our separate daydreams could interlock so beautifully, but I didn't really see how our exchange of confidences and intimacies had anything to do with money or Oriental rugs.

In Yuri's eyes I was, I began to realize, like a boy who fantasies great success with girls—rescuing them from drowning or halting their runaway horses, causing them to fall madly and pliantly in love with him—but dares not visualize a consequence consisting of marriage, children and passionless slippered evenings yawning at TV over a can of beer. If for me our music was going to make us famous, that fame would serve only to make us more desired and more famous—and so on, into Carnegie Hall and Lewisohn Stadium, in tails and smiles. But for Yuri the fame was going to bring him Oriental rugs.

It was disconcerting to learn that he was so practical, but I started with the recognition that he was the better musician and that he was the soloist too. What was more, he took the initiative with my mother, who was a little awed by him, in getting us invitations to perform Schubert, Brahms and Bartok for her clubs and her friends' clubs, for the Soroptimists, the AAUW and the Matinee Musicale Society, some of which got us excused from school, others of which actually paid us. We were big shots in a small way, and I wasn't the only one to realize that I owed it to Yuri. Even my father had to admit that Yuri wasn't doing me any harm, if I didn't get a swelled head from the recitals, which wasn't likely to happen as long as I was merely the accompanist.

One unusually hot June afternoon we were ambling along Cotter Street after a final exam in Spanish, licking at Dairy Queens and sizing up the strolling girls in their thin summer dresses. We came into Yuri's front hallway and looked up to see Helen's broad, soft behind undulating gently at the head of the stairs; she was on her hands and knees, scrubbing the steps. At the sound of our entrance she turned, raising her dripping hand to brush away the dark hair from her forehead, and regarded us with a still childish gravity.

"Hi, Helen," I said.

Then she smiled down at us. "I was trying to do the steps before anybody got home. Where's Yeti?"

Yuri shrugged. "Probably downtown, seeing *Red Shoes* for the fourth time." He stepped over her pail and waved me onward, calling back over his shoulder, "Make us something cold to drink, will you, Helen?"

The rooms were half bare, as usual, the floors strewn with a knocked-over heap of Mr. Cvetic's magazines. Usually I loved entering that apartment, but now it struck me for the first time as somewhat bleak and airless, smelling still of Mrs. Cvetic's cigarette butts. We went on out to the front porch and flopped onto the glider.

I said, "Why do you give Helen such a hard time?"

"You don't mean me, you mean all of us."

I was embarrassed. "I mean, we could have gotten our own drinks from the icebox."

Yuri shrugged again, drawing back his full lips over his teeth.

"Division of labor. My old man works for the rent and the groceries. My mother works for the music and the ballet lessons. Yeti dances and can't spoil her feet, I fiddle and can't spoil my hands, and Helen takes care of the house. What's wrong with that?"

I wasn't quite sure. Maybe, I thought, everything was taken for granted just a little too readily. But Yuri waved away my discomfort.

"Never mind that stuff. You know something? There's room in this town for another kind of music besides rock-and-roll and Schubert. What future is there in Schubert? Fifty bucks a night, two nights a month? All we need is four, five more fiddles, bass, percussion, couple horns, and we're in business. Then, with a booking agent and some stylish arrangements—"

"What kind of music are you talking about?"

Yuri blinked rapidly, as though he were signaling me. "Strauss waltzes, gypsy fiddle music, things people can dance to without being acrobats and hum without being self-conscious. I could be like a strolling violinist, and you could conduct from the piano."

Helen was standing in the doorway with a pitcher of lemonade. She spoke before I did, in a tone that I had never heard her use. "Is that what everybody's been knocking themselves out for?"

Yuri turned on her swiftly. "Who asked you to listen? What do you know? You're fifteen years old, you still think I can go off to Europe and win one of those international prizes and live happily ever after. I'm trying to be practical."

He was, too. At seventeen we weren't ready to organize the kind of society orchestra he had in mind—but in a few years we would be. And in the meantime he knew, better than I, that we simply weren't up to the cut-throat concert world. Given his teaching, his instrument and his practicing, Yuri would at best qualify one day for a first-desk job with the city symphony. In order to supplement his income he would either have to teach ("What a drag! Look at Fiorino!") or play hotel music, which at least had some of the glamour that he thought we had been talking about all these months.

Unlike me, Yuri was daydreaming, I began to see, not about impossibilities but about reality. It troubled me as much as it did Helen, maybe because Yuri was beating me to the cold compromises involved in growing up. And I could not put out of my mind the way the lemonade pitcher trembled in Helen's hands before she set it down by the glider and hurried away.

Yuri spoke no more of the dance orchestra that day or for a long time thereafter. I got a summer job as a camp counselor, and Yuri, who had wanted to go to Tanglewood or Marlboro, had to take a paying job with the Civic Pops Orchestra, which did a summer season in the municipal park.

When we came together again as seniors in the autumn, we were both anxious to make up for lost time. We resumed our duets at once. I had almost forgotten the intensity of the pleasure you could derive from making such music with a friend.

But then, starting as an undiscussed eventuality and looming larger as the year rushed by, there was the prospect of my going away to college. My father, who had managed only a year of college before the depression caught up with him, worked at convincing me that in a Big Ten school "You'll make contacts that will be invaluable to you in later life."

When I made the mistake of repeating that to Yuri, it broke him up. But his mocking laughter jarred me, and I began to think not about how square my father was but about what it might be like, really getting away from Buchanan Street once and for all.

Yuri was bright, school was easy for him, but he couldn't have cared less about going to college. And it wasn't simply sour grapes. I knew his parents would do without necessities to send him to a conservatory, but they hadn't brought him up to face the prospect of being one more poor fish in a great big pond.

"I'm not kidding myself," he said when I raised the subject. "The best I could do after Juilliard, or one of those trade schools, would be an audition for a job with a big orchestra. What's so big about that? I can do better right here with help from people like your mother and without getting gray waiting for a break."

I stared at him. I said, "Are you satisfied to stay here forever? Don't you even want to try to make it in the big time?" I was on the point of adding, What else have we been dreaming about all these months? but something in his face stopped me.

He extended his hands. "Why throw away a sure thing for a mirage?"

He was pleading for more than understanding; he wanted me to tie my future to his. As my best friend, he was hoping against hope that I would turn my back on my father's ambitions for me. It wasn't just that Yuri wanted my moral support and my physical presence. What he wanted even more, it struck me with ferocious suddenness, was the kind of real help from my mother and her friends that would depend on my sticking with him.

I was hurt at Yuri's readiness to use me in this way; I would rather he had come out and said what he wanted from my mother. But that would have involved different admissions on his part, so I held my tongue, and we went on more or less as we had.

More or less, except that even while we were reading duets and rehearsing for recitals, I was studying for my finals and trying to decide among various Big Ten schools. When I finally made up my mind, and then was accepted by several, I didn't run to tell Yuri or his family, as I might have a year earlier. Nor did he bring up the matter with me again.

Yeti too was itching to be out of school. She had been running with a show-business crowd, or the nearest approximation that our town could boast (little-theater actors, modern dancers, and a part-time beatnik group just coming into its own), and after a number of auditions, including one breathless trip to New York, she caught on with the road company of a Broadway musical. She was to join it directly after graduation, and she was trembling with the first real excitement I had ever seen her display.

If Yuri was not particularly impressed, and Helen, smiling very enigmatically for a sixteen-year-old, said nothing, at least their parents seemed pleased. The twins, they decided, were entitled to a big graduation party.

"Listen, boy," Mrs. Cvetic said to me, "you come next Friday night for sure. We're gonna have one hell of a big blowout."

"You couldn't keep me away," I said. "You know that."

"Okay, but this time bring a girl."

I was a little disconcerted. The few girls I could take to movies or concerts wouldn't have known what to make of the Cvetics. So I mumbled something about seeing whether I could dig up a date.

I didn't even try, but on the evening of the party I took the steps up to the Cvetic flat two at a time. In the hallway the noises of many voices talking at once sounded reassuringly familiar; the odors of Mrs. Cvetic's and Helen's cooking smelled familiar too—stuffed cabbage, eggplant salad, savory pudding.

But when I walked in I felt that I had entered a strange house. The noise wasn't coming just from the family but from a throng clustered here and there all through the apartment, which had been decorated like a dance hall with twisted streamers of crepe paper, Chinese lanterns, and life-size pencil drawings of Yeti in her tutu and Yuri with his fiddle.

I recognized some kids from the school orchestra and the glee club.

In addition there were a number of middle-aged strangers, friends of Mr. and Mrs. Cvetic, I guessed, and a gaggle of bony girls and slim-hipped boys from Yeti's ballet school.

It was fairly early, but the air was already exhausted, fogged with smoke, and as I blinked my way through the mob, peering around for Yuri, somebody cracked open a can of beer under my nose and swung it about, lashing a circle of suds onto the bare floor. Girls shrieked, but Mr. Cvetic, ignoring everything, had a classmate of mine pinned to the wall and was exhorting him, as near as I could make out, to eat egg-shells for their mineral value. When he caught sight of me he waved, his hand clutching a stuffed cabbage transfixed with a skewer to a slab of rye bread.

"Hey, go by the dining-room table," he called out amiably. "Helen and the missus have got food there for an army."

He wasn't kidding, but I wasn't hungry. I took a beer and went on to the piano, where I found Yuri, with a new haircut and a new sport shirt, surrounded by a crowd of kids from school. They were egging him on to do an imitation of me accompanying the glee club.

Yuri mussed his hair to approximate mine, and, flinging his hands over the keyboard to make them appear long and scrawny like mine, pounded out the Rudolf Friml medley from *The Vagabond King*. Everybody was laughing. I had to myself, in order not to look like a stuffed shirt, although I didn't think it was all that funny. When Yuri caught sight of me he stopped and held up his hand.

"Here, you do it," he said, making room on the bench. "This is your instrument, not mine."

I was stuck for quite a while after that. The gang pressed more beer on me so that I would give them the cocktail-hour classics that they wanted, but finally it palled and I begged off. I shoved through the knots of dancers and talkers and found myself pushed smack up against Mrs. Cvetic, who was fishing stuffed cabbage out of a Pyrex bowl. She thrust a steaming plate at me.

"Whatsamatta, boy," she asked, squinting to fend off the smoke from her dangling cigarette, "you on a hunger strike or something?"

I made a pass at eating and congratulated her on the party.

"The kids deserve it, they didn't let me down, they worked hard all this time. Besides, you only graduate once, right?" She dug me in the ribs. "So have a good time, the party is for you too."

I wandered on through the apartment, very confused. Mrs. Cvetic was more unselfishly hospitable than my own parents. But was she really doing the twins a favor, making such a big deal about high-school graduation?

At the end of the long hallway I entered the kitchen, intending to leave my plate on the counter and maybe leave the party, since I felt out of place. But as I put down the plate I heard a step behind me, and I turned to face Yuri, who was standing in the doorway, grinning his grin.

"Looking for something?"

"Helen is the only one I haven't said hello to. This is where she punches the clock, isn't it?"

"Stick around, she'll turn up. Can I get you anything in the meantime?"

"Not a thing. Great party." I could see that he expected more, so I added, "I was accepted by two colleges this week."

Instead of asking why I hadn't told him before, he said negligently, "Make up your mind yet?"

"I'm waiting to hear from one more before I decide for sure."

"In any case you're going away. That's it."

"That's it."

I hadn't meant to be flip about what was terribly important for both of us, but Yuri seemed to want it that way. Scratching at the fiddler's rash on the underside of his left jawbone, he said, almost as if it were an afterthought, "I didn't hurt your feelings before, did I? I mean, imitating you at the piano."

"Don't be silly."

"Okay then. Let's split a beer."

I was going to protest that I was full, but something in his face stopped me. I held out a glass, and Yuri poured half a can into it. We drank in silence, not looking at each other.

"Well, I've got to circulate. Anything you don't see, just ask for it."

And he swiveled about and walked out of the kitchen.

I should have left then. But it was true, I told myself, that I still hadn't seen Helen, and she was one person whose feelings I didn't want to hurt. So I wandered through that crowded apartment one last time.

By now the guests had progressed from talking to shouting—about the Korean fighting, which had just broken out, about homosexuals in the ballet and the State Department, about compost heaps and wheat germ—and from dancing to banging beer cans together in rhythmic accompaniment of a monotonous folk singer. Helen was not in sight.

I made my way on through the dining room and the living room to the front porch. The awning was rolled down and the living-room blinds were drawn, and it took my eyes a moment to grow accustomed to the darkness. Then I saw that several couples were embracing against the railing at either end of the porch. I was about to retreat and leave them to their business when I realized that a girl was sitting motionless on the glider, hands folded in her lap. It was Helen.

When she heard me she looked up and smiled and motioned to me to sit beside her. I was a bit uneasy, but she insisted, mouthing the words, "It's all right. They won't care."

I glanced to my right. I was a little shaken to see that the blonde digging her fingers into the hair of the boy pressing her against the railing as though he was trying to shove her over the falls, his leg between hers, was Yeti.

"She won't care either?" I whispered, gesturing at Yeti.

Helen shook her head mildly. "It's just her boy friend."

"But what are you doing here? Don't tell me you're the chaperone."

"It's the only quiet place. I worked pretty hard getting the food ready."

"I bet you did." I had to bring my head closer to hers in order to keep my voice low. "I've been looking for you all evening."

That wasn't strictly true, but it was becoming true as I looked at her. Perhaps because of the heat or the long hours in the kitchen, she had put up her thick dark hair; her face was more mature now, calm, self-assured. She smiled at me again, her cheeks rounding, and she was no longer just Helen; she was someone strange and beautiful.

"I don't think you'll be seeing much more of us," she said, "after this summer."

"What do you mean?" I asked stupidly.

"You'll be going off to college. And then . . . people grow away from each other."

"Not good friends. Good friends stick together." Something made me add, "Besides, I'm not a hundred per cent sure I'll go away. Why can't I go to college here? Right now I'd rather be here with you than any place else in the whole world."

"You mustn't talk like that," she said agitatedly. "Not when you've got the chance to go. Anyway, you'll see. You'll see, when you make new friends you won't need the old ones so much."

Her insistence, stubborn as a child's, was charming; and yet I was touched by a sudden premonition that Helen, unlike Yuri, knew more than I—and always would.

Suddenly her dark eyes filled, and I was in terror lest she begin to weep. "Yuri loves you," she said, "you know that? I hoped you would influence him to be idealistic like you, to use his talent for the best. If it turned out the opposite, and he was the one to influence you . . . it would be better for you if you never saw us again."

"I promise you one thing," I said. "No matter what, I'll never forget the Cvetics. You've been nicer to me than my own family."

"We just like you, that's all."

Encouraged, I added what would never have entered my mind five minutes earlier but now seemed profoundly true and important. "You know something? You're not only the nicest one in the family—" I pressed forward, whispering so that Yeti should not be able to hear— "you're the best-looking."

Helen shivered, as if taken with a sudden chill, and grasped her bare upper arms defensively.

"What's wrong?" I asked. "Are you cold? Here, let me rub you."

I touched her smooth flesh with my fingertips and discovered that it was not cold but blood-warm, not goose-pimpled but satiny. Helen released her grip on herself and raised her eyes to mine.

As we sat there staring at each other, with my palms on her soft arms, we could hear the shuddering sighs of the embracing couples on either side of us, and the rich wet sound of lips and tongues meeting, sticking, parting. Helen drooped toward me, I slid my hands around her back, she raised her hands from her lap and began to caress my temples. When her fingers reached the back of my neck I pulled her to me, overcome as much by the unexpectedness of what was happening as by the beauty of the moment.

Just as our lips swelled and touched, each to the other's, in that instant of exquisite revelation, the porch door swung outward. I opened my eyes to the startling beam of light and raised them to meet those of Yuri, who was standing in silence, his fists clenched, staring at us.

How can I ever forget the look on his face? His glare was compounded of rage, disgust, contempt—and a strange, frightening kind of envy. And in the next instant there glinted in his eyes, I could have sworn, a scheming flicker, a swift calculation of the possible advantage to him of what he saw before him.

Helen sat motionless, not from fear or shock but as if time had come to a stop for her and she did not wish it to start again. Her arms hung free, no longer clasping me; her face was pale but quite composed. It was impossible for me, though, to remain impaled under

Yuri's stare. I arose awkwardly, mumbled something, and shouldered past Yuri and on out of the apartment.

Helen had been right, of course, about me and her family. After I was settled in college I sent her a picture postcard of the bell tower, saying that she would like the quiet, regular, pealing music that it made; but even though I printed my return address, she did not reply. The only acknowledgment I got was a postscript at the bottom of one of Yuri's letters: "Helen asks to be remembered to you."

I wrote Yuri in some detail, but without undue enthusiasm, about my new life. Yuri's occasional letters, on the other hand, struck me as not only provincial (anecdotes about classmates I had hardly known) but increasingly desperate, as if now that I was gone he was discovering, in the blind, lonely thrashing that he preferred to conceal behind a mask of amused contemptuousness, that the times were wrong for what he wanted out of life. I began to think that maybe I had never really understood Yuri.

Then came a last letter in which he told me cryptically that he had joined the Marines. All I could think of at first was that he was trying to beat the draft and in a typically sardonic fashion, fiddling his way through the Halls of Montezuma. But he put it to me in a lower key, in terms of his maybe taking advantage of a new GI Bill for Korean veterans to study conducting "when I come marching home." Maybe he was just saying what he thought might please me or renew my confidence in him. I have no way of really knowing, because after that we lost touch with each other.

It was my father who sent me, many months later, the clipping from the afternoon paper which announced, not without pride, that the gifted young violinist, Yuri Cvetic, who had gone straight from Parris Island to Pusan, had been captured by the Chinese Reds. The best I could do, when I came home in June, was to talk to Yeti and her mother on the phone, for my father's business had turned sour and I had to leave town almost at once for a resort job as pianist with a dance band.

More than once, at the silly hotel by the lake, I reflected on the irony of the fate that found me making a necessary buck out of my music while Yuri was involved in the miserable consequences of a larger decision. I wrote him about this—why not?—through the International Red Cross, because I thought that it just might bring back to his face—even at my expense—that mocking grin.

But he did not reply, and in truth he may never have gotten my letter, for not long after, word came of his death in a prisoner-of-war camp; and I found myself crying, alone in my room, at the idea of his permanent silence. Where had our music gone to?

The papers of that time were full of angry words about the betrayal of the heroic Marines, and in our town the tragic fate of Yuri was coupled with the implication that he must have died a hero's death. I don't know that this was ever substantiated, any more than was the stronger rumor to the contrary when his body was finally shipped home for burial: that Yuri had simply turned his face to the wall and died, as if his capture itself had been a symbolic yielding up of life, which he would not want to have undone any more than he would have wanted to go on living if the joints of his fingering hand had been frostbitten and amputated.

His interment took place on a rare and lovely April afternoon. Yuri was entitled to burial in a military cemetery, but his parents preferred to have him in their own family plot, painfully bought (like his musical education) with their own sacrificial payments. I had just arrived home for Easter vacation, and in fact was not in time for the services; but I borrowed my father's car and hurried on out to the suburbs.

It took me a while to find the cemetery. I got to the graveside just as an honor guard was lowering the flag-draped coffin into the ground. All I could think, as I stood off to one side, away from the family and the faithful friends, inhaling the ineffable fragrance of fresh-turned earth, was that if through some miracle of this heavenly day the dead could draw just one breath, they would burst open their coffins and climb, happily reborn, from their tombs.

I turned to walk away, convincing myself in the usual cowardly fashion that it would be better if I called on the Cvetics later, when they had had the chance to compose themselves. But Helen, walking with a strange doughy-faced young man, caught sight of me, and I could only wait for her to approach. She smiled at me sadly, very white-faced in her mourning costume, and extended her hand with no word of greeting. Her sadness seemed to encompass not just the wasteful death of a young man but, I thought, the tragic quality of life itself for those compelled to go on.

"I'd like you to meet my fiancé," she said to me.

I shook the hand of the young man, who was not only embarrassed but restlessly anxious to get back to his salesman's route before he lost any more commissions.

There was nothing for it then but to await the others, who had not as yet seen me. Mrs. Cvetic, quite bowed over by grief, was being half led, half dragged away from the graveside by her husband and Yeti, whose veiled hat had been knocked somewhat askew by the exertion. As they neared me on the flagstone walk, their figures dappled with the spring sunlight filtering through the river willows, I could hear Mr. Cvetic panting shallowly under his burden and his wife sobbing jaggedly, like a wounded animal, with each step. They stopped to take breath, and suddenly Mrs. Cvetic, in black instead of white, for the first time, raised her head and caught sight of me.

She broke free from the restraining arms and lurched toward me. Before I could move or even think of what to do or say, she had hurled her heavy, sagging body at me, gasping and sobbing.

"My God, my God, my God!" she cried.

I tried to put my arms around her, but she was shaking and crying and pounding at me with her fists. It struck me with a thrill of horror that she was greeting me not with affection but with hatred.

"His best friend!" she screamed. "You were his best friend!"

Clumsily, I strained to pat her heaving back, but she cried loudly, "Best friend, why didn't you stop him? You didn't even try, you didn't go yourself, why didn't you try to stop him? Who's going to play duets with you now?"

Even if I had been able to think of something to say to her, I would not have had the time. Yeti, her head averted, and Mr. Cvetic, shrunken into an unaccustomed Sunday suit and mumbling something either incoherent or in a foreign tongue, took up their burden again, pulling and dragging her by the elbows. Her wails floated back over her shoulder in the spring sunshine of the silent cemetery, and Helen, nodding an apologetic farewell, hastened after her family, her ankles flashing in their black nylons, her escort hurrying along at her side until they had all disappeared from my view.

From my view, but not from my mind. For years I wondered, Was Mrs. Cvetic right? Should I have tried to stop Yuri from going to his death? Yet I must admit that when I think now of the family that changed my life, my feeling for Helen and her fate affect me just as strongly as my feeling for Yuri and his fate. As for the music, it is enough that I hear it in my mind. Where it has gone, along with my youth, I think I know; but where it came from, during those passionate months of performance with Yuri, I doubt that I shall ever know.

ROBERT HAYDEN

(1938, 1942)

The Rabbi

Where I grew up, I used to see
the rabbi, dour and pale
in religion's mourner clothes,
walking to the synagogue.

Once there, did he put on
sackcloth and ashes? Wail?
He would not let me in to see
the gold menorah burning.

Mazuzah, Pesach, Chanukah—
these were timbred words I learned,
were things I knew by glimpses.
And I learned schwartze too

And schnapps, which schwartzes bought
on credit from "Jew Baby.'"
Tippling ironists laughed and said
he'd soon be rich as Rothschild

From their swinish Saturdays.
Hirschel and Molly and I meanwhile
divvied halveh, polly seeds,
were spies and owls and Fu Manchu.

But the synagogue became
New Calvary.
The rabbi bore my friends off
in his prayer shawl.

The Year of the Child

(for my Grandson)

And you have come,
Michael Ahman, to share
         your life with us.
We have given you
         an archangel's name—
and a great poet's;
         we honor too
Abyssinian Ahman,
         hero of peace.

May these names
be talismans;
         may they invoke divine
magic to protect
         you, as we cannot,
in a world that is
         no place for a child—

that had no shelter
for the children in Guyana
         slain by hands
they trusted; no succor
         for the Biafran
child with swollen belly
         and empty begging-bowl;
no refuge for the child
         of the Warsaw ghetto.

What we yearned
but were powerless to do
         for them, oh we
will dare, Michael, for you,
         knowing our need
of unearned increments
         of grace.

I look into your
brilliant eyes, whose gaze
         renews, transforms
each common thing, and hope

that inner vision
will intensify
        their seeing. I am
content meanwhile to have
        you glance at me
sometimes, as though, if you
        could talk, you'd let
us in on a subtle joke.

        May Huck and Jim
attend you. May you walk
        with beauty before you,
beauty behind you, all
        around you, and
The Most Great Beauty keep
        you His concern.

Aunt Jemima of the Ocean Waves

I

Enacting someone's notion of themselves
(and me), The One And Only Aunt Jemima
and Kokimo The Dixie Dancing Fool
do a bally for the freak show.

I watch a moment, then move on,
pondering the logic that makes of them
(and me) confederates
of The Spider Girl, The Snake-skinned Man. . . .

Poor devils have to live somehow.

I cross the boardwalk to the beach,
lie in the sand and gaze beyond
the clutter at the sea.

II

Trouble you for a light?
I turn as Aunt Jemima settles down
beside me, her blue-rinsed hair
without the red bandanna now.

I hold the lighter to her cigarette.
Much obliged. Unmindful (perhaps)
of my embarrassment, she looks
at me and smiles: You sure

do favor a friend I used to have.
Guess that's why I bothered you
for a light. So much like him that I—
She pauses, watching white horses rush

to the shore. Way them big old waves
come slamming whopping in,
sometimes it's like they mean to smash
this no-good world to hell.

Well, it could happen. A book I read—
Crossed that very ocean years ago.
London, Paris, Rome,
Constantinople too—I've seen them all.

Back when they billed me everywhere
as the Sepia High Stepper.
Crowned heads applauded me.
Years before your time. Years and years.

I wore me plenty diamonds then,
and counts or dukes or whatever they were
would fill my dressing room
with the costliest flowers. But of course

there was this one you resemble so.
Get me? The sweetest gentleman.
Dead before his time. Killed in the war
to save the world for another war.

High-stepping days for me
were over after that. Still I'm not one
to let grief idle me for long.
I went out with a mental act—

mind-reading—Mysteria From
The Mystic East—veils and beads
and telling suckers how to get
stolen rings and sweethearts back.

One night he was standing by my bed,
seen him plain as I see you,
and warned me without a single word:
Baby, quit playing with spiritual stuff.

So here I am, so here I am,
fake mammy to God's mistakes.
And that's the beauty part,
I mean, ain't that the beauty part.

She laughs, but I do not, knowing what
her laughter shields. And mocks.
I light another cigarette for her.
She smokes, not saying any more.

Scream of children in the surf,
adagios of sun and flashing foam,
the sexual glitter, oppressive fun. . . .
An antique etching comes to mind:

"The Sable Venus" naked on
a baroque Cellini shell—voluptuous
imago floating in the wake
of slave-ships on fantastic seas.

Jemima sighs, Reckon I'd best
be getting back. I help her up.
Don't you take no wooden nickels, hear?
Tin dimes neither. So long, pal.

JOHN CIARDI
(1939)

Aunt Mary

Aunt Mary died of eating twelve red peppers
    after a hard day's work. The doctor said
    it was her high blood pressure finished her.
    As if disease were anything to Aunt Mary
    who had all of her habits to die of! But imagine
    a last supper of twelve red peppers, twelve
    of those crab-apple size dry scorchers
    you buy on a string at Italian groceries,
    twelve of them fried in oil and gobbled off
    (Aunt Mary was a messy eater)—and then,
    to feel the room go dizzy, and through your blood
    the awful coming on of nothing more
    than twelve red peppers you know you shouldn't have eaten
    but couldn't help yourself, they were so good.

Now what shall I pray for gluttonous Aunt Mary
    who loved us till we screamed? Even poor Mother
    had more of Aunt Mary's love than she could live with,
    but had to live with it. I am talking now
    of a house with people in it, every room
    a life of a sort, a clutter of its own.
    I am talking of a scene in the palm of God
    in which one actor dies of twelve red peppers,
    one has too many children, one a boy friend,
    two are out of work, and one is yowling
    for one (offstage) to open the bathroom door.
    This is not the scene from the palm of God
    in which the actors hold God in their palms,
    nor the scene in which the actors know their prayers—

it is the scene in which Aunt Mary died
    and nobody knew anything, least of all
    Aunt Mary. In her red-hot transformation
    from gluttony into embalmer's calm
    and candlelight, I cried a hypocrite tear.

But it was there, when I had seen Aunt Mary
bloodlet for God, that I began to see
what scene we are. At once I wept Aunt Mary
with a real tear, forgiving all her love,
and its stupidities, in the palm of God.
Or on a ledge of time. Or in the eye
of the blasting sun. Or tightroped on a theorem.
—Let every man select his own persuasion:
I pray the tear she taught me of us all.

The Catalpa

The catalpa's white week is ending there
in its corner of my yard. It has its arms full
of its own flowering now, but the least air
spins off a petal and a breeze lets fall
whole coronations. There is not much more
of what this is. Is every gladness quick?
That tree's a nuisance, really. Long before
the summer's out, its beans, long as a stick,
will start to shed. And every year one limb
cracks without falling off and hangs there dead
till I get up and risk my neck to trim
what it knows how to lose but not to shed.
I keep it only for this one white pass.
The end of June's its garden; July, its Fall;
all else, the world remembering what it was
in the seven days of its visible miracle.

What should I keep if averages were all?

The Gift

In 1945, when the keepers cried *kaput,*
Josef Stein, poet, came out of Dachau
like half a resurrection, his other
eighty pounds still in their invisible grave.

Slowly then the mouth opened and first
a broth, and then a medication, and then
a diet, and all in time and the knitting mercies,
the showing bones were buried back in flesh,

and the miracle was finished. Josef Stein,
man and poet, rose, walked, and could even
beget, and did, and died later of other causes
only partly traceable to his first death.

He noted—with some surprise at first—
that strangers could not tell he had died once.
He returned to his post in the library, drank his beer,
published three poems in a French magazine,

and was very kind to the son who at last was his.
In the spent of one night he wrote three propositions:
That Hell is the denial of the ordinary. That nothing lasts.
That clean white paper waiting under a pen

is the gift beyond history and hurt and heaven.

HOWARD MOSS
(1940)

Horror Movie

Dr. Unlikely, we love you so,
You who made the double-headed rabbits grow
From a single hare. Mutation's friend,
Who could have prophesied the end
When the Spider Woman deftly snared the fly
And the monsters strangled in a monstrous kiss
And somebody hissed, "You'll hang for this!"?

Dear Dracula, sleeping on your native soil
(Any other kind makes him spoil),
How we clapped when you broke the French door down
And surprised the bride in the overwrought bed.
Perfectly dressed for lunar research,
Your evening cape added much
Though the bride, inexplicably dressed in furs,
Was a study in jaded jugulars.

Poor, tortured Leopard Man, you changed your spots
In the debauched village of the Pin-Head Tots;
How we wrung our hands, how we wept
When the eighteenth murder proved inept,
And, caught in the Phosphorous Cave of Sea,
Dangling the last of synthetic flesh,
You said, "There's something wrong with me."

The Wolf Man knew when he prowled at dawn
Beginnings spin a web where endings spawn.
The bat who lived on shaving cream,
A household pet of Dr. Dream,
Unfortunately maddened by the bedlam,
Turned on the Doc, bit the hand that fed him.

And you, Dr. X, who killed by moonlight,
We loved your scream in the laboratory
When the panel slid and the night was starry
And you threw the inventor in the crocodile pit

(An obscure point: Did he deserve it?)
And you took the gold to Transylvania
Where no one guessed how insane you were.

We thank you for the moral and the mood,
Dear Dr. Cliché, Nurse Platitude.
When we meet again by the Overturned Grave
Near the Sunken City of the Twisted Mind
(In *The Son of the Son of Frankenstein*),
Make the blood flow, make the motive muddy:
There's a little death in every body.

NELSON BENTLEY
(1940, 1942)

The Lost Photograph

Lost for twenty years now that large photograph
Of my father in his long room in Golden,
Colorado, in 1901, surrounded
By books and sunlight,

The young teacher from Michigan, his forehead
High and broad, his fine black hair center-parted,
Rugged and hopeful as Lincoln, at his desk,
Shakespeare beside him,

Before he taught at Victor or Cripple Creek
Or had Lowell Thomas as a star student,
Or won my mother's hand away from Ralph Carr
And the music store.

In one corner of the room, piled high with books,
Was the slatted wood, metal and leather trunk
Bought to take all his books and clothes from Detroit
Clear to the Rockies.

On my last night in Michigan, he and I
Climbed to the spare bedroom long used for storage,
Where my mother's dress dummy stood among toys,
Found the old trunk there,

Unmoved since I was born, carefully removed
Teddy bears, dolls, games, and three childrens' clothing,
And carried it with ceremonial joking
Down the long staircase,

Past the ceiling-high cases of well-read books,
Past faded paintings of six great composers,
Past the two old stoves and the battered table,
Out through the kitchen,

Down the back porch where all of our dogs had slept,
Across the yard full of oaks, maples and pine
Where we live in photographs of forty years,
Past the old red barns,

And loaded it into Ramsbottom, the Dodge.
My train was to leave at dawn for Seattle
From the ornate red brick depot in Ann Arbor
Where he had arrived

In 1896. Across Middlebelt,
Beyond the fragrant pastures of horses and Holsteins,
Half a mile away stood Elm Woods, flower-filled
Venus above them.

I could hear far off, down at the Beech crossing,
A Diesel, not an old steam locomotive,
Coming on the Pere Marquette. Then my father,
Seventy-seven,

Standing in the back door in Indian summer
Twilight, his children gone, my mother long dead,
But in his old aura of steadfast love, gave one
Understated wave

As Beth and I drove off into the future.
On the way to Seattle, on the Great Northern,
On the far side of the Rockies, I remembered
The lost photograph.

CID CORMAN
(1947)

The Poppy

On the narrow road
out by a cache of
rocks, clumps of grass,
clover patches,

the car had a flat.
It started raining.
Two goatherds, of no
special age,

in goatskin chaps,
vests of goathide,
strayed over
to catch the operation,

to say hello. No
more than ten minutes;
the goats not stopping
a moment.

Someone picked a poppy,
stuck it in a notch
of the hood
at the windshield.

The wiper all the way
to the coast slashed
and the wind whipped
the flower. By

the time the car
arrived only
an imaginary scarlet
stained glass.

Choices

If suicide is allowed, everything is allowed.
—LUDWIG WITTGENSTEIN

I don't imagine you were considering
the autumn sky, its anticipatory
depths, constellations scattered
across glare like vine maple leaves,
a throbbing punctuation;
or the forest, lacustrine, flooding
each side of the road. Nor
did you notice the air you breathed,
as it rose from warm earth to marry
with the cold, the shock of it
in your nostrils, the brine.
Were the trees indifferent to you?
In the crowd of regrets that clogged
your ears, rushing up, plunging,
with nauseating speed, down,
you noticed no dialogue but your own.

You would have had no thought
for the consciousness behind the steering
wheel of a car, the breath
of a man, younger than you,
perhaps, coasting the county
road, its carefree curves,
toward lamplight, supper with his family,
a welcome of noise. Or a woman driver,
exhilarated, speeding home from her best
job yet, joy frosting her breath
as she sings. And what if,

what if,
the driver has a passenger beside him
on the seat, a child he's picked up
from an after-school game, a boy

with perfect vision, the whites
of his eyes calm as shells with
a knowledge the very young
scarcely recognize in themselves?
Who sees you step out from the roadside
before you actually do so,
sees, with the intuitive quickening
of an animal, in the set of your head,
the set of your shoulders, the intention
you haven't yet fully formulated.

He hears his father shout.
The car stalls, judders, headlights
dipping. It rears, sentient
as a horse, swerves, stops dead.
They stay rigid, your collaborators,
unready for this particular election.

In a moment they will step out of
the car, the safe cave,
and bend over your body. They will turn
you over, your warmth escaping
from tweed like air from a tire.
The silence, the sigh
they will carry away with them
as they carry this night, this year
fastened to their shoulders like a yoke.
Autumn upon autumn it will press
its ridges into flesh and spirit,

until, years later, sleepless
in his old age, in an old house,
October's ambivalence pungent
at the window, the man who was the boy
remembers how the rain began, then,
inaudible as the breath of a newborn,
warm on their eyelids and heads,
how it spattered his father's face
as it lifted toward him, explicit,
transmuted in the car's headlights,
the crescents of his cheekbones luminous
and fragile as porcelain.

Animals

Have you forgotten what we were like then
when we were still first rate
and the day came fat with an apple in its mouth

it's no use worrying about Time
but we did have a few tricks up our sleeves
and turned some sharp corners

the whole pasture looked like our meal
we didn't need speedometers
we could manage cocktails out of ice and water

I wouldn't want to be faster
or greener than now if you were with me O you
were the best of all my days

A Byzantine Place

1 AT A MONDRIAN SHOW

How excited I am!   My piggy
heart is at a traffic intersection

However I run a mirror slaps
me in the face   I'm not tired

of being told I'm beautiful yet
Shall I ever be that ghost of

a chance the right money on
the right nose   Our portraits

hang restlessly and kick their
feet while we run around alas!

2 MY FACE IN THE STREET
That I must do these things
for you find the fortunate bird
and kill where he flies so strong

is there any simple event this
does not answer?   As still
oh my people as still life I'm
your bowl of bread and your
black thought   Do not question
me   Sustain my panic my grope

Poem

At night Chinamen jump
on Asia with a thump

while in our willful way
we, in secret, play

affectionate games and bruise
our knees like China's shoes.

The birds push apples through
grass the moon turns blue,

these apples roll beneath
our buttocks like a heath

full of Chinese thrushes
flushed from China's bushes.

As we love at night
birds sing out of sight,

Chinese rhythms beat
through us in our heat,

the apples and the birds
move us like soft words,

we couple in the grace
of that mysterious race.

ANNE STEVENSON

(1951, 1952, 1954)

Arioso Dolente

(for my grandchildren when they become grandparents)

Mother, who read and thought and poured herself into me;
she was the jug and I was the two-eared cup.
How she would scorn today's "show-biz inanity,
democracy twisted, its high ideals sold up!"
    Cancer filched her voice, then cut her throat.
       Why is it
    none of the faces in this family snapshot
        looks upset?

Father, who ran downstairs as I practised the piano;
barefooted, buttoning his shirt, he shouted "G,
D-natural, *C-flat! Dolente, arioso.*
Put all the griefs of the world in that change of key."
    Who then could lay a finger on his sleeve
       to distress him with
   "One day, Steve, two of your well-taught daughters
       will be deaf."

Mother must be sitting, left, on the porch-set,
you can just see her. My sister's on her lap.
And that's Steve confiding to his cigarette
something my mother's mother has to laugh at.
    The screened door twangs, slamming
       on its sprung hinge.
   Paint blisters on the steps; iced tea, grasscuttings,
       elm flowers, mock orange . . .

A grand June evening, like this one, not too buggy,
unselfquestioning midwestern, maybe 1951.
And, of course, there in my grandmother's memory
lives just such another summer—1890 or 91.
    Though it's not on her mind now/then.
       No, she's thinking of
   the yeast-ring rising in the oven. Or how *any* shoes
       irritate her bunion.

Paper gestures, pictures, newsprint laughter.
And after the camera winks and makes its catch,
the decibels drain away *for ever and ever.*
No need to say "Look!" to these smilers on the porch,
   "Grandmother will have her stroke,
    and you, mother, will nurse her."
 Or to myself, this woman died paralysed-dumb, and that one
     dumb from cancer.

Sufficient unto the day . . . Grandmother, poor and liturgical,
whose days were duties, stitches in the tea-brown blanket
she for years crocheted, its zigzag of yellow wool,
her grateful offering, her proof of goodness to present,
   gift-wrapped, to Our Father in Heaven. "Accept,
    O Lord, this best-I-can-make-it soul."
  And He: "Thou good and faithful servant, lose thyself
     and be whole."

Consciousness walks on tiptoe through what happens.
So much is felt, so little of it said.
But ours is the breath on which the past depends.
"What happened" is what the living teach the dead,
   who, smilingly lost to their lost concerns,
    in grey on grey,
   are all of them deaf, blind, unburdened
    by today.

As if our recording selves, our mortal identities,
could be cupped in a concave universe or lens,
ageless at all ages, cleansed of memories,
not minding that meaningful genealogy extends
   no further than mind's flash images reach back.
    As for what happens next,
    let all the griefs of the world
     find keys for that.

John Keats, 1821–1950

Keats was Miss McKinney's class, 12th grade English,
and we could tell she loved him
by the way she scolded us. "Why is it
you young, spoiled people never look?"

Poetry was what we learned "by heart."
I can still see it, that clammy, Coke-stained textbook's
Ode to Autumn. I think I half believed I was him,
the spirit of Keats come back, in me, to Michigan.

Devoid of thatch-eaves, lambs and granary floors,
Ann Arbor had its river. I hymned the sallows under
violent-coloured maples. Crickets I remember,
and how the fierce gnats' wailing was oracular.

MARGE PIERCY
(1954, 1956, 1957)

Photograph of my mother sitting on the steps

My mother who isn't anyone's
just her own intact and yearning
self complete as a birch tree
sits on the tenement steps.

She is awkwardly lovely, her face
pure as a single trill perfectly
prolonged on a violin, yet she
knows the camera sees her

and she arranges her body
like a flower in a vase to be
displayed, admired she hopes.
She longs to be luminous

and visible, to shine in the eyes
of it must be a handsome man,
who will carry her away—and he
will into poverty and an abortion

but not yet. Now she drapes
her best, her only good dress
inherited by her sister who dances
on the stage, around her legs

which she does not like
and leans a little forward
because she does like her breasts.
How she wants love to bathe

her in honeyed light lifting her
up through smoky clouds clamped
on the Pittsburgh slum. Blessed
are we who cannot know

what will come to us,
our upturned faces following
through the sky
the sun of love.

Colors passing through us

Purple as tulips in May, mauve
into lush velvet, purple
as the stain blackberries leave
on the lips, on the hands,
the purple of ripe grapes
sunlit and warm as flesh.

Every day I will give you a color,
like a new flower in a bud vase
on your desk. Every day
I will paint you, as women
color each other with henna
on hands and feet.

Red as henna, as cinnamon,
as coals, after the fire is banked,
the cardinal in the feeder,
the roses tumbling on the arbor
their weight bending the wood
the red of the syrup I make from petals.

Orange as the perfumed fruit
hanging their globes on the glossy tree,
orange as pumpkins in the field,
orange as butterflyweed and the monarchs
who come to eat it, orange as my
cat running lithe through the high grass.

Yellow as a goat's wise and wicked eyes,
yellow as a hill of daffodils,
yellow as dandelions by the highway,
yellow as butter and egg yolks,
yellow as a school bus stopping you,
yellow as a slicker in a downpour.

Here is my bouquet, here is a sing
song of all the things you make
me think of, here is oblique
praise for the height and depth
of you and the width too.
Here is my box of new crayons at your feet.

Green as mint jelly, green
as a frog on a lily pad twanging,
the green of cos lettuce upright
about to bolt into opulent towers,
green as Grande-Chartreuse in a clear
glass, green as wine bottles.

Blue as cornflowers, delphiniums,
bachelor's buttons. Blue as Roquefort,
blue as Saga. Blue as still water.
Blue as the eyes of a Siamese cat.
Blue as shadows on new snow, as a spring
azure sipping from a puddle on the blacktop.

Cobalt as the midnight sky
when day has gone without a trace
and we lie in each other's arms
eyes shut and fingers open
and all the colors of the world
pass through our bodies like strings of fire.

HENRY VAN DYKE

(1954)

Summer Masquerades

When I arrived, Charlotte Corday and Julius Caesar were smoking pot out in Florian's foyer. I assumed it was Charlotte Corday—she had a Jean-Paul Marat glint in her eyes, and she looked 1792-ish enough. Her cannabis cohort, draped in a toga and crowned with laurel leaves, could have been none other than Caesar himself. Florian Font's invitation to his *Bal Masqué* had clearly suggested everyone come as a character out of *A Midsummer Night's Dream,* but it was mid-August, not midsummer, and nobody took the suggestion seriously. Perhaps somewhere in the four stories of his house on West 10th Street there'd appear a plucky Puck, a discernible Titiana, an Oberon (if not whole batches of them), but as I broke past the reefer freaks in the foyer, I found nothing Shakespearean in the living room; instead I found Cyrano de Bergerac, a Mickey Mouse, a Marie Antoinette, and (perhaps) a Gertrude Stein. I, for the lack of imagination and money, came as Zorro.

But Fedora? Where was Fedora? Surely she'd left Gramercy Park by now. Usually she wore corduroy trousers, which buttoned up in the front, suspenders, brogues. She strode rather than walked. Would a costume gown inhibit her? Normally she spoke in a sort of Ethel Barrymore baritone. Would her new persona prohibit her?

I scanned the crowd, which was quite dense at the far end of the room, but before I could move on to look for Fedora, I was encountered by a drunken Captain Bly and a chatty Miss Haversham. "Hi," a runty little man said, pulling at my cape. "I'm Peaseblossom."

Peaseblossom? Christ, the man was fifty. He had a belly big as a barrel. With a Zorro smile, I nodded goodbye to the trio and pushed my way deeper into the long living room. Right off, three things I discovered: this was a *bal masqué* for middle-aged folk (I was twenty-four); it was an extravaganza for the well-heeled (my summertime work at the *Gazette* paid me peanuts); and Fedora, Fedora de Keogh was in trouble—rather awful trouble.

As a makeshift-job, while I awaited a reply from Grover College concerning a possible position there on the faculty as an art historian, I dabbled in a little writing. Fedora, dear Fedora two floors up from

Mae Britz at 34 Gramercy Park, took pity on my plight and wangled a spot on the *Gazette* for me. I would write a profile of her . . . a tit for tat arrangement. In the course of matters she'd also wangled—she was indeed a great wangler—an invitation to me to attend the midsummer night's affair, by way of explaining to Florian Font, that "for an in-depth article, dear heart, my writer needs to be with me around the clock." (She called everyone "dear heart," with a nicotine croak.) "To catch the flavor, you know." Florian agreed. I wondered. In theory, yes, one needed to know the subject of a profile as well as possible, but after the third day of trailing Fedora around, I suspected she was play-ing games, enjoying the mystery surrounding her, the smoke screens. (Masks! Masks!) Still, I was no better than she. I was using her to bol-ster my secret agenda—my list for *Eccentric Ladies* was now comprised of Mae Browne, Bea Britz, and Winifred Wriothesley. She'd be number four. But God only knew what I'd do with such a list: Incorporate the list into some sort of fiction? Add to the list? Chuck the whole notion as a crazy idea once my *amour-propre* was restored by attaining a po-sition as an art historian?

But Fedora. Some of the basic rumors (I was yet in the midst of ex-ploring, verifying, discarding) were these: She was once an actress, a stage actress of sorts. She was either sixty-three or sixty-eight, or even a generation older than that. She may or may not have understudied Ethel Barrymore in the theater.

Some of the facts (firmly written in my notes) were these: She was di-recting the difficult and talented Carla Respighi. In a revival of Wilde's *The Importance of Being Earnest*. At the Plum Lane Theatre. In the West Village. Out of costume, in real life, Fedora had hectic-scraggly hair—short and silver-black. She had crooked teeth, yellowed from Gauloise cigarettes. She laughed in a Barrymore catarrh. Her friends called her Sapphic; her enemies called her a dyke.

But right now, she was in trouble: it was the business of her gown—a Druid affair. She, who had in recent years little practice in wearing dresses, decided, in her *bal masqué* madness, to appear as Norma, Vin-cenzo Bellini's priestess of the Druids. "You think anybody'll guess who I'll be?" Fedora had asked me earlier. "That I'll be Norma, I mean?" She spoke to me as she stood in front of the long wall mirror at Sylvie's, at the dress shop she had chosen.

Would anybody care? This silent response was not so much cruel as it was an accurate assessment of the masquérading participants: each would be elaborately disguised, too self-absorbed to ferret out the parody of another's masquérade. "But why Norma?" I did ask, quickly regretting even that logical enquiry. Her sharp glance, a prelude to whatever stinging reply she intended, was dissipated by Sylvie's demand. "Toon-awound, Madum," Sylvie said. Sylvie was French. Sylvie had pins in her mouth. "Shhh-til, seed-doo-pway."

I wanted to ask Fedora why didn't she appear at the masked ball as Vita Sackville-West, but I decided that reference might have been as obscure as Norma, so I held my tongue, and Fedora obeyed Sylvie and stood still as the contours of the gown began to take shape. And regal, and Druidish, indeed she did look. Except . . . that Tuscany Knot at the shoulder. Folds and folds of the long priestess gown—six feet three inches of it—seemed to depend upon the Tuscany Knot at her left shoulder. A precarious arrangement, surely. No pins there? No hooks? No chains?

I had not been an alarmist at Sylvie's, and I had every reason to question the security of her Tuscany Knot, for no matter how quaint and inventive, too much hinged upon it; yards and yards, amazonian yards depended upon the security of the Tuscany Knot. But then, why Tuscany, anyway? Was Norma's Pollione Tuscan? And why a knot? What was so Druidish about a knot?

At Florian's at the end of the living room near the canape table, Fedora's Tuscany Knot had not merely come undone as I'd feared; saboteurs were afoot: Marie Antoinette and Marie de Medici, under cover of the revelers' crush, molested Fedora's left shoulder. Then came the awful revelation: a pool of Druiderie fell to Fedora's feet, displaying, above this disaster, inches and inches of an underslip. It was pink, the underslip. It was the pinkness that rankled. It was such a non-Fedora color. And there was so much of it.

Marie Antoinette and Marie de Medicis, royal bloods, giggled. Lucrezia Borgia screamed in delight. Cardinal Wolsey failed to suppress his laughter, his choking sort of bark. Toussaint-Louverture and Phillis Wheatly held on to each other for support.

Fedora stepped out of her pool of Druiderie and, in a shiny pink underslip, pried her way out of the crowd as best she could. I lost her somewhere behind Mae West and Oscar Wilde.

At Fedora's rehearsal the next day, my gestures of sympathy were ignored. She waved a bony, slightly arthritic hand to silence me. She took energetic strides before her assembled group in the Second Avenue rehearsal hall. She was thinking. Planning. The fly of her corduroy trousers had, as usual, come unbuttoned. Finally, she said, "Places everybody" and the actors sought their designated spots, transforming canvas chairs and box crates into love seats and divans. I could easily enough pretend I was looking at a salon in Half-Moon Street in Wilde's *The Importance of Being Earnest;* I could adjust my images of blue jeans and T-shirts from The Gap into fabrics of crinoline and silk, but I could not, no matter with what wattage I turned up my liberal impulses, adjust to the diverse, nontraditional casting.

Lady Bracknell: Carla Respighi had been selected. She fooled few people by declaring she'd not yet passed her fiftieth year, but, to her personal credit (and to the play's harm) she looked too young to portray Wilde's crusty old auntie. Although Carla wanted to think of herself as being zaftig, and had, alas, gone a bit beyond that diplomatic designation, she did have creamy-smooth skin and she possessed luxurious black hair. Her acting fame rested largely on her sensational portrayal of Courage in Bertolt Brecht's *Mother Courage.* Gutsy, I thought of her. Luscious, I thought of her. Lady Bracknell—never. Furthermore, Carla Respighi had not an aristocratic bone in her body.

Algernon Moncrieff: Bracknell's nephew was black. Beauregard Nash. He was handsome, tall, lithe, and walked with a faintly sensuous bowed leg. His voice was all right—a little too studied perhaps. In recompense for his duties as handyman and general factotum, he'd received elocution lessons from her (*air, fare, pear, heir, there*)—"To get the ghetto out of your voice," she'd told him. And indeed, by mid-August he could spin off *jet, gin, gist, azure, seizure,* and so forth, to beat the band. In addition, Fedora had succeeded in sprucing up his fricatives, his diphthongs, and his labials. Still, the play was far too ethnocentric for interracial casting; Beauregard looked about as much like Algernon Moncrieff as I did Wagner's Alberich—and I'm tall and on the skinny side.

Gwendolen Fairfax: Algernon's love interest was Delphine Siegfried, a young beauty who spoke in hard, New York cut-glass tones and owned an exquisite chin—a chin, I fear, she hoped might cover up for her lack of talent, for why else did she pose with it so often. (I had hot-pants for her, but she would not give me the time of day).

John Worthing: Algernon's buddy was Kai Lee, a Eurasian, a startling combination of the beauties of the East and West, but he appeared not even remotely suited for the proceedings in London W., nor in Manor House, Woolton.

Miss Prism sat in a corner, quietly in repose. Of all the cast, she most fit the bill; she might have been Margaret Rutherford's sister.

"All right, everybody!" Fedora barked.

Kai Lee (alias Jack Worthing): Charming day it has been, Miss Fairfax.

Delphine Siegfried (Gwendolen Fairfax): Pray don't talk to me about the weather, Mr. Worthing. Whenever people talk to me about the weather, I always feel quite certain that they mean something else. And that makes me so nervous.

Kai Lee (Jack Worthing): I do mean something else.

Delphine Siegfried (Gwendolen Fairfax): I thought so. In fact, I am never wrong.

Kai Lee (Jack Worthing): And I would like to be allowed to take advantage of Lady Bracknell's temporary absence—

Here everyone in the room came back to the Second Avenue rehearsal hall by way of terrible laughter. It was the kind of laughter that one painfully tries to suppress but once it has burst the dam, cascades of unpardonable mirth spew forth. It was at Carla Respighi's expense. Her absence was not a thing easily accepted; Kai Lee's line, "Lady Bracknell's temporary absence," came off as a sly mockery, for indeed we all could not help but take in Carla's scent (was it *Tabu? Mitsouko?*), and we could all readily see her stretching her zaftig thighs in black tights as if in preparation for performing a pirouette or a grand jeté. Apparently she believed in limbering up body as well as her mind prior to engaging herself in a role. Nonetheless, were such excessive machinations a prerequisite for her asking, eventually, "Prism, where is that baby?" or declaring with regal authority that "a man who desires to get married should know either everything or nothing."

But Carla, never a back-seater, retaliated. As if she'd not in the least been the subject of her colleagues' mean laughter, she said, with plummy conviction: "No, no, that scene's all wrong, my dears. The inflection. The—the projection—"

She left the window ledge, which she had been using as a barre, and came over to the imaginary London living room, ignoring Fedora, and began an impassioned lecture on *aura*, on *beat*, on *interaction*, on *response*. She, after all, was the professional, she implied with each bit of instruction, not they, the mere novices; she, with Brecht, Ibsen, Tennessee Williams, *et al* behind her, knew more of the theatre than Fedora de Keogh, who may or may not have been in a Barrymore play or two—centuries ago.

There might have been some wisdom in Carla Respighi's exegesis, but, I fear it was vitiated by her excess and zeal; we paid more attention to her histrionics than we did the message she showered upon us.

Fedora was livid. She did not like being upstaged, relegated to inferior positions. To boot, she stood on uneasy ground; she'd already been lacerated in the press—mostly by T. Grantly Hunt of the *Gazette*—for her insistence upon multi-racial, non-traditional casting, and she must have felt that any kind of help should be heeded, even if it came from an unwanted source.

When Carla Respighi finished her spiel, Fedora strode back and forth in front of the frozen cast. Beauregard, Miss Prism (I never got her real name straight), and the others stood or sat in stony expectation. Of what? A Fedora de Keogh explosion? A firing of Carla? In about three weeks the play was to preview in the West Village, at the Plum Lane Theatre. A chunk of money was riding on the production, money, it was rumored, largely from Fedora's private coffers. In my Fedora Notebook I had two columns, one headed *Facts* and the other *Rumors*. Under *Facts* I knew Fedora's summer estate up in Rycliff, New York, and her bank account came from her late husband, Willard Keogh. (He had had no "de" in his name. At some point after his death, Fedora had inserted it.) Under *Rumors* I'd scribbled "hobby for a bored, rich woman?" In the last week, my quest for the real Fedora had become as elusive as the quest for Corvo, and it dismayed me to see that some of my entries under the *Facts* side of my Fedora Notebook were beginning to slide toward *Rumors:* i.e., was it fact or rumor that Fedora's downstairs friendly enemy Winifred had secretly sent a large sum of money toward the Plum Lane production? And to complicate matters, Fedora had said, emphatically, with spittle spraying from her rubbery lips, "No tape recorder, or cassette or whatever you call those damned things. Okay?" Oh, but now I wished I had a recorder as she strode before her leading lady, in ominous silence, preparing her tirade.

But—and the moment was shocking—she merely pulled out from her vest pocket a pack of Gauloise Blue and lit one. "That's all for today," she said, in flat tones, in bored tones, managing, as she picked up the Oscar Wilde script, to blow an upward funnel of smoke directly at the No Smoking sign.

Whenever Fedora was depressed—I had not thought this possible—
she said she'd go to get a Fragonard Fix.

"A Fragonard Fix? What, for crissake, is that?"

She leaned back in the taxi seat. "You'll see."

Fragonard. Jean-Honoré Fragonard. Was it to be some food or
drink sensation? Like Peach Melba, or a Caruso Cappuccino? Would
there be a Fragonard Frappe? Fedora told the driver to stop at the
Frick.

She went straight to Room 11 and stood near the empty fireplace. I
heard her sigh, gently, as she stood there to take in the fragrances from
the Fragonard canvases . . . *The Meeting . . . Love Letters . . . The Lover
Crowned.* Tree tops melted into summer clouds. Effulgent tree tops.
Quiet clouds. And the shoulders! Fragonard was full of shoulders.
Shoulders in anticipation. Shoulders of caution. Shoulders of saucy
bliss. And the statues in the paintings—they looked down upon
lovers-about-to-meet, on lovers-having-met, on lovers-in-opulent-
play. Fedora bent her head slightly forward as if she heard music from
a later century—the music of Debussy, or maybe Fauré. Could I hear
it, too? Suddenly, as if I'd come under Fragonard's spell or been mesmerized into seeing what Fedora must have been seeing, the clouds
shifted, made new formations before my very eyes. The tree leaves
shimmered in E major and in C-sharp minor as cherub statues began
to blink. An illusive fragrance floated over the urns, over pedestals. Sun
and shadow played tag. Bits of Poulenc and Ravel now fell through the
shifting clouds and settled upon a patio-garden. Organdy and marble.
Tulle and terraces. And there were always the Debussyan tree tops
melting into Fragonard's fragrant sky.

I began to be embarrassed as I felt all at sea: I'd not expected this
tall, strident, trousered creature to be so beholden to such ephemeral
sentiment. I'd actually *watched* her getting her Fragonard Fix; I'd actually *seen* her blues being chased away.

Like some twenty-four-year-old school boy, I stood there behind
her, shifting from foot to foot, uncertain if by speaking I'd break her
spell. But I needn't have worried; the Japanese took care of that: a
group of five or six tourists had gathered about Fedora, ignoring the
paintings, and stared at her *corps d'amazone* as if she were a character
from a painting from another museum, as if she'd stepped out of a Red
Grooms canvas. One tiny man—from Tokyo? Nagasaki?—came right
up in front of Fedora and snapped her picture, brazen as hell, and

smiled ever so politely, and bowed ever so politely, and said his thanks ever so politely.

"Are cameras allowed in here?" Fedora spat out, nearly making the photographer topple backwards. Then, in corduroy haste, she strode out of Room 11, out to the street. I ran after her.

As we rode down to Gramercy Park, there was silence. By now she had won me over. After participating in her transcendent elevation amongst the Fragonards and then her brutal descent, I had been pushed across the line: she'd become more than mere fodder for my *Eccentric Ladies* list, even if she'd not yet become a friend.

For her? Did I matter? Was she still playing a game, holding up a mask to suit her fancy? She had said, as we got into the taxi, "Come on, let's go home," a phrase that included me, pleased me; but now, as there was no conversation in the taxi, I treated the silence as a gift, a gift mutually enjoyed only by friends. Had I made a breakthrough?

Upstairs, in the turreted 1882 building, sundown rays eased through the park's leaves and settled upon Fedora's window panes. She stood there, looking at the Edwin Booth statue in the center of the park—or maybe she was watching bird-play in the cage at the park's southeast corner. Aimlessly I walked around her living room, estimating the space that Bea Britz's Pleyel piano occupied two stories below. Bea Britz. The terrible Mrs. Britz. Had she really "sneaked" some of her money in to back Fedora's production? To make conversation, to break the silence, I asked Fedora where exactly in the building did James Cagney once live. She did not answer. I had learned that Mildred Dunnock had once lived in the building. Exactly where, did she know? Before her time? And Margaret Hamilton of *The Wizard of Oz* fame? Surely before her time was the residency of the coloratura soprano Emma Thursby, a sort of American Jenny Lind. Thursby, I read, had held both classes and a salon, attended by the likes of Mary Garden, Caruso, and Nellie Melba. Now surely, I prodded her, this folklore had not escaped her; surely she must have heard gossip, tidbits, stories. Not at all?

She'd clammed up. She'd become as impenetrable as her twenty-four-inch interior walls. Finally she left the window and adjusted pillows on her red settee. She pointed to a spot for me to sit in.

She went to make tea.

I'd rather have had scotch.

As I waited, I looked about the room. Hugh Moorish furniture.

Dark woods, highly polished. English prints. Two settees with red velvet pillows. An exceedingly masculine cat—oatmeal-colored, aloof. I imagined that she would raise her hind leg at a fire hydrant. And soon Fedora appeared in the doorway, teacups in hand, and beckoned me to follow her. She'd kicked off her brogues and removed her corduroys. She now stood in terrifying splendor, in a Gustav Klimt gown. It was a brown-russet affair with geometric designs—semi-circles, triangles—sewn into lush folds of brocade and giddy silk. Egyptian eyes poked out from miniature pyramids, and there was just enough blue (cobalt) to enliven the vast desert expanses. On the way to her back room she explained, in low, almost funereal tones, that she'd had the gown for ages—way back when she was in the theatre. It wasn't hers. A stage costume.

"Whose was it?" I asked. "I mean, for what role?"

She could no longer remember much about the origins, she said.

(Oh, come now, Fedora. Masks! Masks! This was not something one forgot—especially a pants-person. But I held my tongue.)

She said she thought it was patterned after a Gustav Klimt portrait in the Osterreichische Galerie in Vienna. And the play? A Molnar? Something by Schnitzler? No matter, no matter, she mumbled.

But it did matter. On which side of the Fedora Notebook would I later make my entry? Under *Facts* or *Rumors*?

She led me into her music room. It was a small, ill-lit place, and doubled as an office-den. In stocking feet, in her Klimt gown, in Sitwell regality, she sat at her piano. An upright. The ivory keys were mostly yellow, the ebony ones unstable. On the stand she opened music by Amy Woodforde-Finden. *Kashmiri Song.* The lyrics came from Lawrence (Violet Nicolson) Hope.

She poked at the folds of her Klimt gown. She sat, shoulders erect. She played. She sang.

Pale hands I loved beside the Shalimar
Where are you now? Who lies beneath your spell?
Whom do you lead on Rapture's roadway, far,
Before you agonize them in farewell?

Oh, pale dispensers of my Joys and Pains,
Holding the doors of Heaven and of Hell,
How the hot blood rushed wildly through the veins
Beneath your touch, until you waved farewell.

> Pale Hands, pink tipped, like Lotus buds that float
> On those cool waters where we used to dwell,
> I would have rather felt you round my throat,
> Crushing out life, than waving me farewell!

The dynamic instructions at the beginning of the song indicated that it should be played and sung *moderato assai con molto sentimento.* It was *sentimento* all right, but Fedora found the accompanying chords too difficult for her arthritic hands, which reduced the rendition of the rather bloodthirsty piece to a stumbling *adagio.*

I wished I might have been a masseur, a healer of her aching hands. I wished I might have played the piano accompaniment for her. But why, why had I been given this glimpse of privacy? I'd been presented a gift of intimacy beyond a profiler's needs. Had her Fragonard Fix been so soured that she needed yet another antidote, needed to indulge in a Musical Medication, despite my presence? And then, at that instance, as if she had heard my unspoken query, and as if she regretted revealing so much of herself, she said, "Go."

"Go?"

"You must go."

"I'll—I'll see you tomorrow, then, huh?"

She stepped into her brogues. She fumbled with the zipper of her Klimt gown. "No. Not tomorrow. Go."

I felt like a rejected lover. I was restless, hurt. What in the hell had I done? And no matter how often I decided that Fedora was loopy, that she was *louche,* that she was a subject not to be taken seriously, I still could not delineate the elusive anxieties her antics had unhinged within me. I even took to hanging about Gramercy Park, hoping to catch her coming or going. I'd pop into nearby Pete's Tavern to rest my weary feet. I also went down to the Plum Lane Theatre but I was not allowed in. Once, from Miss Prism (dashing down Hudson Street to get a sandwich at the deli) I learned that the play was in hot water, that it had gone kaput, that some of the cast—particularly Carla Respighi—had begun denigrating the production, calling it *Oh, Ernie.*

August 22nd: A dress rehearsal.

Invitational.

I was not invited.

Instead, I hung around the *Gazette*'s offices, pretending to work. Amidst my funk and self-pity, a wicked thought came to me: I decided by alerting Fedora to T. Grantly Hunt's planned massacre she might somehow side-step and alter the major ills of her production. I knew Hunt made sneak attacks—viewing a show and reviewing it prior to opening night. Oh, he might tone up or down his piece after the opening, but essentially it would have been written.

In the deserted office I began my skullduggery. I knew that Hunt shunned modern technology—he barely tolerated the telephone—and that he would type out his work rather than use a computer. But his desk drawers would be locked; or would they? Maybe he'd—ah, bingo, there it was in plain sight. I copied the venomous hatchet job, with thundering heart, and fled with the feet of a jewel thief. With a stein of beer at the Riviera Café at Sheridan Square, I read:

No execrations from the lexicon of Oscar Wilde's Wit & Wisdom, from Rousseau's Observations, nor from the trenchant pen of Madame de Sévigné, could adequately pay assessment to the egregious miscarriage currently cluttering the stage at the Plum Lane Theatre.

Wilde, who was a minor genius back at the end of the last century (and this does not mean he was a second-rate genius), wrote *The Importance of Being Earnest* in 1895. This play's orchestrated artificiality—as carefully balanced as a Haydn quartet—rings with paradoxical delights, reversals of the expected, perverse verities: its very meaning (for it is a satire of social manners if nothing else) depends upon the exact nuance in the delivery of each line in the script. To say that Fedora de Keogh's thespians club-footed their way through Wilde's fine-tuned orchestrations would be kindness itself. To say that the marauders have mutilated Wilde's delicate rondo capriccioso is too mild a description of the heinous mayhem you will find in the little bijou theatre downtown in the West Village. To say that the repertory vandals are indulging in the Theater of the Absurd, or the Theatre of the Camp, would mislead you, and give you reasonable cause to file a civil suit against me and this publication for our part in abetting your act of wasting time and money.

In my nearly two-dozen years of theatre-going, I have never encountered such sophomoric inanities, such unmitigated hamming, in the venue of the professional theatre—nor, for that matter, in the auditoria of assorted community colleges. Elephantine cadences reign where the rhythm should snap and sparkle; and, alas, the cast members' scabrous inflections befoul the air.

Chief amongst the perpetrators at the scene of the crime is Carla Respighi whose "uncorseted" Lady Bracknell (both literally and figuratively, I dare say) ought to cause comment on anybody's platform. Miss Respighi, who was given deserved praise in Bertolt Brecht's *Mother Courage,* is, I'm sad to report, a lubricious waddler in this production: her every movement seems more suitable for a denizen of a bordello (the madam?) than it does for Lady Augusta Bracknell.

Must the scurrilities of this production lie at the feet of Fedora de Keogh? One must assume so; she is listed on the program as director and producer. An entrepreneur she may be, but directing, I fear, is not her metier.

As for the other actors in this show (which, if you must know, is now being called *Oh, Ernie,* according to the gossip mongers), their performances might be rated on a scale of zero to 10. With quite valiant attempts, most are able to reach a minus -1 mark. Except for Beauregard Nash. Mr. Nash is not an actor. In this vehicle he is not even an also-ran. Stage presence and good looks do not an actor make. (The fact that he is black, that the cast is indeed multi-social-ethnic-or-what-have-you is entirely another matter. If you have not already been sufficiently discouraged, and should you read further, you may see my comments on this below.)

Delphine Siegfried exhibits herself. Her chin. Her well-sheathed hips. And although these attributes are lovely to view, the play in question is not exactly *Ziegfeld's Follies*—though, God knows, what Fedora de Keogh's intention will be if, as is rumored, she really does change the title of the play to *Oh, Ernie.* (Quite frankly, my observations here are based upon a late preview, but I trust you will deem them as a valuable reconnoitering service.)

Miss Siegfried plays the role of the Hon. Gwendolen Fairfax, but, oh, dear me, she delivers her lines with all the clarity of a clerk at Macy's. Nonetheless, she is shoulders above Kai Lee (in the role of Jack Worthing) who seems to wish he were playing the lead in *The King and I.* (Wrong play, fella.)

Imitative, too, is the actress who plays Miss Prism: she (Amanda Stone) outdoes Margaret Rutherford with her mugging jaw, her "endearing" sputterings. Miss Rutherford, bless her, must be lying in an unquiet grave.

As for the plot of this spectacular bit of incompetence . . .

I waved to the waiter. I ordered a double brandy.

. . . multi-racial casts are fine and dandy for interactions at First Avenue and 42nd Street, there at the United Nations, but the idea rarely works upon the stage, and in this case, in the Wildean milieu of Half-Moon Street, W. and Manor House at Woolton, it is a disaster. Mrs. de Keogh's Equal Employment Opportunity principles, admirable as they are, ought to be reasonably applied. This particular display of brotherhood and good will is a sad miscalculation.

My biographical dictionary indicates that Vyvyan Holland, one of Oscar Wilde's sons, died in 1967. Did Mr. Holland leave any heirs? If so, cannot those heirs sue Fedora de Keogh for her flagrant desecrations?

Somewhere in Act Three, Delphine Siegfried says to her intended, Kai Lee: "If you are not too long, I will wait here for you all my life."

Fool.

—T. Grantly Hunt

I rushed over to Fedora's. Impatient with the elevator, I bounded up the iron-marble-tile stairs. I showed her Hunt's review.

After reading it, and standing perfectly still for a moment, she then pounded an arthritic fist into her opened hand. "He thinks he'll fuck me up, does he?" Outside it had begun to rain against Fedora's windows, and her cat, Brandenburg, growled his consolations. At the liquor cabinet, I dug out some rum. I'd expected, under the circumstances, that I'd stay and commiserate, scheme, plot; that I'd help her find a way out of the thicket; but instead she planted a rum-wet kiss on my forehead and said, "You've been a big help, Clay, but you must go."

"So you're going to dump me again, huh?"

"Dear heart, I—I must do this alone." She walked over to the window to look at the rain.

Brandenburg followed. She came back and leaned against the ugly escritoire. Brandenburg stood beside her. "I must do this thing alone—I must—Oh, Hunt thinks the play is bad, does he?"

"The production," I ventured.

"Bad? He's not seen bad yet, the bastard."

Reluctantly, I prepared to leave. "You're planning to do what, Fedora? What exactly?"

She appeared not to have heard me. She spoke as if solely addressing herself: "Bad? T. Grantly Hunt's not seen bad yet." Her Gauloise lips trembled. "I'll give him bad so bad that it'll be good. Just wait."

I left her staring at the rain. Brandenburg saw me to the door.

September 4th: Despite my second trip to Coventry, I learned of three developments in Fedora's world: (1) Opening Night had been postponed. (2) The production's title had been officially changed to *Oh, Ernie.* (3) Pirandello had entered the proceedings.

On the first account, no one was surprised; a play in trouble needed time for amendments, doctoring.

On the second account, I wondered had Carla Respighi had her way, or had Fedora's scheme for revisions circled around the theory that badness, exaggerated badness could, perversely, be deemed good, i.e., could produce saleable high camp.

On the third account, I'd play errand boy: upon request, I sent Fedora a copy of Pirandello's *Six Characters in Search of an Author.* (Prior to my compliance to this request, I asked her on the phone what she planned to do with the Pirandello play. "Just send it, Clay, don't ask me questions, just send it." Miffed, I sent her (by way of the doorman) *Sei Personnagi in Cerca D'autore,* but her silence and my guilt prompted me to leave with her doorman the English translation of the play; I even threw in a critical study of the work to boot.)

September 7th: Wilde-thoughts filled my head. Fedora was making a musical out of the play? Would she use a banjo? A piano? Beauregard (Algernon) and Lady Bracknell (Carla Respighi) would perhaps do a tango, a slightly incestuous tango? Miss Prism's plaintive song of remorse would be *I Left a Baby in a Handbag?*

Would somebody tap dance?

Would the chorus line's reprise be *All's Well That Ends Wilde,* and then, when the cheering subsided, would the chorus line reappear with *All's Wilde That Ends Well?*

Damn Fedora.

September 10th: All morning I read Wilde's play. Tightly wrought. Music of a string quartet. I read Pirandello: "security of perception," he says, "is mere illusion."

September 12th: Saturday. Opening Night. I was too nervous to go, too afraid. I drank a lot of coffee, then, in a caffeine stupor, I finally went out to get the *Gotham Times*. With fumbling fingers I found Frank Armer's review. He said:

> Although it would seem an unlikely enterprise—the resurrection of two weather-beaten fossils and welding them again as new—this is exactly what has happened down at the Plum Lane Theatre and I am pleased to report that the result is a happy one. How exactly the director, Fedora de Keogh, has managed to make Oscar Wilde's *The Importance of Being Earnest* and Pirandello's *Six Characters in Search of an Author* into a crafty vehicle for theatrical madness, I am hard put to tell you—it would be far better to simply go and let reason take a back seat to non-stop hilarity. Mind you, there is no important message in this uplifting farce, and stay at home if you require redeeming stuffing to make acceptable what some may consider naught but soft porn.
>
> As a first preparation for visiting this outré, sometimes faltering, but largely brilliant work, one must forget the drawing-room wit of Wilde; one must forget the investigation of the real and the non-real of Pirandello; the hybrid piece you will find when you see the de Keogh concoction will offer you only distilled laughter—silly laughter perhaps, but it is nearly non-stop. When one does pause for reflection, it is apparent that we are being offered a sly spoof of theatrical conventions, of the avant-garde; and portentous theories, of whatever ilk, are left smashed in the wake of the work's ferocious satire.
>
> A major portion of the play's success must be attributed to the dynamic performance of Carla Respighi, an actress recently acclaimed for the portrait of Courage in Brecht's *Mother Courage*.
>
> I shall not even attempt to give you a synopsis of the convoluted plot; its course is devious and treacherous; and in any case the story line serves only for the "improvised" machinations of the brilliant cast. I say "improvised"—and in so doing I give the group and the director my highest praise. Indeed the variations on the Wilde and Pirandello play are as intricate as a Swiss watch; the actors exhibit skill at its pinnacle as they recite highly orchestrated lines, as if the lines were just that moment thought of. And it is Miss Respighi who is most adept at giving the impression of improvisation as she changes from the personage of Lady Augusta Bracknell—starch, hauteur, accent, all of it—into an earthy,

near-slatternly actress who fights with the other actors over her lines, fights with the director, screams bloody hell about the pacing, the lighting.

It is a tribute to Fedora de Keogh that we forget that it is she who has devised these "improvised" lines for Miss Respighi to utter. And utter them she does with the insinuation of a Mae West and the passion of an Anna Magnani. An incongruous combination? Quite. But Miss Respighi, by some theatrical magic, makes it work.

Oh, Ernie, will continue its run at the Plum Lane on into the new year, until mid-January, but I daresay it'll be around much longer.

—Frank Armer

The elevator ride up to Fedora's apartment seemed to take longer than usual. Inch by inch as I rode upward, I thought of Pirandello: "security of perception," he says, "is mere illusion." But how precisely, I burned to know, had Fedora paid homage to the playwright's theorem, exacting thereby such a bountiful blessing from Frank Armer in the *Gotham Times*. And, too, had she found some way to *use* Pirandello as she'd used the Fragonard paintings at the Frick, as she'd used the Woodford-Finden song while costumed in her Klimt gown? Would the face she'd present at the door be the true Fedora, or would it be a Fedora even less true than the one behind her masks, her myriad ploys? *Security of perception is mere illusion.* . . . Still, there would be one certainty: Sunday morning sunlight would be racing through the park leaves to reach her window panes. Brandenburg would be gazing into this same sunlight, blinking smugly with some arcane knowledge. There would be the faint aroma of almond-polish from the Moorish monstrosities in her living room. And tea, no doubt, would be in the making.

At the doorway she said, "Ah, dear heart." As soon as she spied my Fedora Notebook, she took it from my hand and placed it—dumped it—atop the hall table as if it were an unneeded umbrella on a sunlit day. Then, smiling with Gauloise teeth, she strode with a Scaramouchian swagger across her Moroccan rug to fetch some rum and Darjeeling tea.

LAURENCE LIEBERMAN
(1955, 1958)

Carib's Leap

Heyling Charles, alias Pali Wali, recounts how his mother died
  last year, this very week,
   at age seventy-six; mine two years back, to the day,
    just six weeks shy of her eightieth birth
  month—*too soon, too too young,* we sigh in vocal duet: together,
    five beers downed
   apiece, we stand on the cliff ledge overlook
    at CARIB'S LEAP, and mourn
     the demise
     of mothers. . . . I shake off
    the municipal seas mists, while we survey
    a diversity
of stones in this small graveyard—flanking the Sauteurs public
  grade school: a few larger slabs, markers
crowning the plots of turn-of-the-Century prominent
   citizens, seem half-dislodged
from their moorings in loose untended sod. One tall rectangle,

       engraved with gold script, nods,
        as if top heavy,
      from the cliff skull's receding hairline: grave
         of the town's one-time
   Minister of Finance. Now we make
      a half-hearted attempt, Heyling Charles and I,

to prop up the loose fake-marbly column, incised with tributes
   of ornate Romanesque scrawl
  lauding the one civil servant who always balanced
  de town's shaky budget, keeping de blue
collar worker citizentry's payroll checks solvent, and town monies
  in de black.
  We pile up mossy rocks around the tombstone
   brushing loose dirt and gravel
    in earthen
   cracks—to steady the mount.

We take turns. One shoulders the Pisa-angled
  tablet upright,
while the other stuffs firm landfill in gaps under the base. . . .
  Our moms, too, were shrewd and frugal
money jugglers—we the legatees of such thrift:
  both *only* sons, both orphaned
in middle age, but no less devastated by that parental void

          than if we'd been teenagers.
            O we are half
        teens, still, half Mid-Century lads! And today,
                boy half swallows man,
    as we tipsy two, asway, invoke a Spirit
            of our mothers—both snatched from us by *Strokes.* . . .

And here stood they, all arms twined in a last communal embrace,
      some forty-odd survivors
  of the Carib tribe, men, women, small babes & toddlers
    in whatever proportion (no one knows
    the exact number), their Spaniard pursuers clamoring at their backs.
      Whatever Fate
    beckoned—slaughter by musket fire, burnings
      at the stake, or most dreaded
        enslavement
      to those fish-belly-faced
  Conquistadores—they chose, all of One Voice Howl
      in the trade winds,
    same winds as today, to die   and yes, *die out*   in one Mystic
      synchronized bold LEAP of defiance
    to the naked rocks below. They knew their family
      multitude of spirits, the clan
Over-Soul, would *fly up,* while their hand-clasped lean bodies gored

          on the horned rock pinnacles
            below, and soar
        into a life beyond, a life forevermore remote
                from *terrible   nonsense,*
    terrible   nonsense (Pali Wali's words,
          himself an unbookish man) *of   dem   White   Barbarians.* . . .

Gull screech. Two frigatebirds lunge for the feathered small game
            overhead—the prolonged shrieks
      may be Caribs adrift on the wind updrafts, or perhaps
         they may be our two mothers, in chorus,
      quavering   *it's alright   we, too, are at peace   spared life's
         last   terrible*
   nonsense   here we are   O we do continue
      just as you last remember
            us   only sons
         our beauty intact   you know
   how it grew ever stronger in Age   peaked....
            My mom, but two days
   before she died, had her hair done up spiffy by her favorite
      beautician. We sat in the Cuban-Chinese
   family diner awaiting our entree. The chef's twelve-
         year-old petite daughter,
who served us, kept staring and staring at Anita, always finding

                  more pretext to come back, ever
                     back, to our table.
            Water refills. Extra Fortune Cookie (my first
                     fortune strip drew
      a blank) . . . At last, she could contain
                  herself no more, and blurted out: *Senora, you are*

so beautiful, your hair, so beautiful, I've never seen anyone look so,
      so, so . . . Mother looked puzzled
   and mildly annoyed. *O what can she possibly mean*
      by that? she asked the mute tablecloth.
   But who *could* explain? I merely repeated the child's plain words,
         they were true,
      and from me, her only son, she would accept—
         if vaguely—their drift. . . .
            Drab schoolhouse
         to one side, Catholic Church
      across the path, the horror and violence
         of Old Grenada's
   darkest day seem effaced, dulled, by the bland civic exteriors.
         And below, the many thick shrubs and sea-
   resistant low trees seem to shroud those jagged rocks,

to blunt all rugged pointy spires
that burst open soft bellies, ribcages and thighs of the self-flung

families, crushed limbs or skulls
like so many soft-
rinded melons hurled at the sharp cutting edges. We
may suppose they aimed
themselves—like practised Sky Divers
or parachutists—at the most keen-rimmed silhouettes

flashing below, honed by the sea's whetstone to a razor's hairline
cutting edge, their bodies looping
in glory of their last aerial dance, last dream flight.
And yes, we do see them steering their plunge
to greet, headforemost, the punishing raw angles of rock, welcoming
that Great Howl
of speediest death, the surest brain-crushers
most dear, O yes, most fiercely
sought after. . . .

NANCY WILLARD
(1955, 1956, 1957, 1958)

The Ladybugs

It's true. I invited them into my home,
four thousand ladybugs from the Sierras.
I paid for their passage.
I paid for their skilled labor.
I was desperate when I read the notice
in a mail-order catalog showing flea zappers
and organic devices for vaporizing mold.

Are pests killing your trees and shrubs?
Ladybugs are the answer.

They arrived, famished and sleepy,
in a muslin bag slim as a pencil case,
or a reticule for opera glasses,
or very small change.
For once in my life I read the instructions
for sending my private army into the world.

The ladybugs will want a drink
after their long journey.
Sprinkle the sack before releasing them.

I shook handfuls of water over them.
Drops big as bombs pounded their shelter,
a mass baptism into our human ways.
They did not buzz or beat their wings,
but as the warmth of my house woke them,
I saw a shifting of bodies, of muscles rippling,
like waves adjusting themselves to a passing boat.

Do not release the ladybugs during the heat of the day
or while the sun is shining.

Under the full moon I carried my guests
to the afflicted catalpa waving its green flags.
I untied the bag. I reached in and felt a tickling,
a pulsing of lives small as a watch spring.

I seized a handful and tossed them into the branches.
They clung to my hand for safety.
Their brothers and sisters,
smelling the night air,
hung on my thumb, my wrist,
and my arm sleeved in ladybugs, baffled, muttering
in the silent tick of their language.
Where are we? What does she want of us?

Do not release too many at one time.
A tablespoon of ladybugs on each shrub
and a handful on each tree should keep them
pest-free. Keep on hand, always, a small bag
of ladybugs in your refrigerator.
Do not freeze.

I have made my abode with the ladybugs
and they have chosen me as their guardian,
because the meek shall inherit the earth,
because I found one at rest in the porch
of my ear, because I did not harm the one
that spent the night under the deep ridge
of my collarbone, or the one that crossed
my knuckles like a ring seeking
the perfect finger.

Swimming Lessons

A mile across the lake, the horizon bare
or nearly so: a broken sentence of birches.
No sand. No voices calling me back.
Waves small and polite as your newly washed hair
push the slime-furred pebbles like pawns,
an inch here. Or there.

You threaded five balsa blocks on a strap
and buckled them to my waist, a crazy life
vest for your lazy little daughter.
Under me, green deepened to black.
You said, "Swim out to the deep water."
I was seven years old. I paddled forth

and the water held me. Sunday you took away
one block, the front one. I stared down
at my legs, so small, so nervous and pale,
not fit for a place without roads.
Nothing in these depths had legs or need of them
except the toeless foot of the snail.

Tuesday you took away two more blocks.
Now I could somersault and stretch.
I could scratch myself against trees like a cat.
I even made peace with the weeds that fetch
swimmers in the noose of their stems
while the cold lake puckers and preens.

Friday the fourth block broke free. "Let it go,"
you said. When I asked you to take
out the block that kept jabbing my heart,
I felt strong. This was the sixth day.
For a week I wore the only part
of the vest that bothered to stay:

a canvas strap with nothing to carry.
The day I swam away from our safe shore,
you followed from far off, your stealthy oar
raised, ready to ferry me home
if the lake tried to keep me.
Now I watch the tides of your body

pull back from the hospital sheets.
"Let it go," you said. "Let it go."
My heart is not afraid of deep water.
It is wearing its life vest,
that invisible garment of love
and trust, and it tells you this story.

KEITH WALDROP
(1958)

Transparent Like the Air

spirits love
houses and also

certain exemplary places

(such as the rotten
pilings off
India Point)

without necessarily controlling
the intervening spaces

they are nothing

they have not returned

(a primitive
sign meaning "neither . . . nor")

they do not
need to return I am
still here I

can bear only
the figures light
delineates not
the light itself

(unstable, un-
determined, in a
state of final ruin where
ontology seeps in)

clear things
with dark
addresses

certain stones give
birth to other stones

(bodies we label
heavy) some

split into thin
flakes tightly
embedded a

liquid

petrified

animals
fallen down shafts the
marrow of their bones

frozen to this
selfsame

stone
(opaque

and then the flash
of a bird's wing) I

go down the column

X. J. KENNEDY

(1959)

To Dorothy on Her Exclusion from the Guinness Book of World Records

Not being Breedlove, whose immortal skid
Bore him for six charmed miles on screeching brakes;
Not having whacked from Mieres to Madrid
The longest-running hoop; at ducks and drakes
The type whose stone drowns in a couple of skips
Even if pittypats be counted plinkers;
Smashing of face, but having launched no ships;
Not of a kidney with beer's foremost drinkers;

Fewer the namesakes that display your brand
Than Prout has little protons—yet you win
The world with just a peerless laugh. I stand
Stricken amazed: you merely settle chin
Into a casual fixture of your hand
And a uniqueness is, that hasn't been.

Old Men Pitching Horseshoes

Back in a yard where ringers groove a ditch,
These four in shirtsleeves congregate to pitch
Dirt-burnished iron. With appraising eye,
One sizes up a peg, hoists and lets fly—
A clang resounds as though a smith had struck
Fire from a forge. His first blow, out of luck,
Rattles in circles. Hitching up his face,
He swings, and weight once more inhabits space,
Tumbles as gently as a new-laid egg.
Extended iron arms surround their peg
Like one come home to greet a long-lost brother.
Shouts from one outpost. Mutters from the other.

Now changing sides, each withered pitcher moves
As his considered dignity behooves
Down the worn path of earth where August flies
And sheaves of air in warm distortions rise,
To stand ground, fling, kick dust with all the force
Of shoes still hammered to a living horse.

At Paestum

Our bus maintains a distance-runner's pace.
    Lurching on tires scraped bare as marrowbones,
It whisks us past a teeming marketplace.
    We shun life. What we're after is old stones.

Pillars the Greeks erected with a crane
    Went up in sections as canned fruit is stacked.
An accurate spear could pierce a soldier's brain
    Before he'd even known he'd been attacked.

Bright fresco of a wild symposium
    With busy whores, nude boys, a choice of wines—
("And where in Massachusetts are you from?")
    Abruptly, snowdrifts clasp the Apennines.

"Wouldn't you think him practically alive?"
    Says someone of a youth fresh out of school
Painted upon a tomb, who makes a dive
    Into the next world's waiting swimming-pool

Lunch is a belch-fest: rigatoni, beer.
    A saw-toothed wind cuts paths through flat-topped pines.
Weathered white temple columns linger here
    Like gods who went away and left their spines.

PATRICIA HOOPER

(1960, 1961, 1962, 1963)

In the Backyard

This morning a hawk plunges
straight for the squirrel at my feeder
and leaves only
its signature: blood on the snow.

All morning it circled the yard,
then dove, stunning itself
on the glass sky of my window,

and in minutes returned, braving
the thin, perilous channel
between hedgerow and house. I was watching
its path as it fell, its persistence,

and the squirrel, how it dashed
for the downspout, finding itself
motionless under the heat
of the hawk's body,

the claws in its rib cage, the sudden
tearing of wind as it rose
over the fence, the feeder,

the tops of maples and houses.
All morning it stays with me, not
the squirrel's terror, the hawk's
accuracy, but only

how it must feel to be lifted
out of your life, astonished

at the yard growing smaller, the earth
with its snow-covered fields tilting,
and what must be your shadow
flying across it, farther
and farther below.

Narcissus

Near the path through the woods I've seen it:
a trail of white candles.

I could find it again, I could follow
its light deep into shadows.

Didn't I stand there once?
Didn't I choose to go back

down the cleared path, the familiar?
Narcissus, you said. Wasn't this

the flower whose sudden enchantments
led Persephone down into Hades?

You remember the way she was changed
when she came every spring, having seen

the withering branches, the chasms,
and how she had to return there

helplessly, having eaten
the seed of desire. What was it

I saw you were offering me
without meaning to, there in the sunlight,

while the flowers beckoned and shone
in their flickering season?

MAX APPLE
(1963, 1970)

Bridging

At the Astrodome, Nolan Ryan is shaving the corners. He's going through the Giants in order. The radio announcer is not even mentioning that by the sixth the Giants haven't had a hit. The K's mount the scoreboard. Tonight Nolan passes the Big Train and is now the all-time strikeout king. He's almost as old as I am and he still throws nothing but smoke. His fastball is an aspirin; batters tear their tendons lunging for his curve. Jessica and I have season tickets, but tonight she's home listening and I'm in the basement of St. Anne's Church watching Kay Randall's fingertips. Kay is holding her hands out from her chest, her fingertips on each other. Her fingers move a little as she talks and I can hear her nails click when they meet. That's how close I'm sitting.

Kay is talking about "bridging"; that's what her arched fingers represent.

"Bridging," she says, "is the way Brownies become Girl Scouts. It's a slow steady process. It's not easy, but we allow a whole year for bridging."

Eleven girls in brown shirts with red bandannas at their necks are imitating Kay as she talks. They hold their stumpy chewed fingertips out and bridge them. So do I.

I brought the paste tonight and the stick-on gold stars and the thread for sewing buttonholes.

"I feel a little awkward," Kay Randall said on the phone, "asking a man to do these errands . . . but that's my problem, not yours. Just bring the supplies and try to be at the church meeting room a few minutes before seven."

I arrive a half hour early.

"You're off your rocker," Jessica says. She begs me to drop her at the Astrodome on my way to the Girl Scout meeting. "After the game, I'll meet you at the main souvenir stand on the first level. They stay open an hour after the game. I'll be all right. There are cops and ushers every five yards."

She can't believe that I am missing this game to perform my functions as an assistant Girl Scout leader. Our Girl Scout battle has been going on for two months.

"Girl Scouts is stupid," Jessica says. "Who wants to sell cookies and sew buttons and walk around wearing stupid old badges?"

When she agreed to go to the first meeting, I was so happy I volunteered to become an assistant leader. After the meeting, Jessica went directly to the car the way she does after school, after a birthday party, after a ball game, after anything. A straight line to the car. No jabbering with girlfriends, no smiles, no dallying, just right to the car. She slides into the back seat, belts in, and braces herself for destruction. It has already happened once.

I swoop past five thousand years of stereotypes and accept my assistant leader's packet and credentials.

"I'm sure there have been other men in the movement," Kay says, "we just haven't had any in our district. It will be good for the girls."

Not for my Jessica. She won't bridge, she won't budge.

"I know why you're doing this," she says. "You think that because I don't have a mother, Kay Randall and the Girl Scouts will help me. That's crazy. And I know that Sharon is supposed to be like a mother too. Why don't you just leave me alone."

Sharon is Jessica's therapist. Jessica sees her twice a week. Sharon and I have a meeting once a month.

"We have a lot of shy girls," Kay Randall tells me. "Scouting brings them out. Believe me, it's hard to stay shy when you're nine years old and you're sharing a tent with six other girls. You have to count on each other, you have to communicate."

I imagine Jessica zipping up in her sleeping bag, mumbling good night to anyone who first says it to her, then closing her eyes and hating me for sending her out among the happy.

"She likes all sports, especially baseball," I tell my leader.

"There's room for baseball in scouting," Kay says. "Once a year the whole district goes to a game. They mention us on the big scoreboard."

"Jessica and I go to all the home games. We're real fans."

Kay smiles.

"That's why I want her in Girl Scouts. You know, I want her to go to things with her girlfriends instead of always hanging around with me at ball games."

"I understand," Kay says. "It's part of bridging."

With Sharon the term is "separation anxiety." That's the fastball, "bridging" is the curve. Amid all their magic words I feel as if Jessica and I are standing at home plate blindfolded.

While I await Kay and the members of Troop 111, District 6, I eye St.

Anne in her grotto and St. Gregory and St. Thomas. Their hands are folded as if they started out bridging, ended up praying.

In October the principal sent Jessica home from school because Mrs. Simmons caught her in spelling class listening to the World Series through an earphone.

"It's against the school policy," Mrs. Simmons said. "Jessica understands school policy. We confiscate radios and send the child home."

"I'm glad," Jessica said. "It was a cheap-o radio. Now I can watch the TV with you."

They sent her home in the middle of the sixth game. I let her stay home for the seventh too.

The Brewers are her favorite American League team. She likes Rollie Fingers, and especially Robin Yount.

"Does Yount go in the hole better than Harvey Kuenn used to?"

"You bet," I tell her. "Kuenn was never a great fielder but he could hit three hundred with his eyes closed."

Kuenn is the Brewers' manager. He has an artificial leg and can barely make it up the dugout steps, but when I was Jessica's age and the Tigers were my team, Kuenn used to stand at the plate, tap the corners with his bat, spit some tobacco juice, and knock liners up the alley.

She took the Brewers' loss hard.

"If Fingers wasn't hurt they would have squashed the Cards, wouldn't they?"

I agreed.

"But I'm glad for Andujar."

We had Andujar's autograph. Once we met him at a McDonald's. He was a relief pitcher then, an erratic right-hander. In St. Louis he improved. I was happy to get his name on a napkin. Jessica shook his hand.

One night after I read her a story, she said, "Daddy, if we were rich could we go to the away games too? I mean, if you didn't have to be at work every day."

"Probably we could," I said, "but wouldn't it get boring? We'd have to stay at hotels and eat in restaurants. Even the players get sick of it."

"Are you kidding?" she said. "I'd never get sick of it."

"Jessica has fantasies of being with you forever, following baseball or whatever," Sharon says. "All she's trying to do is please you. Since she lost her mother she feels that you and she are alone in the world. She doesn't want to let anyone or anything else into that unit, the two of you. She's afraid of any more losses. And, of course, her greatest worry is about losing you."

"You know," I tell Sharon, "that's pretty much how I feel too."

"Of course it is," she says. "I'm glad to hear you say it."

Sharon is glad to hear me say almost anything. When I complain that her $100-a-week fee would buy a lot of peanut butter sandwiches, she says she is "glad to hear me expressing my anger."

"Sharon's not fooling me," Jessica says. "I know that she thinks drawing those pictures is supposed to make me feel better or something. You're just wasting your money. There's nothing wrong with me."

"It's a long, difficult, expensive process," Sharon says. "You and Jessica have lost a lot. Jessica is going to have to learn to trust the world again. It would help if you could do it too."

So I decide to trust Girl Scouts. First Girl Scouts, then the world. I make my stand at the meeting of Kay Randall's fingertips. While Nolan Ryan breaks Walter Johnson's strikeout record and pitches a two-hit shutout, I pass out paste and thread to nine-year-olds who are sticking and sewing their lives together in ways Jessica and I can't.

II

Scouting is not altogether new to me. I was a Cub Scout. I owned a blue beanie and I remember very well my den mother, Mrs. Clark. A den mother made perfect sense to me then and still does. Maybe that's why I don't feel uncomfortable being a Girl Scout assistant leader.

We had no den father. Mr. Clark was only a photograph on the living room wall, the tiny living room where we held our monthly meetings. Mr. Clark was killed in the Korean War. His son John was in the troop. John was stocky but Mrs. Clark was huge. She couldn't sit on a regular chair, only on a couch or a stool without sides. She was the cashier in the convenience store beneath their apartment. The story we heard was that Walt, the old man who owned the store, felt sorry for her and gave her the job. He was her landlord too. She sat on a swivel stool and rang up the purchases.

We met at the store and watched while she locked the door; then we followed her up the steep staircase to her three-room apartment. She carried two wet glass bottles of milk. Her body took up the entire width of the staircase. She passed the banisters the way semi trucks pass each other on a narrow highway.

We were ten years old, a time when everything is funny, especially fat people. But I don't remember anyone ever laughing about Mrs. Clark. She had great dignity and character. So did John. I didn't know what to call it then, but I knew John was someone you could always trust.

She passed out milk and cookies, then John collected the cups and washed them. They didn't even have a television set. The only decoration in the room that barely held all of us was Mr. Clark's picture on the wall. We saw him in his uniform and we knew he died in Korea defending his country. We were little boys in blue beanies drinking milk in the apartment of a hero. Through that aura I came to scouting. I wanted Kay Randall to have all of Mrs. Clark's dignity.

When she took a deep breath and then bridged, Kay Randall had noticeable armpits. Her wide shoulders slithered into a tiny rib cage. Her armpits were like bridges. She said "bridging" like a mantra, holding her hands before her for about thirty seconds at the start of each meeting.

"A promise is a promise," I told Jessica. "I signed up to be a leader, and I'm going to do it with you or without you."

"But you didn't even ask me if I liked it. You just signed up without talking it over."

"That's true; that's why I'm not going to force you to go along. It was my choice."

"What can you like about it? I hate Melissa Randall. She always has a cold."

"Her mother is a good leader."

"How do you know?"

"She's my boss. I've got to like her, don't I?" I hugged Jessica. "C'mon, honey, give it a chance. What do you have to lose?"

"If you make me go I'll do it, but if I have a choice I won't."

Every other Tuesday, Karen, the fifteen-year-old Greek girl who lives on the corner, babysits Jessica while I go to the Scout meetings. We talk about field trips and how to earn merit badges. The girls giggle when Kay pins a promptness badge on me, my first.

Jessica thinks it's hilarious. She tells me to wear it to work.

Sometimes when I watch Jessica brush her hair and tie her ponytail and make up her lunch kit I start to think that maybe I should just relax and stop the therapy and the scouting and all my not-so-subtle attempts to get her to invite friends over. I start to think that, in spite of everything, she's a good student and she's got a sense of humor. She's barely nine years old. She'll grow up like everyone else does. John Clark did it without a father; she'll do it without a mother. I start to wonder if Jessica seems to the girls in her class the way John Clark seemed to me: dignified, serious, almost an adult even while we were playing. I admired him. Maybe the girls in her class admire her. But John had that hero on the wall, his father in a uniform, dead for reasons John and all the rest of us understood.

My Jessica had to explain a neurologic disease she couldn't even pronounce. "I hate it when people ask me about Mom," she says. "I just tell them she fell off the Empire State Building."

III

Before our first field trip I go to Kay's house for a planning session. We're going to collect wildflowers in East Texas. It's a one-day trip. I arranged to rent the school bus.

I told Jessica that she could go on the trip even though she wasn't a troop member, but she refused.

We sit on colonial furniture in Kay's den. She brings in coffee and we go over the supply list. Another troop is joining ours so there will be twenty-two girls, three women, and me, a busload among the bluebonnets.

"We have to be sure the girls understand that the bluebonnets they pick are on private land and that we have permission to pick them. Otherwise they might pick them along the roadside, which is against the law."

I imagine all twenty-two of them behind bars for picking bluebonnets and Jessica laughing while I scramble for bail money.

I keep noticing Kay's hands. I notice them as she pours coffee, as she checks off the items on the list, as she gestures. I keep expecting her to bridge. She has large, solid, confident hands. When she finishes bridging I sometimes feel like clapping the way people do after the national anthem.

"I admire you," she tells me. "I admire you for going ahead with Scouts even though your daughter rejects it. She'll get a lot out of it indirectly from you."

Kay Randall is thirty-three, divorced, and has a Bluebird too. Her older daughter is one of the stubby-fingered girls, Melissa. Jessica is right; Melissa always has a cold.

Kay teaches fifth grade and has been divorced for three years. I am the first assistant she's ever had.

"My husband, Bill, never helped with Scouts," Kay says. "He was pretty much turned off to everything except his business and drinking. When we separated I can't honestly say I missed him; he'd never been there. I don't think the girls miss him either. He only sees them about once a month. He has girlfriends, and his business is doing very well. I guess he has what he wants."

"And you?"

She uses one of those wonderful hands to move the hair away from her eyes, a gesture that makes her seem very young.

"I guess I do too. I've got the girls and my job. I'm lonesome, though. It's not exactly what I wanted."

We both think about what might have been as we sit beside her glass coffeepot with our lists of sachet supplies. If she was Barbra Streisand and I Robert Redford and the music started playing in the background to give us a clue and there was a long close-up of our lips, we might just fade into middle age together. But Melissa called for Mom because her mosquito bite was bleeding where she scratched it. And I had an angry daughter waiting for me. And all Kay and I had in common was Girl Scouts. We were both smart enough to know it. When Kay looked at me before going to put alcohol on the mosquito bite, our mutual sadness dripped from us like the last drops of coffee through the grinds.

"You really missed something tonight," Jessica tells me. "The Astros did a double steal. I've never seen one before. In the fourth they sent Thon and Moreno together, and Moreno stole home."

She knows batting averages and won-lost percentages too, just like the older boys, only they go out to play. Jessica stays in and waits for me.

During the field trip, while the girls pick flowers to dry and then manufacture into sachets, I think about Jessica at home, probably beside the radio. Juana, our once-a-week cleaning lady, agreed to work on Saturday so she could stay with Jessica while I took the all-day field trip.

It was no small event. In the eight months since Vicki died I had not gone away for an entire day.

I made waffles in the waffle iron for her before I left, but she hardly ate.

"If you want anything, just ask Juana."

"Juana doesn't speak English."

"She understands, that's enough."

"Maybe for you it's enough."

"Honey, I told you, you can come; there's plenty of room on the bus. It's not too late for you to change your mind."

"It's not too late for you either. There's going to be plenty of other leaders there. You don't have to go. You're just doing this to be mean to me."

I'm ready for this. I spent an hour with Sharon steeling myself. "Before she can leave you," Sharon said, "you'll have to show her that you can leave. Nothing's going to happen to her. And don't let her be sick that day either."

Jessica is too smart to pull the "I don't feel good" routine. Instead she becomes more silent, more unhappy looking than usual. She stays in her pajamas while I wash the dishes and get ready to leave.

I didn't notice the sadness as it was coming upon Jessica. It must have happened gradually in the years of Vicki's decline, the years in which I paid so little attention to my daughter. There were times when Jessica seemed to recognize the truth more than I did.

As my Scouts picked their wildflowers, I remembered the last outing I had planned for us. It was going to be a Fourth of July picnic with some friends in Austin. I stopped at the bank and got $200 in cash for the long weekend. But when I came home Vicki was too sick to move and the air conditioner had broken. I called our friends to cancel the picnic; then I took Jessica to the mall with me to buy a fan. I bought the biggest one they had, a 58-inch oscillating model that sounded like a hurricane. It could cool 10,000 square feet, but it wasn't enough.

Vicki was home sitting blankly in front of the TV set. The fan could move eight tons of air an hour, but I wanted it to save my wife. I wanted a fan that would blow the whole earth out of its orbit.

I had $50 left. I gave it to Jessica and told her to buy anything she wanted.

"Whenever you're sad, Daddy, you want to buy me things." She put the money back in my pocket. "It won't help." She was seven years old, holding my hand tightly in the appliance department at J. C. Penney's.

I watched Melissa sniffle even more among the wildflowers, and I pointed out the names of various flowers to Carol and JoAnne and Sue and Linda and Rebecca, who were by now used to me and treated me pretty much as they treated Kay. I noticed that the Girl Scout flower book had very accurate photographs that made it easy to identify the bluebonnets and buttercups and poppies. There were also several varieties of wild grasses.

We were only 70 miles from home on some land a wealthy rancher long ago donated to the Girl Scouts. The girls bending among the flowers seemed to have been quickly transformed by the colorful meadow. The gigglers and monotonous singers on the bus were now, like the bees, sucking strength from the beauty around them. Kay was in the midst of them and so, I realized, was I, not watching and keeping score and admiring from the distance but a participant, a player.

JoAnne and Carol sneaked up from behind me and dropped some dandelions down my back. I chased them; then I helped the other leaders pour the Kool-Aid and distribute the Baggies and the name tags for each girl's flowers.

My daughter is home listening to a ball game, I thought, and I'm out here having fun with nine-year-olds. It's upside down.

When I came home with dandelion fragments still on my back, Juana had cleaned the house and I could smell the taco sauce in the kitchen. Jessica was in her room. I suspected that she had spent the day listless and tearful, although I had asked her to invite a friend over.

"I had a lot of fun, honey, but I missed you."

She hugged me and cried against my shoulder. I felt like holding her the way I used to when she was an infant, the way I rocked her to sleep. But she was a big girl now and needed not sleep but wakefulness.

"I heard on the news that the Rockets signed Ralph Sampson," she sobbed, "and you hardly ever take me to any pro basketball games."

"But if they have a new center things will be different. With Sampson we'll be contenders. Sure I'll take you."

"Promise?"

"Promise." I promise to take you everywhere, my lovely child, and then to leave you. I'm learning to be a leader.

Hazard Response

As in that grey exurban wasteland in *Gatsby*
When the white sky darkens over the city
Of ashes, far from the once happy valley,
This daze spreads across the blank faces
Of the inhabitants, suddenly deprived
Of the kingdom's original promised gift.
Did I say kingdom when I meant place
Of worship? Original when I meant
Damaged in handling? Promised when
I meant stolen? Gift when I meant
Trick? Inhabitants when I meant slaves?
Slaves when I meant clowns
Who have wandered into test sites? Test
Sites when I meant contagious hospitals?
Contagious hospitals when I meant clouds
Of laughing gas? Laughing gas
When I meant tears? No, it's true,
No one should be writing poetry
In times like these, Dear Reader,
I don't have to tell you of all people why.
It's as apparent as an attempted
Punch in the eye that actually
Catches only empty air—which is
The inside of your head, where
The green ritual sanction
Of the poem has been cancelled.

November of the Plague Year

Unwilling to turn and glimpse the blind exorcist's face,
Unconditional suspenders of disbelief,
Back-to-Normals shop to live, drive to shop

So a busy world spins by my window again
Till buying hour stops, and night noise
Falls through the white rain and hangs there.

Sky glows red with last few searching tracer lights,
Infant tenement memories and other spectral
Mystery silhouettes, shifting in the mind

Between the first and last breaths, a blank disassembling.
Between the first flashback—a brick airshaft,
Carlight Zero diving, wartime voices distant—

And the evaporation of the tribe, replaying
The great mobilization of ghosts
In the grey area, somewhere before dawn.

How long? The shadow of a doubt moves
Across a door in the imagined dark
Of the ancient cranium, under a patriot sky.

ROSMARIE WALDROP

(1963)

Leonardo as Anatomist, Repeatedly

To raise the ribs to dilate the chest to expand the lung to indraw the air to enter the mouth to enter the lung.

He plays on a tendon, decentered, opening the lungs of his name. Deluge. Unmoved by muscle, by act of will or without. By raising hopes in a calm and elegant direction.

In the evening, fleshy excrescence dilates a point on the lower lip where it flowers in an unmistakable "no" displacing breath.

Fat extends the fin-de-siècle from dinner to dinner. Witness the joint. Of the bone which this dotted line is attached.

What if smiling expands the chest westward? Or property is threatened as an organ touches visibility, as there is no vacuum, as a pair of bellows?

To thicken the space with reverberations rather than imprint the sinewy force of pigment. To spur a feminine ending.

Rings under his eyes, clairvoyant. Otherwise unlit.

To raise the ribs to dilate the chest to expand the lung to indraw the air to enter the mouth to enter the lung.

LAWRENCE JOSEPH
(1970)

Unyieldingly Present

Near the curb beside the police lines
a pool of blood, the gas tanks of the cars

in the garage on West Street
exploding, an air tank, its out-of-air

alarm going off, pops, and is skidding.
That woman staring into space, her dress

on fire. What transpires in
a second. On an intact floor

a globe of the world
bursts like a balloon. A ceiling-mounted

exit sign is melting. Facile equivalences
are to be avoided. Hell the horrific

into the routine. Glass and metal
can be identified, not the atoms

of human ash. I set down thoughts. Sequences
of images, of emotions, dissolved

in a mass, encoded in the brain.
The depth or the width of the hatred measured?

From so high up the time it takes for those
who are falling. Is it that reality, disjointed,

cannot be discerned, or that consciousness,
disjointed, cannot discern it?

The message I am communicating,
this beam of focused energy, no, I said,

no, I am not going to allow anything
to happen to you. I summon up

in my mind a place where my thoughts will find
yours—no, nothing is going to happen to you.

An issue of language now,
isn't it? There are these vicious circles

of accumulated causation.
Irreal is the word. I know of no

defense against those addicted to death. God.
My God. I thought it was over, absolutely

had to be. What am I supposed to feel?
Images that, after that, loop in the head.

Looming ahead, in the smoke, that man
at the railing can't breathe.

I'm having trouble breathing, he says.
You saw it? I saw it. I'm frightened.

This is about—which states of mind? Solid brown
and gray, a muddy mass of debris,

of powder. There is a strip of window glazing
hanging from—what kind of a tree?

What isn't separated, what isn't
scribbled, what will not be metamorphosed,

reduced, occurring, it will be said,
unyieldingly fixed, unyieldingly present . . .

The Needle

Grandmother, you are as pale
as Christ's hands on the wall above you.
When you close your eyes you are all
white—hair, skin, gown. I blink
to find you again in the bed.

I remember once you told me
you weighed a hundred and twenty-three,
the day you married Grandfather.
You had handsome legs. He watched you
working at the sink.

The soft ring is loose on your hand.
I hated coming here.
I know you can't understand me.
I'll try again,
like the young nurse with the needle.

Happiness

There's just no accounting for happiness,
or the way it turns up like a prodigal
who comes back to the dust at your feet
having squandered a fortune far away.

And how can you not forgive?
You make a feast in honor of what
was lost, and take from its place the finest
garment, which you saved for an occasion
you could not imagine, and you weep night and day
to know that you were not abandoned,
that happiness saved its most extreme form
for you alone.

No, happiness is the uncle you never
knew about, who flies a single-engine plane
onto the grassy landing strip, hitchhikes
into town, and inquires at every door
until he finds you asleep midafternoon
as you so often are during the unmerciful
hours of your despair.

It comes to the monk in his cell.
It comes to the woman sweeping the street
with a birch broom, to the child
whose mother has passed out from drink.
It comes to the lover, to the dog chewing
a sock, to the pusher, to the basket maker,
and to the clerk stacking cans of carrots
in the night.
              It even comes to the boulder
in the perpetual shade of pine barrens,
to rain falling on the open sea,
to the wineglass, weary of holding wine.

Three Small Oranges

My old flannel nightgown, the elbows out,
one shoulder torn. . . . Instead of putting it
away with the clean wash, I cut it up
for rags, removing the arms and opening
their seams, scissoring across the breast
and upper back, then tearing the thin
cloth of the body into long rectangles.
Suddenly an immense sadness. . . .

Making supper, I listen to news
from the war, of torture where the air
is black at noon with burning oil,
and of a market in Baghdad, bombed
by accident, where yesterday an old man
carried in his basket a piece of fish
wrapped in paper and tied with string,
and three small hard green oranges.

RONALD WALLACE
(1970)

Redundancies

I've always wanted to have
backups for everything—
two houses, two cars,
two computers, two kids.
I'd have two wives, two
hearts, if I could. So don't
tell me I can't have
"the aesthetics of beauty"
as the title of the next chapter of
my life. Where beauty is
concerned, I would double
my money, have two
for the price of one.
I've never had a problem
with second chances, second
opinions. The tautology of repetition
has a certain interest, a certain
charm (Got you? Got you again?)
Perhaps it has something to do
with *being,* the ontology of being;
or *knowledge,* the epistemology
of knowledge. Let me repeat,
again: On each diurnal day
I look for some teleology
of purpose. Why not be doubly
satisfied, twice blessed?
I would make a gift of
this present. I would consider
my choice of options. I would
examine the theology of
religion, the inspiration of
breath, the optics of vision.
I would be twice
the man I am.

SmackDown!

It's all an act, isn't it?
When Love gets up and struts its stuff,
flexing its pecs and biceps,
its gaudy, improbable muscles,
we all know it's choreographed, fake.
So when the ringside announcer claims
Kid Valentine's all heart
and Captain Romance is,
and has always been, champ,
we know better. We're no country
bumpkins, we weren't born yesterday,
you can't put that stuff
over on us, we say, as we
sit back on our haunches and scoff.
But wait! Why's that tag team,
Desire and Lust, thrusting its attributes
out at us, taunting us, mouthing off?
And why is the camera now swiveling—
Oh my!—its bright eye in our direction?
We're too old for such foolishness,
we think, but—*Good Lord!*—you're
the babe in the too-tight tank top, I'm
the hunk in the red satin trunks,
and we're up out of our seats now,
all cartoon breasts & sequins,
all forearms & crotch,
all latex & spandex & pomp,
wondering just how we got here,
and who's got the script,
and will we luck out,
and get smacked down for the count?

GARRETT HONGO
(1975)

On the Origin of Blind-Boy Lilikoi

I came out of Hilo, on the island of Hawaii,
lap-steel and dobro like outriggers on either side of me,
shamisen strapped to my back as I went up the gangplank
to the City of Tokio running inter-island
to Honolulu and the big, pink hotel on Waikiki
where all the work was back in those days.
I bought a white linen suit on Hotel Street
as soon as I landed, bought a white Panama too,
and put the Jack of Diamonds in my hatband for luck.
Of my own, I had only one song, "Hilo March,"
and I played it everywhere, to anyone who would listen,
walking all the way from the Aloha Tower to Waikiki,
wearing out my old sandals along the way.
But that's okay. I got to the Banyan Tree
on Kalakaua and played for the tourists there.
The bartenders didn't kick me out or ask for much back.
Zatoh-no-bozu, nah! I went put on the dark glasses and pretend I blind.
I played the slack-key, some hulas, an island rag,
and made the tourists laugh singing hapa-haole songs,
half English, half Hawaiian. Come sundown, though,
I had to shoo—the contract entertainers would be along,
and they didn't want manini like me
stealing the tips, cockroach the attention.
I'd ride the trolley back to Hotel Street
and Chinatown then, change in my pocket,
find a dive on Mauna Kea and play chang-a-lang
with the Portagee, paniolo music with Hawaiians,
slack-key with anybody, singing harmonies,
waiting for my chance to bring out the shamisen.
But there hardly ever was. Japanee people
no come the bars and brothels like before.
After a while, I give up and just play whatever,
dueling with ukulele players for fun,
trading licks, make ass, practicing that

happy-go-lucky all the tourists seem to love.
But smiling no good for me. I like the stone-face,
the no-emotion-go-show on the face,
all feeling in my singing and playing instead.
That's why Japanee style suits me best.
Shigin *and* gunka, *ballads about warriors*
and soldier song in Japanee speech.
I like the key. I like the slap and barong *of* shamisen.
It make me feel like I galvanize
and the rain go drum on me,
make the steel go ring inside.
Ass when I feel, you know, ass when I right.
Ass why me, I like the blues. Hear 'em first time
from one kurombo *seaman from New Orleans.*
He come off his ship from Hilo Bay, walking downtown
in front the S. Hata General Store
on his way to Manono Street looking for
one crap game or play cards or something.
I sitting barber shop, doing nothing but reading book.
He singing, yeah? sounding good but sad.
And den he bring his funny guitar from case,
all steel and silver with plenty puka *holes all over the box.*
Make the tin-kine sound, good for vibrate.
Make dakine shake innah bones sound,
like one engine innah blood. Penetrate.
He teach me all kine songs. Field hollers, he say,
dakine slave g'on use for call each oddah
from field to field. Ju'like cane workers.
And rags and marches and blues all make up
from diss black buggah from Yazoo City,
up-river and a ways, the blues man say.
Spooky. No can forget. Ass how I learn for sing.
Farewell to my baby,
Farewell to my love.
The guards they taking me,
One convict in the rain.
I going far across the sea, you know,
And I no go'n' be home again.

JAMES HYNES
(1976)

"Nelson in Nighttown"
An excerpt from *The Lecturer's Tale*

Nelson Humboldt, the hero of *The Lecturer's Tale,* is a failing English professor at the University of the Midwest in Hamilton Groves, Minnesota. At the beginning of the novel, Nelson loses his job teaching composition, and a few minutes later, adding injury to insult, he loses his right index finger in a freak accident. After the finger is reattached, he discovers that he can make people do whatever he wants with the mere touch of it. At first he uses his finger simply to get his job back, but as the story progresses, he uses his magic touch to become a player in the department. Now Nelson has been deputed to rid the department of a troublesome faculty member, a faux-Irish poet named Timothy Coogan, who is suspected of writing anonymously anti-Semitic and homophobic poison-pen letters. The department's uneasy ruling troika—the chair Anthony Pescacane, a flashy postmodernist; Victoria Victorinix, a queer theorist; and Morton Weissmann, the department's last remaining canon-mongering traditionalist—have just decided that Professor Coogan must go, and if he won't jump, he must be pushed. Nelson encounters him that same evening on a street corner, and the poet, who affects an Irish accent and calls himself "the Coogan," agrees to accompany Nelson for a drink . . .

Nelson and the Coogan are drinking pitchers of dark, bitter Guinness in Slieve Bloom, an Irish bar, under the sign of crossed keys. The Coogan's known here, but they serve him anyway. There's music on a Friday night, a gaunt man on guitar and a bony, big-nosed woman on fiddle, and without leaving the booth he shares with Nelson, the Coogan shouts out a request. He sings along with the first stanza of "The Wild Colonial Boy," then weeps through the next seven verses as Gaunt the Guitar and Bony Big Nose harmonize.

"He dies in the end," the Coogan whispers wetly, halfway through the song. "But he takes the bastards with him."

Numb Nelson is chiefly aware of the room reeling. Out of the booth and off to the jakes for a piss, and the uneven, creaking floorboards rock from side to side like a rough passage from Larne to Stranraer. At the urinal Nelson's nose directs him to a pair of graffiti.

Juneau, Alaska, reads the first.

No, reads the reply, *but if you hum a few bars, I can fake it.*

Nelson considers the Unanswered Question, the one he means to ask the Coogan. If he can only remember what it is.

"Why am I here?" he asks the greasy, clammy, snot-bespeckled wall.

Back at the booth, sliding in with a hiss of polyester parka, he asks it again, "Why am I here?"

The Coogan does a classic spit take, spraying a fan of Guinness warmed to 98.6 degrees Fahrenheit. Christ, thinks Nelson, did I say that out loud?

"Well there's an intelligent fuckin' question." The Coogan belches. "I'll bet ye keep yer students in stitches, a sharp-witted fella like yerself."

"But why *am* I here?" gasps Nelson, his parka glazed in imported beer. "I can't remember."

"It's existential doubt now, is it?" The Coogan wipes his mouth with his palm. "If that's what ye want, I'll give ye existential doubt."

The Coogan lifts his glass and leans forward.

"I should've been an Elizabethan, Kinch," he whispers. "Even if it meant being a bloody Englishman. *There* were poets, by Christ. Ben Jonson laid bricks and soldiered some and went to fuckin' prison. Kit Marlowe spied and whored and died in a barroom, stabbed to death in the forehead. They were after fighting over the check, don't ye know. Now *that's* a poet's death."

He drinks, swallows, smacks his lips.

"Whereas the worst that'll happen to me," he gasps, "is I'll lose my fuckin' tenure. It's a pusillanimous time to be a poet, Kinch. I ought to be ashamed of myself."

Nelson hears a little crystalline *ping!* like the chime of a wine glass, but there's only two foamy beer glasses and an empty plastic pitcher on the table. You *ought* to be ashamed, thinks Nelson, meaning the Coogan, then claps his hand over his mouth. Did I say that out loud?

The Coogan bangs on the table with the pitcher.

"Molly!" he bellows. "Molly Molly Molly!"

The music stopped some time ago, Gaunt and Big Nose are nowhere to be seen. When did that happen? A waitress is standing a step back from the end of the table, arms akimbo.

"Who's Molly?" she says.

Good question, thinks Nelson. She doesn't look Irish, she looks Hispanic, with black hair and dark eyes and olive skin. She stands with her lips pursed, her hip canted, her little apron across her darling lap like a loincloth. Darling lap. Nelson claps his hand over his mouth. Did I say that?

"He's Kinch," says the Coogan, pointing at Nelson. "Sharp as a fuckin' knife is Kinch." He adds, in a hoarse stage whisper, "But don't ask him about his mother."

The waitress swings her level gaze to Nelson.

"Mum's the word," she says.

A breathless pause. Nelson and the Coogan catch each other's eye and erupt into laughter. Nelson laughs so hard he snorts Guinness through his nose.

"And how's that Hebrew husband of yours?" the Coogan says to the waitress.

Ping! Something swims up out of the sea of beer behind Nelson's eyes, and for a moment he can almost glimpse what it is. It's something to do with Hebrews. That, and the Coogan's shame.

"Maybe you guys have had enough," the waitress says.

"Not lately," says the Coogan, and he leans out of the booth to make a feeble lunge for the waitress's ass. She steps nimbly back and the Coogan catches himself, barely, by the edge of the table. She glances back at the bar.

"Oh Jaysus." The Coogan is nearly prone on his seat, peering one-eyed over the edge of the table. "Is he after watching us, Kinch?"

"Who?"

"The barman, ye jejune Jesuit," hisses the Coogan. "Stately, plump whatsisname."

Nelson turns to look, and the Coogan hisses at him again.

"Don't be so bloody obvious about it!"

So Nelson looks at the ceiling. He looks in his glass. He looks at his watch. He looks at the empty stage. Then, with a wide yawn, he looks at the bartender standing at the end of the bar, his hands on the bartop. A big fellow, and he's watching.

"Well?" The Coogan is nearly under the table.

"Yes," whispers Nelson. "He's watching us."

The Coogan lifts his head and ducks down again.

"O shite and onions, Kinch, it's Blazcs Boylan! The man himself!"

The Coogan propels himself out of the booth, nearly horizontal. He's all elbows and knees, bulging at all angles through his vast black overcoat like two weasels fighting in a sack. Nelson manages a more grace-ful, polyester-hissing exit, but once upright Nelson dares not take a step, because every direction from where he stands is *down*. The room wheels around him on a pivot, and the Coogan passes him once, roar-ing, then the bartender passes, cracking his knuckles. Nelson is lifted and propelled down the slope of the barroom floor on his toes. He sails out the door into the snow, skidding sideways like a hockey player.

"K.M.R.I.A.!" howls the Coogan, sailing out after him. "Kiss my royal Irish arse!"

In the bitter, frosty cold, they clutch each other for support, their single blue shadow staggering in the streetlight along the pavement, a rough beast, a hunchbacked, two-headed, four-legged thing. The freezing haze roughens Nelson's throat and tightens his skin. Is the Coogan holding him up, or is he holding up the Coogan? Is there a difference?

"Irish women," the Coogan pants. "They'll cut ye so quick yer half drained before ye know yer bleeding."

"Funny," Nelson says, trying to master the use of his feet, "she didn't look Irish."

"Black Irish." The Coogan peels himself off Nelson a finger at a time. "The worst kind. Daughter of a fair Limerick colleen and some dusky Spanish sailor washed up from the Armada, a commingling of bloodlines ye can trace all the way back to fuckin' Morocco."

"Did I mention," says Nelson, "that my wife is Irish?"

"I had a wee Jewish girl once." The Coogan stands free at last. "Speaking of Mediterraneans. A mouth like velvet she had, so. She could suck a billiard ball through thirty feet of garden hose."

Nelson's ears are pinging again, or is it just the cold?

"Why did you say she was Jewish?" he says.

"Because she *was*." The Coogan staggers up the sidewalk. "She was of the Hebraic persuasion. She was Judeo but not Christian. The fuck difference does it make?"

In slow motion, in the misting cold, the Coogan turns and swings his hamfist at Nelson. Nelson ducks in slow motion. He finds himself propped against a wall, his parka caught on the rough red brick at his back.

"There was a time, Kinch," the Coogan is saying, waving his finger at Nelson from inches away, "when teaching poetry was a license to fornicate."

He wobbles, an inflatable clown who cannot fall over.

"Every semester, another crop of virgins." He lifts his eyes to a golden past. "I'd look out over that classroom full of sweet young faces and I'd pick one out like I was picking a chocolate out of a box. It was a perquisite of the job. Like free books. Like summers off. Like a fuckin' parking space."

He sighs heavily, and even in the freezing air, Nelson can feel the brewery blast of the poet's breath.

"Nobody complained. Nobody noticed. Nobody got hurt. Twas a fair exchange. Good value on the dollar. The young ladies could tell their grandkids that they lost their cherry to a real Irish poet, and I got more pussy than Mick Jagger."

The Coogan digs his thick fingers deep into Nelson's parka.

"There once was a poet named Tim," he says,

Who whored all his life after quim.
> But the feminist crowd
> Said, "Tim, that's not allowed."
Now Tim's chances for quim are quite slim.

The Coogan's eyes have a pleading, liquid gleam, but he isn't seeing Nelson at all. Waves of the Coogan's murderous breath wash against Nelson's face, while behind Nelson's eyeballs there's a steady pulse that goes *ping! ping! ping!*

"I have two daughters, sir," Nelson manages to say, and an alarm goes off in his head. What time *is* it? Where am I? Bridget will want to know. Talk about your sharp Irish women.

"Then ye'll want to be keeping them from the likes of me." The Coogan focuses at last on Nelson. "Don't teach yer daughters poetry, Kinch, that's my advice."

He turns away, but reaches back one-handed and peels Nelson away from the wall.

"No lollygagging, Kinch!" he cries. "Off we go, slouching toward Bethlehem! March or die, Kinch, march or die."

Down darker streets away from the student bars and yuppie saloons, where gloomy industrial buildings stand behind cyclone fence and razor wire. Streetlights are half as frequent as before, and half of those are smashed. Breathlessly they enter the sickly yellow light of a nameless workingman's bar, a squat, clammy, windowless box of cinder-

block. Flickering neon signs advertise blue collar beers with blunt Teu-
tonic names—Hamm's, Schlitz, Pabst. The only heat's a roaring gas
burner over the door. Grey-faced men of indeterminate age slump in
shapeless flannel coats at the bar. Nelson and the Coogan slump as
well in one of the two booths at the back, under an undusted Stroh's
sign that hasn't been lit since Nixon was president.

The flinty bartender brooks no brouhaha from anybody.

"Glenfiddich?" inquires the Coogan, not sounding too sure about it.

"Jim Beam," says the barkeep, and the Coogan buys the bottle entire, to keep on the man's exceedingly narrow good side.

A bottle and two chipped glasses on the sticky, beer-ringed tabletop.
No more undergraduate friskiness. The giddiness of beer is over. It's
time for serious drinking, when a man can crawl up his own funda-
ment and vanish quietly, without a trace. In keeping with the dress
code, the Coogan sits red-faced in his coat, stewing in Kentucky bourbon and his own sweat.

"You hate me, don'tcha, Kinch?"

His deadened gaze. His murderous breath across the table.

"But I *don't*," protests Nelson, pretty sweaty himself in his lurid
parka. "It's the truth."

He just doesn't want this man near his daughters, and that's the
truth too. The distant pinging in his brain.

"The truth," says the Coogan, his accent a good deal less distinct than
before. "That's rich."

He erupts into a wheezing laugh, which ends only when he downs
the contents of his glass.

"Easy," says Nelson. He lifts the bourbon and tries to top up his
glass, the Coogan's glass, both their glasses, the mouth of the bottle
turning and turning in a widening gyre about the lip of his tumbler.
At last bottle meets tumbler with a clink and bourbon splashes out,
some of it in the glass.

"But you do," the Coogan insists. "Hate me. That's why you're here,
init? It's your nature, as the frog said to the scorpion. Not just you,
Kinch, but the whole useless, Jesuitical lot of ya. Morons. Vermin. Cu-
rates. Cretins. *Crrritics.*"

The Coogan begins a wet, hacking cough that goes on for some time.
Some small figure in Nelson's brain sits before a greenish sonar screen,
which goes steadily *ping . . . ping . . . ping* while the figure searches the
depths for an echo. He should have approached the Coogan that first
moment on the curb, when Nelson could have taken the poet by the

hand, man to man, and said to him . . . what? Something surfaces for a moment, then dives again into the darkness.

"Plato was the first," the Coogan wheezes. "To hate poets, I mean. Showed us to the border of his tinpot republic and told us to *piss off.* Unless, of course, we wrote him hymns to the gods and songs of praise to famous men. Otherwise, it's on your bike, paddy. No poets need apply."

Ping! Is that an echo? Something down there in the deep?

"Nobody trusts *Plato* anymore," Nelson insists, his gullet burning. Whoever said bourbon was smooth was a fucking liar. "He's phallo . . . he's phallogo . . . he's . . ."

Nelson reaches for the bottle and misses.

"But you're still after reading the bastard, aren't ya?" Coogan lurches forward. "It's the same fuckin' argument, you've just tarted it up with new jargon. A poem can't ever just be a poem, it has to *enlighten,* it has to *empower.* It must represent the Hottentots in the most flattering fuckin' light. It must transgress the hegemonific fuckin' discourse. In other words, a poem must do *fuck all,*" shouts the Coogan, "but what it does best."

His rising voice catches the unforgiving eye of the barman, but the Coogan falls deflated back in his seat.

"Beauty and truth, Kinch," the Coogan says. "Beauty and truth. All the rest is bumper stickers."

The Coogan lifts the bourbon and gauges the level against the sickly light. He holds his glass to the light as well and unerringly aims the bottle into it.

"Bugger Plato," he mutters, and giggles like a schoolboy. "But then he'd've enjoyed that, wouldn't he? The old sod."

Ping! That's something! Up she rises!

"To the ould sod," Nelson says, lifting his glass, trying to change the subject.

But the Coogan's not listening. He's swirling Jim Beam against the light, Dr. Jekyll judging the proportions.

"I'm your tamed poet," he says. "Your artist in captivity. Old Ezra was the last poet in the wild, and you put him in a fuckin' cage. After which we poets learned our lesson, and found ourselves a nice cage each and handed the likes of you the bloody key. In exchange for what? Lifetime employment and summers off."

He drinks, one burning gulp. Winces, eyes watering.

Ping! Ping! Ping! goes Nelson's sonar. Something the Coogan said has set it off, and this time Nelson thinks he catches the shape of it swimming up out of the waves behind his eyeballs. It's Pound. The Coogan mentioned that old anti-Semite, Ezra Pound.

"The pure products of America used to go crazy." The Coogan belches. "Now they do committee work."

Not to mention, thinks sobering Nelson, that crack about that old bugger, Plato.

The Coogan pours another, holds the glass between himself and Nelson and closes one eye.

"I had a member of my tenure committee tell me I was a minor poet. A minor poet."

He peers through the amber glass with one liquid eye.

"To my *face*," roars the Coogan, slamming the glass on the table. Bourbon erupts volcanically out of his glass. The bottle and Nelson's tumbler thump on the tabletop like clog dancers.

Thar she blows! Ahoy the great white whale! Nelson presses himself back in his seat, shocked another quarter inch toward sobriety. The barrel-chested bartender, his face set like old concrete, comes around the bar. The shapeless men scarcely turn to watch.

"You two." The bartender twists a rag between his massive hands like he's killing a chicken. "Get out."

The Coogan slides halfway out of the booth, stops, and reaches for the bottle. The bartender clamps him by the wrist and squeezes until the Coogan lets go.

"I paid for that bottle," the Coogan says, rubbing his wrist.

"You paid for the booth." The barman's eyes are like gunslits. "I let you drink from the bottle."

The Coogan stands, barely. Nelson hisses out and edges all the way around the massive bartender. The Coogan's eyes are full of need and self-pity, and Nelson can tell he's considering a grab for the bourbon.

"Come on," Nelson says, trying to turn him away by his shoulder.

"Take your hands off me!" The Coogan leaps back, putting the bartender between himself and Nelson. "Murderer!"

Now Nelson's stone sober. He remembers why he's here. Vita's letter is still nestled inside his parka, and for the first time since they started drinking this evening—or was it last evening?—he feels the weight of it against his heart. His finger throbs.

"That man's my executioner!" The Coogan clutches the bartender from behind, turning him toward Nelson. "He's been sent to kill me!"

"I, I, I . . ." stammers Nelson.

The bartender flips his rag over his shoulder, freeing his hands. Nelson backs away.

And the Coogan, with no one watching, snatches the bourbon from the table, breaks surprisingly nimbly around the bartender, and dashes for the door.

The barman lunges, knocking Nelson sideways and breathless. He catches the Coogan by his coat and reels him in, the Coogan's feet scrabbling against the gritty linoleum, the bottle clutched to his chest. The barman turns the poet and slams a fist into the Coogan's gut. The bottle drops and smashes. The Coogan doubles over silently and nearly falls, except that Nelson catches him under the arms and hauls him gasping and groaning, backwards toward the door.

A fine, steady snow hisses through the freezing air. A rubbled lot under a single harsh light, bordered by water-stained brick wall on one side, by darkness on the other three. Shattered concrete, broken glass, shards of tin, twisted lengths of rebar, all blurred and blunted by a thick layer of snow. Two men, one holding the other, furrow the drifts, lurching and twisting as broken bricks shift under their feet. The man in the slippery parka breathes hard, supporting his companion, his breath misting steadily. The man doubled over in the overcoat blows out pale clouds at irregular intervals. He clutches his gut with one hand, and he flails feebly with his other at the one holding him up. At last, almost by accident, he catches the man in the parka in the face with the back of his hand, and the parka lets him go. The overcoat falls heavily to his knees, threatens to topple over, rights himself with his knuckles in the snow. On all fours, hunched almost like a runner at the block, he retches, a thin, clear stream that plunges steaming through the snow.

He wipes his mouth with the back of his hand, then pushes himself back on his knees, breathing out clouds of vapor. He looks up. The man above him is lost in the glare of the overhead light.

"*Murderer,*" gasps the Coogan.

Nelson stands steady and clear-headed above him. Nelson's skin, clammy from sitting in bars with his parka on, is tightening around him in the cold like a black leather glove. Only his finger is warm. In the glaring overhead light, the snow all around, in the air, on the ground, sparkles like diamonds.

"That little wop sent you to do me in, didn't he?" The Coogan's accent is gone now. His voice is thin, he can't manage anything more than a whisper. "You're here to *make my day,* isn't that right?"

Did he? thinks Nelson. Am I? He says nothing.

"Nobody ever expects the Spanish Inquisition," the Coogan says, laughing hoarsely. He looks up at Nelson.

"You're my judge, jury, and executioner." He smiles. "Don't be so surprised. You've the soul of a Jesuit torturer, every fucking one of you. It's the hallmark of your parasitical profession. Blindness and insight, isn't that it? We're the blind bastards, and you've got all the insight. You set yourself up as little paper gods, and you judge *everybody*. You judge your students. You judge your colleagues. You judge each other's useless fucking books."

He coughs, a feeble honk lost in the cold.

"But most of all you judge *us*," the Coogan says, watching Nelson sidelong, "the poor artists, the idiot savants who create the grist for your fucking mill."

"Everybody's innocent," says Nelson, "until proven guilty."

The grip of the cold tightens around Nelson, and he can feel it squeezing his heart. He has little pity left for this poor, sodden, foul-mouthed, lustful, bigoted drunk. This man kneeling in the snow is a threat—to the department, to his colleagues, to his students, to Nelson's innocent young daughters. The Coogan watches Nelson's hand with a narrow interest as Nelson reaches into his parka and produces Vita's letter. He unfolds it, crisp and crackling in the frozen air.

"Did you write this?" His finger burns.

The Coogan glances wearily at the letter. He pinches his lapels together with pale fingers and looks away through the snow glittering through the lamplight.

"It's Pound's fate turned on its head, isn't it? You're going to drag me out of my cage and let me die in the wild. Where I've forgotten how to live." He's breathing hard, blurring his face with his own steam. "Same conniving crew of murderers, though. Pound was done in by the Italians and the Jews, and so am I. Victorinix is in on it, too, isn't she? Our own little road company Gertrude Stein. It's the one thing all three of them can agree on. Screw the poet."

His shoulders start to shake under the vast coat. He expels little chugging clouds of steam. He's laughing.

"There was an unfortunate mick," he wheezes,

Who made much too free with his dick
    An Italian and Jew
    And a lesbian, too
Gave that mick the short end of the stick.

The Coogan's hacking with laughter. Nelson refolds the letter along its knife-edge creases, slides it silently into his parka again. He can't feel his hands, or rather, he seems to manipulate them from a distance. His burning finger seems to float entirely free of him, of its own accord. Distantly, he's aware of the action of every muscle, the cold charge of every nerve impulse. He steps toward the Coogan. The snow crunches under his boot.

The Coogan starts violently at the sound, tumbling sideways onto his backside. He crawls crabwise away from Nelson through the snow, backwards across the broken field, gasping.

"You think we're arrogant," pants the Coogan, "but we're not. We're the humble ones. Always have been. Right from the start, from Caedmon on. The first poem in English, and it's all about how God creates everything. We create nothing. Especially poetry. We're only stewards. Vessels for the Word of God. That's what you can't stand. Proof that there's a higher authority than literary critics. *Agh!*"

The Coogan yelps, yanks a hand out of the snow, collapses onto his back. He looks at his hand, holds it up for Nelson to see. He's cut himself on something sharp under the snow. His blood is as bright as a flower.

Nelson pauses, looming over the poet.

"You're full of passionate intensity, Kinch, I can see that." The Coogan closes his palm, clutches it to his chest. "But hold on for a moment. Listen."

His chest heaves under his coat. He closes his eyes. He speaks.

Loss of our learning brought darkness, weakness and woe
on me and mine, amid these unrighteous hordes.
Oafs have entered the places of the poets
and taken the light of the schools from everyone.

He opens his eyes. Tears are squeezing down his cheeks. Nelson is crouching over him now on one knee. The Coogan begins to tremble.

"Where's your humility, Kinch? Only the arrogant look at all of creation and see nothing but words, words, words. The worst tragedy in life, don't you know. We are all of us in the gutter, Kinch, but some of us are looking at the stars."

He heaves himself up one last time out of the snow and digs his fingers into Nelson's parka.

"Lift your eyes, you Jesuits!" he cries. "And ask yourselves the question, what is the stars? What is the stars?"

Nelson takes him by the wrists and squeezes until the Coogan releases his grip. There's a stain of blood on Nelson's parka. The Coogan collapses full length, head to toe, as though he intends to make an angel in the snow. He's staring up into the sky, but there are no stars to be seen in the glare of the lamp, only the flakes, silver and dark, falling obliquely against the lamplight.

"Out of key with my time," murmurs the Coogan, "I strove to resuscitate the dead art of poetry." His blue lips work soundlessly for a moment. "Wrong from the start."

Nelson's on one knee beside him, head bowed. He might be praying, or administering final unction, but he looks over his shoulder and sees nothing through the faintly falling snow, nothing beyond the thick drifts over the wreckage in the yard, only darkness all around. The blows and buffets of the world, Nelson thinks, have so incensed me, I am reckless what I do to spite the world. The flame in his finger soars and he takes the Coogan by the hand, flesh against flesh, neither man feeling the other's touch, and tells the poet what he has to do.

MELANIE RAE THON
(1980)

Punishment

In 1858, the slave called Lize was hanged in Louisville, Georgia, for the murder of her master's son. I was twelve that day, and now I'm ninety, but I still see her bare feet, scratched and dusty from being dragged down the road. Those feet dangle among leaves so green they writhe like flames. I stand in the garden. The perfume of gardenias makes me dizzy enough to faint.

From where I hang, I see a woman thrown from a ship because her child don' come. She screams too loud and long. The others lift her over the rail, let her fall. They all touch her. They all say: I'm not the one. I see the mother of my mother, standing naked on a beach. The men look her over, burn a mark on her thigh. She squats in a cage for fifteen days. Flies land on her face. She don' swat them away. I see the bodies chained in the holds of ships. Each man got less room than he got in the grave. They panic, break their own ankles, smother in their own waste. They jump if they get the chance. Black sea swallow a black man. Nobody stop to find him. On the distant shore, I see a runaway stripped of his own skin like a rabbit, torn limb from limb. To teach the others. I see Abe's head. I crawl on my hands and knees, look for his ears. But Walkerman takes them. Did you see how long a man bleeds? Did you see how his head festers in the heat, no way to clean those wounds though I wash him morning and night.

Mama died of a five-day fever we couldn't break with wet towels and ice baths. She left her baby squalling with hunger. That's why Father brought Lize to the house, to keep Seth alive. My brother, four months old, still wrinkled and nearly hairless, was going to have a full-grown woman slave of his own.

Mama would not have abided seeing Lize close to her boy. Father owned more than thirty Negroes, but Mama kept an Irish girl, Martha Parnell, to brush her hair and make her bed, to wipe the vomit off the floor during the weeks when her belly first began to swell, to rock the baby during the days when she lay dying. Mama wouldn't have no nigger woman upstairs, touching her child, fondling the silver-handled mirror on her dresser or cleaning the long, light hair out of her comb.

She said they were dirty, first of all, and they had appetites dangerous to men; she didn't want Seth getting used to the smell of them. Only Beulah, the cook, two hundred and twenty pounds and fifty-seven years old, was allowed to stay in the house while Mama was living. And Beulah was allowed to care for me, to wash the blood from my scraped knees when I fell in the yard, to lay cool rags on my head when my temperature flared, to cradle me in her huge arms when I shook with chills.

Every day, Mama sat for hours listening to me read from the Bible, making me repeat a verse a dozen times, until every pause was perfect and every consonant clipped. She smiled and closed her eyes, her patience endless: *Again, Selina.* But she couldn't bear my small wounds or mild afflictions. She had no tolerance for suffering; my whimpering drove her from the room and made her call for Beulah to come with her root cures. And I was not permitted to hold the precious mirror or brush my mama's hair either. She said I was too rough, too clumsy— seven years' bad luck—I brushed too fast, only Martha Parnell did it right: *Yes, Martha, that feels nice.* I hid in the shadows of the doorway. *Yes, like that, good girl Martha, just another hundred strokes.* Mama's honey hair caught the light, shot back a thousand sparks of gold fire. Martha said, "My mam told me the angels have yellow hair, Missus." She stopped to press the silken strands to her mouth and nose, forgetting Mama could see her in the mirror. "Stop that," Mama said, "I don't have time for such silliness." Martha raised the brush, gripped it like the stick she'd used to beat the stray dog in the yard, but she brought it down gently, brushing again—a hundred strokes, just like Mama said—before she coiled that angel hair into two thick braids and pinned them tight, high on Mama's head.

Martha couldn't make Seth take the bottle after Mama died. She was a spinster at twenty, a girl who never ripened, her hips narrow as a boy's and bone-hard, her breasts already shriveled before they'd blossomed. Her body offered no comfort to man or child. Father cursed the sight of her, abused her for the foolish way she cooed at the baby, making him cry harder till he was too hoarse to wail and only squeaked. She dipped her finger in warm milk, but Seth was not fooled. Only Beulah could soothe him, holding him on the great pillow of her lap, quieting him with hands so fat and smooth she seemed to have no bones. She gave him a bit of cloth soaked with sugar water. He suckled and slept. Still, my father's only son was starving; that's what drove him down to the slaves' quarters, looking for Lize.

The man come to the shack. He say, my boy's hungry. He pulls my dress apart at the neck, looks at my breasts like I'm some cow. He say, looks like you got plenty to spare.

Secretly I was glad to hear my father rail at Martha Parnell, calling her a worthless dried-up bit of ground, threatening to send her scrawny ass back to Ireland if she didn't find some way to make herself useful. At my mother's funeral, she tugged on my braids and hissed in my ear, "Looks like you're no better'n me now, Miss Selina. Nothin' but a motherless child with no one but the devil to keep her safe from her daddy. Don't I know. Eight of us. Mama and the ninth dead and me the oldest. Just you watch yourself, little girl, and lock your door at night." My lack of understanding made her laugh out loud. People turned to stare. When Father caught my eye, my face burned, blood rising in my cheeks as if I'd just been slapped.

Martha's only pleasure was bringing sorrow to others. Her lies cost Abe his ears. Mama was nearing her sixth month when it happened. She yelled when a door slammed too hard, fretted when the heat got too heavy—she was a walking misery, despising her own bloated body, its strange new weight, its hard curves. When Martha claimed Abe cuffed her jaw and shoved her down, Mama's judgment was swift and cruel. He was going to be an example. "Can't let these boys get above themselves," she said.

I pleaded for mercy. Martha was always calling Abe, telling him to fetch her some water, fetch her some eggs. One day she'd say, "Help me move this rockin' chair, Abe." And the next day, she'd make him move it back to where it had always been. She ran her fingers through her dry, colorless hair; she batted her stubby eyelashes and never thanked him.

I knew she led him into the grove, looking for mushrooms, she said; but as soon as the trees hid them, she grabbed his wrist and pushed her face against his, mouth wet and open for the kiss he would not give. Scorned gentleman, proper husband of another woman, he knocked the girl to the ground and fled.

Spitting blood from her bitten lip, Martha came complaining to Mama. False and fearful, she whispered she was lucky to have her virtue intact. "Just think what he might'a done if I hadn't kicked him and run."

No one truly believed her, not even Mama, and least of all my father. Still, the orders were given. Three other slaves held Abe down in the barn, and old Walkerman, Father's overseer, took a knife to Abe's head. His howls filled the yard. The green twilight pulsed with the throb of his veins. I sat on the porch, racked by dry sobs. Mama said, "Quit that fussing. It's for your own good. If he thinks he can get away with slapping Martha, maybe he'll go after me next—or you. Slaves must be obedient to their masters on earth, with fear and trembling, just as we are obedient to the Lord," she said. "I want you to find that passage and memorize it for tomorrow's lesson."

Father gave me a swat to the back of the head. He said, "What would people think if they heard you crying over some nigger boy, Selina?"

In the barn, a man lay facedown in his own sticky pool of blood. On the veranda, Father kissed Mother's radiant hair, sat down beside her and laid his hand on her belly. "My son," he said.

"I can't make that promise," Mama told him.

That night I stood at my window and saw my father run toward the grove, a bundle in his arms. His high black boots caught the moonlight, flashed in the dark. I followed him deep in the trees. Limbs snagged my hair; shrubs tore at my dress. I saw the girl-child, naked on the ground, saw him raise the shovel, heard the dull crack, metal on bone, a pumpkin cleaved open to spill the seed. My father dug a shallow grave for my sister. She was small enough to hold in his two broad hands, but he let her drop, unwanted runt, the shoat that will starve because it's weaker than the rest, so you kill it and call yourself merciful.

When I woke, the image hovered between dream and memory. I too prayed my mother's child would be a son.

I saw Abe chopping cotton in the fields, his skin so black it blazed blue at noonday. For weeks he wore a bandage around his head, and I pretended his ears were growing back, that when he unwrapped himself in the evening, he could feel the first nubs, and soon, very soon, the whorls would bloom to full size, firm in the curves and fleshy at the lobes, perfect ears. I touched them in my sleep, peeled away the crust of dried blood, pressed my lips to the fine lines of his scars until they disappeared. I clambered to the edge of sleep to wake hot and tangled in my sheets, my hair damp with sweat, my chest pounding. *Yes, I was the one he hit; yes, I was the one who told.*

After Lize came, my brother ate day and night. He shrieked if she set him down. She couldn't go to the toilet alone or wash her face without bouncing him on one hip. If she tried to talk to Beulah while she nursed, he'd start to whine and then to wail. He needed every inch of her and every breath. Mama hadn't had enough milk for him. After months of hunger, he was determined never to want for anything again. He seemed to know his power already, four-month-old master, king, little man. Green-eyed Lize, flesh-full from cheek to thigh, gave him her body and did not complain.

Lize, I do not believe you loathed my brother. You showed a certain kindness toward him, and fed him well. Soon he grew fat. His fine white hair fell out in patches and the hair that grew in its place was coarse and dark, glossy as my father's hair.

Sounds new to me rose out of the night air. Whippoorwills repeated their own names, a sleepless dirge; the wings of insects clicked and buzzed, a swarm in the yard, hissing in the dirt. Even the earth carried a sound, a distant stamping, a thunderous herd of wild horses.

Abe call at my window. I say, go away. I say, havin' no ears ain't bad enough? You want to die too? But he keep callin' so I go down. He tell me, the boy don't eat. He say, won' take no milk-wet finger. Your own baby gon' die, Lize, and you lettin' some white man's child suck you dry. He cryin' there in the bushes like some fool. I say, what you want me to do? I say, that white boy shake the house with his screamin' if I go. Your baby get one good meal 'fore we all dead.

Later, there were other sounds. One night, before I learned to hide, before I learned to pull the blankets over my head and press my palms against my ears, I heard a muffled cry in the kitchen and crept down the back stairs, shadow of myself.

The man pushed me up on the table. He slap me when I yell. One smack break my nose. Nobody notice bruises on a black-skinned woman, that's what he think. He say, why fight? I never knew no nigger woman who didn't like a white man better'n her own kind. I close my eyes. He don't take too long.

I stood mute, though I saw her skirt bunched up around her waist, and my father's pants dropped to his knees. His black boots were dull and brutal in the dim light, but the pale globes of his buttocks made him ridiculous, a child caught pissing in the woods, his tender flesh exposed.

I remembered my mother's caution, her voice in my skull: *A nigger woman's appetites are dangerous to men.* And I believed, because she spoke to me so rarely. *God is light. In Him there is no darkness.* Still I was afraid, hearing Martha Parnell whisper: *Nothin' but a motherless child with no one but the devil to keep her safe from her daddy.* The son of Noah saw his father drunk and naked and did not turn away. So Ham was cursed, forced to be a slave of slaves to his brothers—because his brothers were good, because his brothers walked backward to their father and covered his nakedness without looking. *Read it again,* Mama said, *slowly Selina, open your vowels.*

The morning I woke with blood on my sheets, I wept half the day, until Beulah came to me, held my hand between her two soft hands, and explained the life of a woman to me. Later she laughed with Lize in the kitchen, shaking over the joke of me, mouth wide, pink tongue clicking: *Silly white girl, cryin' over a bit of blood,* and then, the terrible words again: *Motherless child don' know nothin'.*

Fool or not, I stole a knife from the kitchen, hid it under my pillow, slept with one eye open.

I heard the table scrape across the floor, heard my father cuss. No one was laughing now. I scuttled down to the bottom of my bed and buried myself beneath the heavy blankets. I almost wished to smother, to have him find me there in the morning and repent.

Abe came to me that hot night. I was blue-veined and pale. In the grove, I knelt beside him and touched his dark back, making his muscles mine. I laid my hands on his chest, drained him until my skin was black and he turned white and woman in my hands.

They bury my boy 'fore I know. I go down to the shack. Don' wake nobody. Don' want to see the husband all weepy eye, ear place bloody I know 'cause he pick the scabs when he not thinking. I find the heap of ground. I dig in the loose dirt. Don' take me long, be not bury deep. I hold my baby next to my naked breast. Eat, I say. I wipe the dirt from his eyes, dig it out of his nose and ears, pull a clot from his mouth. He smell bad and I cry and cry but I don' make no sound. I say, God, You ain't nothin' but a dark horse stamping on my soul.

My brother's tiny coffin had flowers enough to drown him: gardenias and orchids, lilies so white I was afraid to stare, afraid my gaze would stain them. The gravestone was twice the size of Seth, its four carved names too great a burden for a six-month-old boy to bear.

When they come lookin' for me, I don' tell no lies. I say, I smothered him between my own breasts. He beat and beat at me with those tiny fists, but I hold him tight till he go limp in my arms. I hold him tight, then I put him in his basket, rock him all night.

Lize, I condemned you for the murder of my brother, execrated you for your bold confession when lies might have kept you alive. You were dangerous to men in ways my mother never dreamed. *What fellowship has light with darkness?* Devil in a woman's shape, you kept me pure, but I thought you deserved to hang, unnatural woman, I'll say it plain: death for death, justice simple and swift.

I never risked my father's curse, never spoke of the ring of bruises on your wrists the day you died or the scratches on my father's face, though I knew well what these signs meant.

At dusk, Abe cut her down, lifted her in his powerful arms as if she weighed no more than a child. Beulah followed, her face a map of sorrow, rivers of blood in the lines of her cheeks, broad forehead a desert to march, bodies laid out in the sun, mountains to rot behind her eyes.

In the shack, the women washed the body in silence, no sound but the wringing of rags and drip of water. They rubbed her until her skin shone, until her feet were beautiful and clean, toes dark as polished stones. They dressed her in white, wrapped her hair in gauze, folded her hands across her chest.

At nightfall the keening of women rose from the shack. Their moans raised Lize up to the arms of God and He took her, begged *her* for forgiveness—poor, betrayed murderer.

The cicadas screamed in the heat of day, the buzz of their wings a wild cry. A constant, rising hum and hiss swelled in waves, a torrent surging through the endless days of summer. In the morning, I'd find their shells belly-up on the steps, a horde that had tried to invade the house each night, and each night failed.

The cotton fields steamed. All day the Negroes chopped, backs stooped, knees bent. All day they coughed, choking on cotton dust. When they stood to clear their lungs, Walkerman cracked his whip, crippled them with a shout. Even the women with bellies bulged enough to burst worked until the sun struck them down and they had to be carried to the shade. Walkerman waved salts under their noses. If they woke, he put them back to chopping until they fell again.

My father festered, grew foul with self-pity. The best part of him, his beloved son, was dead. The sound of his boots on the porch scattered us like mice, sent us all skittering to separate corners of the house. At night, he paced the hallway, and I tossed, gripping the knife whenever his shadow darkened the line of light at the bottom of my closed door.

Martha Parnell still owed Father five years for her passage to America, but in August he sold her time to Walkerman for a single dollar. In the first month, she lost three teeth to his fists, paying at last for Abe's ears. By the fifth month she was swollen up like a spider, her great load teetering on spindly legs. As soon as one child stopped suckling, another began to grow. Her third pushed at her dress when the war started and Walkerman and my father went off to fight.

Walkerman never did come home. Even his body disappeared, was buried with a dozen others in a common grave or left to rot on the road, bloated and black with worms. Martha was free but had no money and nowhere to go. She stayed long enough to see my father's fields scorched, long enough to see the fine house fill with dust and start to crumble. One day she told me she was going to find Walkerman. I imagined she felt some misguided sense of devotion and wanted the father of her children to have a Christian burial. But I was mistaken. "Have to be sure the bastard's really dead," she told me.

My father lost his legs and his mind in that war. I nursed him for ten years, saw his nakedness daily and could not turn away as the good sons of Noah had. His chest shrank, his eyes fell back in his skull, his hair turned white and fine as a child's. Only his hands were spared. Huge and gnarled, they flailed at the air, cuffed me when I came too near, clutched me in his fits of grief. When he wept, he did not call to Seth or my mother. No, he mourned only for his own legs, kept asking where they were, as if I might know, as if I had hidden them.

Though I knew he could not stand, sometimes I saw him at my bedroom door. His boots gleamed. "Touch me," he wheezed, "I'm cold."

To save what little money I could for train fare to Chicago, I buried him in a four-foot box and marked his grave with a wooden cross. The big man fit in a boy's coffin, and I believed I had nothing left to fear.

I fled the South to take a job as a teacher at a Catholic school. Father would have detested me for that: tasting their bread, drinking their wine, letting it turn to body and blood in my mouth. My constant sins were the lies I told, pretending to be Catholic. Mornings I woke at five to pray. At each station of the cross I murmured: *Hail*

*Mary, full of grace. The Lord is with thee. Blessed art thou among women.
And blessed is the fruit of thy womb, Jesus.*

In the chill of those lightless winter mornings, I almost believed in this God who could change Himself to human flesh and die for me. But alone, in my room, the prayers that rose in my heart called out to another god. There were no crosses, only the leafless trees beyond my window.

All these years I have lived in one room, cramped and dim, a place I chose because it did not burden me with spaces to fill. There were no hallways to swarm with drunken soldiers, no parlors to become hospital rooms for the one-armed men, no banisters to polish, no crystal to explode against the wall when my father raged, no trees near enough to scrape the glass with frenzied hands, no scent of gardenia in the spring to make me sick with memory.

Still, there was room enough for my father, withered in my daydreams, spitting gruel back in my face when I tried to feed him, but tall and thick through the chest at night, stamping with impatience, his boots loud as hooves on bare wood. There was room for my brother, his puling cries when he was hungry, and then, his unbearable silence. And there was always room for you, Lize. For seventy-eight years I have watched you hang.

My brother and I were the last of my father's line. Your blood spilled on the ground and flowed like a river to the sea. Ours dried in my veins. You died for my silence. Untouched by a man, unloved by a child, I never mourned the slow death of my body, but now I see this is your just revenge.

All day she sways in the wind, her body light with age. By night she roams the streets. Her bare feet leave no mark in snow. I have seen her often and prayed she would not know me. Tonight, I duck into an alley. Garbage is piled high; the shadows are alive, crawling with rats. Lize follows. She has no age, but I am a fleshless woman, bones in a bag of skin. *Murderer,* she whispers. I am too frail to flee. *I see you watchin' your daddy and me.* She pins me to the wall. *You don' say nothin'.* Her knee jabs my brittle pelvis; the bones of my back feel as if they'll snap. *You kill me, and my child too.* She holds my arms, outstretched. I dangle in her grasp, toes barely touching the ground, legs weak as clay pocked by rain. *You take Abe's ears,* she says, *I can't find them.*

"No, Walkerman tacked them to his wall," I say.

You cry to your mama, tell your lies.

"No, that was Martha."

Whitewoman, you all look the same to me. You all kill us with desire.

I crumple to my knees, alone in the alley. "I never touched him," I say "only in a dream." The wind whistles down the canyon of brick, repeating Lize's last word. I sob between two garbage cans. The smell is sweet and foul, gardenias rotting in the heat, but I am cold, so cold.

I curl into a ball, tight as a fist, small as an ear. The snow is falling. Rats sniff my ankles and scurry away. I am not even food enough for them. Voices hover. Hands stroke my face, hands softer than my mother's hands, fingers tender as Beulah's—Mother never touched me that way. Soon enough the voice is human. The hands shake my shoulder, call me back from the dead.

"Honey, what you doin' in this alley? You lose your way?" The woman's dark face is close to mine, her breath warm with whiskey. "Let Ruthie help you, honey," she says. "Tell Ruthie where you live."

At first I am afraid, Lize. I think it is you in disguise, come back fat as Beulah to torture me again. But no, this woman knows nothing of my crimes. She is condescending and kind. In her eyes I am harmless, my white skin too withered to despise. She helps me find my way home, half carries me up the stairs, sets me in my chair by the window and covers my legs with a blanket. She asks if she can heat some soup, but I say, "No, please go."

From where I hang, I see all the brown-skinned children. You think your death can save them? Your father's blood runs dark in the veins of my children. Your father's blood clots in the heart, bursts in the brain. Your father's blood destroys us all again and again.

"Forgive me," I whisper. The fog of my breath turns to frost on the windowpane. Chill has turned to fever. I cannot kneel or stand, so I sit at my window and wait.

Listen, Lize, I am a desiccated shell of a woman, a cicada you could crush with one step. Put your weight on me, and be done with it. I am old enough and prepared to die.

She does not answer. Her eyes are always open, bulged and blind. She never looks at me. At dusk, Abe comes and cuts her down. I follow her all night, calling her name down unlit alleys. I hear her breath when she stops to rest. But she is a cruel god, she who becomes flesh only to be crucified again and again. At dawn, I am still alive. At dawn, Walkerman ties a noose. Everywhere the silent snow is falling, melting on bare trees until their bark is black and shiny as wet skin. Soon, the men will drag Lize down the road, haul her up, and let her fall. I will see her wrists tied, her blouse torn; I will see her bruised and battered feet. And I will sit, just as I do now, mute witness to her endless death.

Terra Form

Elizabeth woke too early again on Saturday morning. She sat up, opened the curtains and looked out. It was a bright day in early spring. The branches of the maple tree in the front yard were shocking against the white house across the street. Beyond the white house were fir trees and soft blue sky. Each thing—tree, house, fir trees, sky—was defined and distinct according to the elegant and beautiful character of this planet. But to Elizabeth they seemed undifferentiated: a single vast organism breathing slowly and deeply outside her window, as dense as her own body, full of tissue, blood, bones, all the tiny things you can't see that keep everything going. She felt like a space traveler staring out of her capsule, an invader blind to her own world. She closed the curtain.

Elizabeth was pregnant. She was only six weeks pregnant but still she felt it powerfully. She felt like an hourglass being crazily tipped back and forth, except instead of sand the glass was filled with homunculi, all screaming and clawing and holding each other for balance—some bravely trying to assist the others—as the glass swung top to bottom. She was 42 years old and she had not expected to get pregnant. For most of her life she hadn't wanted it, not one bit. There were certain terrible moments when she wasn't even sure she wanted it now, and this morning was turning into one of those moments.

It was as if there was a tiny, faceted sensor in her brain that stored terrible information where she wouldn't have to think about it—except that her unstable system had triggered an alarm and the sensor gone crazy, sending an unbroken shriek of warning in the form of grotesque images, each surging into each other with the sickening truth of dreams:

A starving polar bear collapsed on its side, so emaciated it looked more like a dog than a bear. The sun had gotten too hot too fast and melted the ice it hunted on. It lifted its head and let it fall again. Five-year-old girls grew breasts and pubic hair because of pesticides that mimicked estrogen. Parents gave them drugs that produced symptoms of menopause and then had to take them to therapy in order to cope with their emotions.

Millions of Africans died of AIDS, leaving millions of orphaned children. A magazine printed a photograph of a dying African woman. She lay in an empty room on a cot covered by a piece of cloth. Her skeletal body was exhausted by its slow descent through layers of suffering, and her eyes stared up from the pit. But her spirit came up through her eyes in full force. Her spirit was soft and it was powerful, and it could hold her suffering, and it would stay with her until she fell into darkness.

Thousands of Americans died of AIDS too. They also died of diet drugs, liposuction and anorexia. Their pictures were in a magazine too. They were smiling from wedding photos, school yearbooks, family albums. Their eyes were bright with happiness and want; one woman looked nearly out of her mind with happiness and wanting of more of it, and terror of being without it. "I'd rather die than be fat!" cried a nineteen-year-old anorexic. And then she died.

Elizabeth's heart pounded. She groped over her night table for the packet of crackers she kept there to calm her stomach. The salty biscuit was dry in her mouth, and she had drunk the water she had put on the table the night before. Muttering irritably, she rolled from bed and went to the bathroom to drink from the tap. She bent over the sink and slurped the cold, faintly metallic water running sideways into her mouth, visually tinged with the tiny toothpaste flecks on the faucet.

She remembered the first time he had said it: "I want to make you pregnant." They were fucking, and the words opened a scalding pit in her imagination. He wanted to see her breasts swell with milk, he wanted to feel her giant belly from behind. She pictured herself swelling, straining until her body showed its fleshy seam, slowly bursting, screaming as she broke open. Her mind abject before her body, her words dissolved, her personality irrelevant. They had made it a fantasy of abjection, sometimes his, sometimes hers. They made sounds of pretend abjection, grunts and bestial moans, making fun and playing. Except that something earnest and yearning started creeping into the sounds, then something fierce, like a roar—and then it had happened for real.

She stood and wiped her mouth. She imagined ice plant growing over the ground with impossible speed, its fleshy leaves glistening with vesicles, growing hungrily and busily, devouring the earth and feeding it too. It was a signal from another part of her brain, saying "But wait! Look at this!" She pictured Matt pointing at the ice plant and giving a roar of triumph and solidarity. "It grow!" he would roar. "Life good!" She would roar back, they would crouch down with their legs apart, raise up their fists and jump around roaring. They did this when they were happy and excited; they did it a lot. If they were in public, and couldn't roar, they instead made faces of bestial satiety and uttered quiet grunts of affirmation.

She grunted to herself as she turned off the water and left the room. She thought of going to Matt's room to get under the covers with him and decided she wanted a snack first. She put on her thick socks and went downstairs. The curtains were still drawn so the house was dim and a little cold. She put on the tea kettle and looked into the refrigerator. She had been thinking bread and cheese, but when she saw the tinfoiled remains of the Chinese food they'd had the night before—crispy Peking duck!—she began to salivate. She took out the container and peeled back the tin-foil; the crisp, fatty meat was irresistible. She got herself a glass of cranberry juice for sweetness, poured salt on the meat and sat at the kitchen table eating crispy duck with her fingers in a trance of pleasure. She felt like she had when she was eight years old and had for some reason come home from school a few hours early and found that her mother wasn't home. Because she was alone, she got a chicken drumstick from the fridge, salted it and ate it while watching cartoons on TV. It was a wonderful sensation of independence and solitude and salt.

Then came her family, crashing in. Her father a boiling tumbleweed, her mother a wet amoeba of love, her sister a geyser of pain squeezed off with a tourniquet of madness and will. When people asked her to describe her family she said, "They're like people who've been sent on a camping trip with a tent and no stakes." What she meant was, there wasn't anything wrong with them; she always thought that if they could be placed in a more congenial enviroment—say, in another solar system where they would not be bound by the personality requirements and bodily structure of human beings, they would do extraordinarily well. Somewhere, for example, where you didn't need a tent.

She especially thought this of her sister Angela: a beauty at nine, with a tender mouth and huge gray eyes full of gravity and joy, she was obese by age fifteen, with the affectless face of a wood totem. The story Elizabeth always told: When Angela was in high school, a psychologist came to visit her science class in order to demonstrate psychology to them. He gave each student a deck of cards and told them to arrange them in a pattern, so that he could explain what the patterns meant at the end of the exercise. He went around the class, analyzing everyone according to their card pattern. When he came to Angela, he stood and frowned. "What did you do?" he asked her. She could not tell him. He re-shuffled her cards and told her to do it again. She did, repeating the pattern. He shook his head. "I have never seen anything like that before," he said, and then went on to the next student. The teacher made a face. "It figures," she said.

The physical flavor of crispy duck ran together with the emotional flavor of her sister and her handful of unwanted cards; pain with sweetness. Memories came to her like several different tastes all at once, hard to sort. She remembered lying on the thin maize carpet of her childhood home, feeling the furnace make the floor hum slightly as the warmth came up through it. It was like feeling her mother's body through her sweater. One Thousand and One Strings was playing on the stereo. Listening to One Thousand and One Strings felt like flying through a peaceful sky filled with light, limitless yet absolutely safe. It made you picture everything moving outwards in an endless, revelatory triumph. She put her face down eye-level with the floor; the small house grew vast, and the thin maize carpet became a happy traveler, live as a rippling field in a Technicolor movie, rambling through the bedrooms, the living room, Daddy's private room. The music was all smooth, like pudding in the mouth, and the carpet was rough and nubbly, with bare patches and lumps under the legs of Grandmother's table. She got up on the couch and lay against Mama. Mama was rough and nubbly too, with tiny watery noises in her stomach, and secret voices all trying to talk to Elizabeth while Mama listened to music and read her magazine. Her mother didn't know about the voices, even though they were hers. They said things without words, and because we live in a world of words, nobody listened and because nobody listened Mama forgot about them herself. But Elizabeth was new in the world of words; she had recently come out of her mother's body, and she couldn't help but listen. The voices saw this, and they reached for her.

Some of the voices were sad and scared. Others were gentle and intrepid as the sky in One Thousand and One Strings. Some were all rage, like a flailing ax, rage at everything, including Elizabeth. Others were delighted and loving, like children themselves, wanting to play. Some were a hole of need, a hole made of sucking, tactile voices that clutched at Elizabeth and tried to pull her in. Elizabeth was afraid of the voices; they were a tangled knot she did not want to get lost in. So she went past them, whistling and looking straight ahead like a traveler in a haunted place. She sent her attention further down, searching for the solid thing underneath them all; her mother's furnace, running deep inside her, sending warmth and power and blind, muscular love.

Elizabeth sat in her cold kitchen, six weeks pregnant with a faint acrid nausea in her mouth. She heard another voice, a voice inside her now, the sound of her sister screaming. Angela had screamed at night and was told to shut up, to stop being a baby. They did not realize that she had spinal meningitis. When they finally did realize it, they took Angela to the hospital, where she screamed for mama not to leave while mama waved good-bye.

Now Angela was thirty-eight, and her voice sounded like a scream had gotten stuck in it. It was jagged and too bright except when it sounded half-dead. She'd been on welfare since she'd gotten fired from a chain pharmacy for stealing drugs, moving from one SRO hotel to the next. She came in and out of their lives like a figure in a dream, calling from pay phones to ask for money. Except for the previous year, when she had been hospitalized after a stroke bashed in one side of her face and made her walk with a limp. Then they knew where she was, and went to visit her. Their mother tried to get Angela to come live with her but Angela said she preferred her freedom.

Angela had been overjoyed to hear that Elizabeth was pregnant. "I think its really going to ground you," she said. Then she paused and Elizabeth heard her through the pay phone, working for breath after the long sentence.

"She didn't feel the furnace," thought Elizabeth. "That was the problem. She got lost."

She put away the food and headed up the stairs to Matt's room.

Probably their friends wondered about their having separate bedrooms; possibly some of the married ones envied the arrangement. It had been a condition of their moving in together, and Elizabeth was grateful to Matt for understanding, even sharing her special need to not have his corporeal reality pressed upon her at all times. Of course, this special need would be literally pissed on by the approaching infant, who would soon—again, literally—be pressed upon her at all times *starting from the inside*. Her first feeling about this was one of soft, blind opening, like a viscous plant efflorescing in a nature show. Then the hourglass tipped. She felt lost in the middle of her mother's voices, except that they were her voices now, a winding knot that she could not sort, yelling one thing, then another.

She opened Matt's door; he was still asleep, she could tell even though he was faced away from her towards the wall. She crouched on the floor with her hands planted in front of her and made a monster face. They liked to do that: sneak up, crouch, make a face and wait for the other person to see. She waited. He stirred but he didn't turn. She uttered a soft guttural sigh. You could deliver a baby squatting on the floor. You could fuck that way too, and once they had, him behind her. He'd said "Do you want a baby? Do you want a baby?" and there was the scalding pit. She made a noise like a cow with a hot ass. She was joking, but she was liking it too. She pictured a woman kneeling with her butt in the air, her face dissolved in want, bellowing "just give me a baby!" All the middle-aged, Pilates-trained, surgically-enhanced, middle-aged women progressing in their therapy and loaded with fertility drugs, finally letting it all out. The queen throwing her fit. She bellowed like a cow with a crown on its head, charging through the forest.

She emitted a sultry little noise at Matt's sleeping form. He lifted his head and turned, an affable dog with rumpled skin and sleepy eyes, answering her with his own noise, a doggish question mark on the end of it. She came off the floor and into the bed, under the covers with their chests touching. Even half asleep, his body was busy with the sniffing, scratching, licking, proudly trotting energy of a loyal pack animal.

"Matt," she asked, "do you remember Elsie the cow?"

"Sort of. What was she?"

"The cow on the carton of milk. She had big soft eyes and she wore a crown." Mama took the milk in from the chute in the kitchen where the milk man delivered it for breakfast. A slur of Mama in her flannel robe, moving in the kitchen.

"She didn't have a crown," said Matt. "I remember. She wore a garland of flowers." He paused. "Her husband was Murgatroid the bull."

He ran his hand down her body, slipping it into her pajama bottoms to feel the rough hair on her crotch.

"I'm in a horrible mood," she said.

He hesitated, then withdrew his hand.

"I feel like we're living in an enemy world," she said. "Or I am anyway."

"Enemy world how?"

"I'm thinking about Angela. How she was destroyed by the world."

"She isn't destroyed. We just talked to her."

"She's destroyed."

"She's homeless. She's not destroyed."

"Oh come on!"

"Anyway, you aren't Angela."

"But I'm like her."

"No, you're not. You have friends and you're able to—"

"I don't really have friends. I'm able to perform socially better than Angela. I understand the codes better. I know the ways you're supposed to arrange the cards." Matt of course had heard the story.

"What about Liane?"

"Liane? Are you kidding?"

"Well, she was your friend for awhile."

"But she turned on me." She was vomiting self-pity, and she couldn't stop it; the hourglass had turned into a carnival ride where they spin you upside-down and then make you hang there. Besides, it was true! "People are always turning on me. I've never had a real friend except Doreen, and she's in Texas. And anyway, she's crazy."

"People turn on each other," said Matt. "I've turned on people, so have you."

"I know," she said. "That's what I mean. The world is so ugly. I feel like I'm another species, like my whole family is another species and now I'm creating another one. Why? They killed my father and they're killing my sister, and those fuckers at the office would like to kill me if they could. In a primitive society, they'd stone me. Why would a baby want to be here?"

The ride flipped around again and everyone screamed. Matt was sitting up looking like a concerned middle-aged man who'd never made a bestial noise in his life.

"Beth," he said. "Your dad died of cancer and Angela, well, if she wants to kill herself, that's her choice. And what are you talking about, the people in the office? You were really liking them last week."

How to explain? She did like them, even Liane who had last month joined forces with the bitch who'd tried to get her fired. Just last week she had sat in a meeting looking at them all in wonderment; it seemed as if their discontented, ironic personalities were flimsy costumes they could barely keep in place, and that she could see beneath the absurd make-up and false noses just enough to intuit the innocence and strangeness flashing, deer-like, beneath. Even the sweet personalities seemed a garish imitation of the real, the hidden sweetness she could sense the way she had sensed her mother's purring furnace.

But now they just seemed like pigs. Even worse, it seemed like they were deliberately choosing to turn themselves into pigs made of complex masking, with entire layers made of barbed-wire and booby traps, anything to hide and pervert the tender thing beneath.

"Your co-workers are not going to stone you. You're too tough and besides, you're pregnant—once they know that, they'll cut you a lot of slack."

"Yeah, you're probably right. It'll all get better when they can ID me as one more stupid cow." She stood up. "Just a minute."

Quickly, she went back down the hall to the bathroom. A light sweat broke on her forehead as she knelt before the toilet. She lifted the lid, leaned forward and puked. When she and Angela were little and they got sick, Mama would sit with them and stroke their backs while they puked into a yellow bucket. There were no crazy voices, just her strong, warm hand. Elizabeth's mind followed the example of her mother's hand, and was gentle with her puking body.

When she was finished she felt calm, dense and heavy. She rinsed her mouth and sat on the edge of the tub. She pictured a dense, heavy demon, a creature of flesh and stone, sitting with its chin in its hand. She imagined herself inside it, the whole room inside it. Matt was there too, in another room. Somewhere in it was the office and everybody that worked there, somewhere else was her mother, making tea and watching television. They might be in the liver section, where they were saturated with bitterness and bile, or they might be near the heart, saturated with the tremendous, singing energy of blood. Wherever they lived, they went about their lives, amid the inner organs of the demon. Outside, something else was happening, but that's not where they were.

"Earth," she thought. "Physical life."

She pictured her child, the size of a fingernail, deep in her own demon body. She pictured him questing through it, as if through a living mountain, guided by a strand of gossamer, finding his way out.

She went back to the bedroom and sat on the bed.

"I'm sorry," she said. "I know I'm being weird."

"Well," he said, "I was sort of wondering. Do you want to kill them?"

"Who?"

"Like the people at work. Anybody, everybody."

"No," she said. "I don't want to kill them. But I'd like to replace them."

"With what?"

"I don't know." She considered a moment. "Maybe cartoons?"

He threw back his head and laughed, and she loved him laughing, as if her self-pity were a cartoon with a wonderful character that you liked no matter what. Now she was only half in the mucky rich inside of the demon and half in a place of light and shimmering particles. She shifted back and forth between the two places, enjoying both of them. She pictured their child, age two or three, sitting in a sunny room, rubbing both hands in finger paints, palms down, smearing the heavy paper with wonderful purple and red mud. He would like the mucky richness too. Or maybe not. He might be finicky and ethereal, all light and surface. He might think she was gross! She smiled and got under the blankets with Matt. They put their arms around each other, and each sensitive hair of her personality extended to feel each sensitive hair of his.

"What kind of cartoons?" he asked.

"I don't know. Something nice for him to play with."

"Maybe Pokemon?"

"Yeah. Maybe those."

Matt put his hand on her belly. She put her hand on his; they made soft lowing noises of herd animal recognition. She tried to recall the ice plant, but instead she got pictures of the people who'd died of diet drugs or liposuction, their eyes wanting more and starving to get it. They were made to want like the plants were made to grow. Their want was as persistent as roots through concrete, twisting and turning, finding every way to want and every way to satisfy and then wanting again. It suddenly seemed to her that if you untwisted the want, you would see a different version of the growing. If one was terrible, so was the other. Her father used to say, "I hate nature. Nature is trying to kill us, and if we didn't fight it twenty-four hours a day, it would kill us. I wish they could just pave the whole damn thing over so all you'd have to do would be hose it down every once in awhile." She smiled; her father had been funny.

"You know," said Matt. "I wouldn't blame you if you did want to kill people. I think it's pretty normal. I was thinking of killing Ted Agrew just last night."

"Who's he?"

Matt produced plays in a small theater, and the people he worked with came and went.

"The director of that company, Blue Bug. You met him, he wears ridiculous glasses and he tells horrible sex stories, like dogs ejaculating on women's faces and stuff."

"Oh, yeah."

"I imagined coming up behind him and stabbing him in the back of the neck with an ice pick."

"You couldn't do that Matt, you're too short."

"I could too!" He sat up and made the face of a retarded psychopath, one hand clutching an imaginary ice pick. "Like this!"

They laughed and pressed against each other. But this time the closeness agitated instead of comforting her, and she pulled away.

"The thing about Angela." She frowned and lay on her back. "My parents always said she was a cry-baby, and she was. But it was like, it was like she wasn't wired like everybody else and so they couldn't help her grow up. Because she couldn't receive their signals."

"Ummm!"

"That's what I mean about enemy world. Not that people are actively trying to kill her. Just that they can't recognize what she has and so it's rotting. Like Africa. It's so beautiful and its spirit is so big. And it doesn't do any good. It's dying anyway. Because the world doesn't know that spirit anymore."

They were quiet a moment. The heat came on and the vent behind Matt's bed began to ping and tick. Elizabeth considered all the things that worked without thinking; machines, plants, bacteria, bugs, the hearts of mammals. She pictured a vending machine: a waxed paper cup rattling into place and thin, sugary hot chocolate streaming into it.

"I feel it too sometimes," said Matt, "the enemy world thing. In a different way. I feel like a small tugboat chugging through hostile waters. I cast my search light up on the hill—and there's Ted Agrew's smirking face, illuminated and staring down."

"But people aren't your enemy," said Elizabeth. "People like you. You don't have these alien feelers coming out of your forehead. You have this earthy thing that makes them feel safe. They don't realize you want to stab them in the neck with an ice pick."

"Then the baby will have it too. He'll have that and the feelers. He'll have everything. And as soon as he's old enough, we'll send him to African dance class so he'll find out about African spirit."

"But it won't help if *he* knows about it, that's not the point. The world is killing Africa. It doesn't care about the dances."

Matt sighed. "You're just being self-indulgent now. The world is not killing Africa."

"But it is! That's what I'm saying. The climate that has been created by other cultures is antithetical to the spirit of Africa. Africa is being spiritually suffocated. That's why they're getting AIDS and having those wars."

"Okay," said Matt. "Okay. We'll arm the house like the Swiss Family Robinson and stay in."

"Then they'd just get us for being crazy."

Matt was silent for so long that she thought he might be fed up. She considered apologizing, but she was suddenly too tired. A cloud covered the sun; the room became soft and dim. Matt put his hand on her stomach. He sang: "Roses love sunshine / Violets love dew / Angels in heaven / Know I love you." He kept singing, except instead of words he sang soft little syllables: "ma ma ma MA ma—"

Tenderness opened inside her with erotic force. It was impossible to close herself to it. Strangely, she thought of her co-worker and former friend, the treacherous Liane. She thought of her asleep, her ovaries cycling through, making blood and eggs while her head dreamed, innocent of treachery. She thought of her own body building flesh and bone, tiny nails and teeth and an unknowable, electrical brain. She pictured Angela, holding her arms up like she was calling something down from the sky. The hair on Elizabeth's arm stood up. The eye on the collapsed side of her sister's face looked out as if from a secret, exalted place. She was calling all her hidden power from the world beyond the stroke to bless her sister's baby.

The cloud moved off the sun and a pool of light spilled across the floor, full of trembling shadows: nervous little branches, a preening bird, a flying bird, water dripping off the roof. The rippling shadows of heat and air. She imagined herself and Angela and Matt as motes of light. She imagined Christopher—because suddenly she knew his name—working his way through the warm density of her body to the light, following the cord that guided him to her. Because she wanted him. She wanted him.

LAURA KASISCHKE

(1981, 1982, 1983, 1984)

Black Dress

I could go no further than that first line:
Spring comes even to the closet.
The words like little iron blossoms on a vine.

The parks full of people under a heathery sky.
The music of silverware, of violins.
Near the road, a woman paints

the pickets of her fence with blinding light.

When Herod sat down at the dinner table, the roasted
bird flew from the platter crying, "Christ lives! He is alive!"

It's spring, even at night.
The mushrooms damply reflect the stars.

All manner of pale flesh, opened up like eyes. Moonlight

on the jellyfish. In the dark grass the startling
muteness of a child's
white rubber rat.

But the closet. Even

in spring, the closet's a blind hive. A black dress

hangs at its center—like Persephone, it's

the closet's prisoner, and its queen. *Never forget,* it sings.

I saw you then. I saw it all:

After the funeral, the riotous dance. After the wedding, the long
weeping and kneeling in the bathroom stall.

Oh, there are birds the world's entirely forgotten
(winter, amnesia)
singing again to the comings
and the goings, the bright
and empty flashes,
the openings and closings. *Sweetheart,*

I'm leaving. Honey, I'm home. But that

black dress hangs always and omniscient in its single thought, its

accumulating mass—a darkness
tucked into another darkness: where I wore it first,

and where I'll wear it last.

Clown

It was summer, and the clown had come
to the same restaurant to which we'd come
for a piece of strawberry pie.
Big white smile.
Wig of fire.

The sun had begun to set
with a piece of gold in its mouth.
There were devils in the dumpsters eating flies.
What's that? the three year old asked.
I said, *She is a clown.*

Time had begun to pass so fast I felt
as if the weekly newspaper came to our house every day, yet
I had a photograph of myself
in which I'd blown my bangs back, wanting
to have wings like an angel, or Farrah Fawcett

when what I had was hair
that made me look in this photograph
like a girl who'd lived for a while
in another century, on a distant planet.
Someday my children would laugh.

She's not a woman, the three year old said
of the clown. There were
white seeds blowing around in the evening breeze
without a plan, landing their fluff-craft in
the Big Boy parking lot, onto the hoods of cars.

A man puts a gun to your head and demands
your child, what should you do? That's
the kind of early summer night it was.
The kind of night in which, perhaps,
you have a last moment.

to look around and laugh—at
the child, and the clown, and the pie, and the fact
that if each atom could be collapsed
into a sphere no bigger than its core, all
of the Washington Monument could be crammed

into a space no bigger than an eraser.
How modest were your desires!
In the order of things, it's true
a clown is last, but all of us are futile
when it comes to want

and stupid to look at in a restaurant.

ALYSON HAGY

(1984)

Sharking

I know some fellows who believe fishing is more than recreation and more than a bad habit. I even know a dozen stand-up guys who'd rather drop line in a mud puddle than play eighteen holes at Pebble Beach. Soulmates, those guys. But I've never been one to claim fishing is the be-all and end-all. I've got a grown daughter married to a chief petty officer up in Norfolk; she and her kids are worth the sunrise to me. And the love of a woman—I mean the real skingrain kind of love—that's surely the blood equal of solitude on the water. When I drive down to the pier with my coolers and my gear and my all-night shark-radar mood, however, I don't care to be interrupted.

Now that I'm retired, I go for shark maybe thirty times a year. Big Al was the one who got me to tally my excursions; he's damn competitive that way. Still, the days when I seriously counted brook trout and salmon and tequila shots and hard-ons are pretty much behind me. It doesn't make sense to apply that kind of bullshit to snagging sharks. Sharking is primarily attitude. Like climbing a mountain to meet one of those mysterious lama monks, something like that. You got your rituals, you keep to yourself. Sometimes you hook a beauty, but mostly, almost always, you don't.

Frankie, the guy who's running Frisco Pier this season, is good about my quirks. I pay my four dollars just like everybody else only I stay out all night, even after he shuts down at two, and that's fine with him. I've never had any trouble with the help here—they're ex-navy lots of times, or ex-cons, sometimes just ex-schoolteachers happy to bum around again like they did when they were eighteen. Frankie is solid, and he'll make change for the cigarette machine if you want it. He knows I'm good for free beer, too, which pleases him since he doesn't like to sneak it from the snack bar.

On a weeknight I'm pretty much guaranteed my spot at the end of the pier, just past the utility shed. Tourists beat me there on occasion, but they don't stay. They get restless if a fish doesn't latch onto their bait after about ten minutes. Besides, Frankie tells them their luck will be better midpier where the surf begins to break, which is mostly true. He knows I like my elbow room. He also knows I'll get it—at the southern corner, best place to keep my line clear—one way or another.

I can be downright gentlemanly once my bait's in the water and the sky's gone dark and hovering. But I'm a big man, wide enough to cover the top of a Coleman cooler with one haunch. The beard, the black cap, and the smeary Indonesian tattoos give some tourists the idea I might be a biker, so they sidle clear. Others, especially those whiny-type dads trying to teach their sons to fish, they got something else to prove, some need to hang out over the everlasting end of the pier like they're Columbus on the edge of the world. So they get too close to the rods I set up to catch my bait, they tangle their lines with mine, then swear at themselves or wise-eye me like I'm some bum on a park bench. In either case, they pretty quickly leave. Sometimes because of the bowie knife I pull to cut the tangled lines. Sometimes because the babble I produce as I hunker down on my cooler, a beer in each hand, doesn't dovetail with their idea of a family vacation.

So I aim for a perfect evening. A Tuesday in early May, three weeks before the tourist season cranks up. Wind out of the north, five to ten knots. Clear sky, and Big Al is nowhere in sight. Chances are he's on the pier at Nags Head because he's a lazy coot who won't steer his ass another hour south to Hatteras Island to take me on. Am I complaining? I am not. The night's a joke when we're both rigging floats, swapping tales about the mako the charters have brought in, or the hammerheads the surfers have skedaddled from. I don't like how I get sucked into it, verbal sparring of the lowest, toothiest sort, but it's a weakness of mine. One of several.

Besides the folks on the beach, the only company I've got is fifty yards back where a lanky, careful-moving couple in bill caps and dark green work clothes are bottom-fishing with cut mullet. I like their looks. They've each got a tackle box, they hardly speak a word, their eyes are focused on the scalloped water of the middle distance. The woman's had a good day; I saw her bagging fillets when I passed by. The man, well, maybe he hasn't caught a damn thing, but I can tell by the set of his head that he'd never think of complaining. He might consider trying another spot tomorrow, or the day after, but he's too aware of his good fortune to bitch and moan. I like to see people inhabiting their fishing time like that—you know, living right in it. Gives me hope that the world may yet learn to leave us all alone.

I lay out the pieces of my rig like I'm a mechanic, or maybe a gourmet chef. The tide has shifted, but I've got an hour before I need to drop my float and there are preparations to be savored. The hook—a six-inch single barb—and the three-foot steel leader are old, though you wouldn't know that by looking. I keep things polished. I got one white garbage bag, a spool of catgut thread, 800 yards of 80-pound test on a top-of-the-line Daiwa reel, and my best St. Croix rod. The St. Croix's short and thick around as a longshoreman's thumb, looks more like an instrument of punishment than anything else. In my second-string cooler I've got a four-day-old amberjack, stinkingest piece of bait I've had all season.

So I'm at it, a heavy man working light on his feet. Stuff laid out on a pair of striped bath towels, each thing in its place. I re-oil the reel. I finger the leader for chinks or flaws. I back off and crack open a beer just so I don't rush. That's when I see her, a wisp of a woman clearing the glare of the halogen lights posted every twenty yards or so. She's got a bucket in one hand, rod in the other. She's walking that slow, self-absorbed walk, heel to toe, no hip swing, and I see exactly how it's going to be. She's going to set up in my outpost, right on my sea-splashed fang of a world, and I'm going to have to deal with it.

She stops short when she sees me, takes in the clutter of my passion and flattens her lips. In her forties, I'd guess. Too thin for my taste, but dressed practically in a yellow shirt, jeans, a pair of boys' tennis shoes. Got a blue windbreaker knotted around her waist and a bandanna on her head. She looks me in the eye just once to be polite, then threads her way around my stuff to set up in the northern corner. I can't figure right off what she's after—puppy drum, maybe—but it's clear she'll stay out of my way. I peg her as one of those edgy divorced types who like to see if they can hack loneliness in the dark.

I get back to business. Rig the pole, check the wind, blow the garbage bag up like it's a balloon and tie it off with catgut. Then the best part—lifting that vile jack from the cooler and running the hook through its gristly eyes. My homemade float will carry that sucker out with the tide a couple hundred yards before the catgut melts and drops the bait in deep water. And there she'll lay, grand and sour and available.

The waiting is the heart of it, of course. My companion knows that. She baits her own hook deliberately and without distraction. She never even looks at me, barely nods at the sightseers who wander out after their seafood and wine dinners in the village. Out of respect for her concentration, I don't holler when I drop my masterpiece over the rail. I just roam back to my cooler, spritz open a cold one, and take a gander at the stars, which make me think of the pale sky over Okinawa, which leads me to consider the slow fade-out of my marriage. No regrets. The wife and I both wrung what we could from twenty-five hopscotch years in the navy. Then she bailed to live with her sister in West Virginia. I see our daughter and grandkids more often than she does, but I'm not fool enough to think that makes me a better person.

I wonder if my lone friend in the corner has children. I watch her for a few minutes—my float is finally out of sight in the black draw of wind and water—and I make guesses at her life. No rings on her fingers that I can see, so I decide there's an asshole left behind in a good brick house somewhere, a drinker maybe, middle-aged guy scared of his own life. She's a fine person, I decide that too, though I can't quite say why she gets my vote. Then I notice the bandanna, how it folds and flips in the breeze, how it reveals uneven tufts of downy hair all over the back of her skull, and I rethink her history with the knowledge that the score has been less in her favor all along.

She'd dyed that brave hair platinum blond, bless her, a fact that nearly makes me laugh. Skinny, sick, a stubborn sense of humor—I reckon she deserves a night like this, with the timbers shivering under her feet and the wind singing off the guide wires. All the nights she wants. I watch her lean into the chest-high rail as her bait does a free fall. When she sets the line, her shoulders and back relax, and I see her hips begin to sway. One, two, three. One, two, three. It's a thing I haven't noticed before. How the rhythm of the surf beneath us, the way she hears it, has her waltzing above the waves.

Seeing this makes me restless, so I stand to check my line, which doesn't need to be checked. I'm wondering how I'd be doing in the Texas hold'em poker game at Eddie's in Virginia Beach, when I hear a commotion on shore. Hell. One look tells me all I need to know. Four or five guys have piled up a bonfire and are set to create some mayhem. I can tell they're drunk by the hee-haw quality of their laughter. Their faces are like orangish half-moons from this distance, staggering planets around a sparking sun. No problem. I'll tune them out. Which I do until a crescendo of shouting causes me to take another look. By God, I get acid in my throat then. The punks are muscling an inflatable raft into the surf, two guys clinging to the sides, and I know they're planing to row some bait into my territory and poach on my shark.

If I'm lucky, they'll capsize before they clear the surf. If I'm unlucky, they'll get out there and cross my line and cause big trouble for all of us. I grab the gut-smeared rail and shake it with my hands, wishing I had a rifle so I could pop a hole in that oversized doughnut of a raft. I don't quite swear out loud, but I hear a rattling scrape behind me and sense the woman looking at me, at my quivering temper, wondering why I'm suddenly so out of whack. She's right. *You're right,* I think. Where's my God damn poise and equilibrium?

I don't like how I feel—flummoxed, out-maneuvered—but I manage to let go of the rail.

Enough time passes for me to get halfway through a cheddar cheese and mustard sandwich. Then I hear a sound that doubles the coils in my guts and takes me back fifteen years, to when a steam pipe blew on the supply ship I was assigned to and scalded the unlucky sods working nearby. Deep pain and panic. I can't see much, just a couple of dark figures zigzagging from that bonfire to the surf, but I assume the worst. The idiot raft has gone over in the waves.

I'm down the pier in half a minute, over the rail by the snack bar before Frankie has even gotten out the door. "Call Leon right now," I say. "Get him up here." Frankie's face is thick with sleep and confusion, but he understands the important part. Two deputies with lifesaving equipment can be here in three minutes, and we might need them.

I pump my legs through sand. The first guy, arms straight out in front of him, rushes up to meet me like I'm a long-lost cousin. He's wet to the waist and shivering, though not from cold. The second guy comes in behind me like he's been up to the parking lot or something, looking for help that isn't there. They're both hopping from foot to foot, saying something about Wayne and Talbot and the raft, though it's all coming out in hoarse fragments that don't help me a bit. I don't know what I'm going to do, of course. I'm overweight and don't swim that well, regardless of my years on the pitching decks of the U.S.N. I take it as a good sign that I'm absorbing a lot of detail with Kodak-type clarity, like the fact these fellows are both wearing shirts from the University of Tennessee, though it's hard not to connect those neon orange shirts to the general stupidity of the situation.

We all three trot into the surf up to our knees. There's some shouting coming from beyond the white fringe of the breakers, but it's impossible to tell how desperate it is. The story I've got by now is that Wayne and his brother were in the raft. Then Talbot, who was fishing from shore, hooked something big and heavy, a thing he swore was a shark, and the boys rowed over to see what it was. That's when the yelling started. Maybe the raft capsized, maybe it didn't. All they know is that Wayne and his brother, who doesn't appear to have a name of his own, are wearing life jackets and both know how to swim. Talbot, who is drunk enough to worry even these two locos, decided to follow his fishing line to the source of the trouble. According to the report I'm getting, Talbot's never soaked himself in anything bigger than a bathtub.

God almighty. The first thing I say is, Boys, maybe it's best we wait for the law. Your friends will be washing up around our ankles any minute.

Second thing I say is, Do you have a flashlight?

They do. Talbot's got one with him too, though he apparently hasn't managed to turn it on. I assess the situation one more time. The surf's not *that* rough, but the current is strong. I turn on the light and, guessing at the raft's drift, hightail it down the beach about two hundred yards. One Tennessee guy stays near the bonfire to flag down Leon when he arrives; the other one follows me like a duckling after its nettled mother.

Of course I'm a hard-hearted SOB, so I still manage to think about my bait and how it's lying out there unattended, how my night's a ruin. These fellows have trifled with the ocean and with me—the way I see it, they've only got one strike left. I wade in, waves smacking at my thighs and chest. I haven't been in salt water this deep since I slipped off a dock in the Philippines, many, many whiskeys ago. Go from sandbar to sandbar, I tell myself, keep your own damn head above water while you try to pinpoint that raft.

They find *me*, of course. Two ratty-looking boys in life jackets, their long rock 'n' roll hair plastered to their foreheads and necks. One of them's got a cut-up arm, but they're safe, been trying to swim the raft in against the tide, which hasn't been easy. They look surprised as hell to see me, and hangdog grateful. What about Talbot, I ask, shouting into the wind that's picked up again, where is he? The brothers look befuddled, then a little weepy. The one I think of as Wayne, who looks most likely to have that name even in his present condition, stops dog-paddling with his free hand and grabs at the front of my shirt. Tells me I must be crazy, mistaken. There's only them two with the raft. Talbot would never come out yonder, he says. He don't know how to swim.

By now Mr. Tennessee Shirt Number One has joined us and we're set to drag that raft to dry land. Or we will be, once the Three Musketeers stop spitting and slapping fives. Talbot, they pant. Talbot, man, we got to find him. I can see a wheel of lights beyond the pier now, the tiny lighthouse flashes of the rescue van. We may get lucky, I think to myself, and be out one drunk fisherman instead of three. Tugging on

the raft is going to flare up the bursitis in my left shoulder, I'm thinking that too, when Mr. Tennessee Shirt who's stumbling beside me
says, What if a shark got hold of Talbot after he got hold of it? He looks
behind him as he says this, then back at me with eyes the size of line
spools. He wants me to tell him it can't be so.

I ask the soggy brothers, Did you all see what Talbot had on his line?
No, Wayne says, they never got that far, a breaker flipped them. His
brother, who has got the cut arm and a mustache with maybe five hairs
in it, appears relieved they missed their chance. Probably hooked a
lunker drum, I say. Naw, says Tennessee Shirt, no way. The drag was set
tight and the line played on out. Whatever he had was damn big. Tennessee's hands fly off the raft to measure just how big and his eyes are
filled with braggart's pride for his buddy until he remembers why he's
staggering through the strongest undertow on the Atlantic coast, losing his shoes to the devil's kiss of the tide. Then it's like the bones in
his long hillbilly neck have collapsed and his chin's at his chest in
prayer or cruel sobriety, I can't tell which.

Don't worry, boys, I say. He probably just snagged one of them Nazi
subs sunk offshore during the war. It won't harm him none.

Wayne snorts and sticks out his jawbone so I'll know he gets the
joke. I have less luck with his brother, who practically crawls back into
the raft to get his legs out of the thundering, ghostly water. My main
point is well-taken though: We can't do toot for Talbot until we get our
own selves back to land.

Ten minutes of coughing and dunking and we're in. Frankie's Jeep
is working its way down the beach while Leon sweeps the water with a
portable searchlight. I can't help but notice how much that light re-
sembles the Atlantic moon, slightly bluish, slightly creamy, when it
sails across these same sands on a silent night. The pier's gone dark
too, though I can't figure why Frankie thought dousing the lights
would be a help. All I know is I'm sorry I'm not up there playing captain on my black skeleton of a ship. I don't look forward to what
Frankie and Leon are going to find.

The Jeep stops about 500 yards south of where I've fallen to my
knees. I spit and wheeze salt water into my beard, allowing myself a
cuss or two in honor of lost stamina and lost youth. The other three
sound as whipped as I am but take off down the beach anyway.
They've got to get to their buddy. I admire their dog-pack loyalty. It's
part of what got me through my six-month cruises in the Pacific. Part
of what helps one man tolerate another.

By the time I limp my way to the scene, I find Leon in the posture I've anticipated, on his knees by the victim's swollen face, his movements hindered by his stiff, glowing vest and loaded equipment belt. Leon's a local boy who did four years with the Coast Guard in Oregon before getting on with the Dare County Sheriff. I know him because his dad runs a good charter boat. He looks at me, then flicks his serious eyes to a slick grayish lump behind him in the sand. God almighty.

Talbot caught himself a ray, a big one, and that's at the heart of this whole fiasco. Of course it takes a shitload of ignorance to mistake a ray for a shark, though I've seen it happen more than once, especially in daylight when a flapping wing looks like a dorsal fin to a tourist. I can just see the look on Talbot's face when his rod bent, him all wicked with drink and pride, just scared enough to get bullying. He thinks the only big, bad creatures in the sea are sharks—the dumb ass. I note he managed to foul-hook the poor thing as well, which is why Leon has brought it to my attention. I pull my knife and kneel by the ray's blunt, cowlike nose. Locate the hook by hand since it's buried on the underside of a wing, then cut it loose with a sizable chunk of rubbery flesh besides. Like most ocean critters, the ray can't make a sound, even in agony, and I'm halfway pleased about that. The noise coming from behind me—whispering, sobbing, the occasional chunk and clang of medical equipment—is plenty enough.

I ship the ray back out to sea, its five-foot span quickly buoyant in the fanning glitter of water. Tennessee Shirt Number One helps me—the ray must weigh near seventy pounds—and it's then he tells me that Talbot's still alive, passed out more from alcohol and fatigue than from water in his lungs. "They want to take him on up to the clinic in Nags Head," he says. "So I reckon they'll do that. We thank you for your help."

"You're welcome to it," I say, running my fingers through air until I realize my hat's missing, washed away during our crazy water dance. "Maybe do me a favor next time you all come down this way—" And I start to tell him to stick to trout fishing, for Chrissake, and leave the bigger game to wised-up, busted-up bastards like me. But I don't. I go back to the old rules. No judgment, no chitchat.

"Yes, sir," he says with good church manners, finishing my thought for me. And he thanks me again. I nod to Leon and his partner, who are lifting Talbot into the back of Frankie's Jeep. Old Talbot will puke in there, I'm sure of it, and Frankie will be mad as hell. It'll add an extra hoot to the story he'll be telling in the snack bar by lunchtime, however, which is worth the time it'll take him to scour his floor mats. Frankie loves his stories. I lumber off into the night as solo as can be, my body aching from skin to bone, and the last words I hear come from Wayne's brother, who's asking Deputy Leon what he knows about them sneaky Nazi subs.

She's still there, by gosh, fishing with no more company than the milky starlight. I make out her yellow shirt the same time I make out the stripes of my towels, which are still flat on the pier under the weight of extra tackle and beer cans. I wonder if she's had any luck. I wonder if she knows what happened out there, beyond her ken. I wonder if she cares. Figure I'll ask her as much after I check my orphaned line, maybe bend the rules one last time and offer her a drink. So I lift my St. Croix from where it's nestled tight in its premium corner and . . . nothing. Line's been snapped clean off. I can feel the loose filament whipping back toward my mouth, my eyes.

"I heard it run," she says, her voice smooth with the lull of an accent I can't quite place. "Went real fast for five, ten seconds. I was worried you'd lose the rod."

But you didn't pick it up? This is the unforgiving question that breaks into my mind. I take a step or two toward her, the St. Croix in one fist, my other hand lost in the salty mat of my hair as it searches for my cap.

"I watched it for you," she says, turned around so she doesn't have to speak over the sharp ledge of her shoulder. "I did that, in the time I had." I see she's no longer waltzing, and I also see, or think I see, that she's younger than I first thought. Or maybe I get that from the lack of hair at her temples. She's not joking with me, though, and she's not shy. Her words are steadily matter-of-fact, just like I like them.

"Think I had a shark?"

One side of her mouth pulls tight, and I see dry wrinkles there, etched from worry and pain. "I think you had trouble, and I'm sorry."

"Yeah. Trouble." I lay my rod at my feet and turn away. It appears I had a rare chance and it didn't stay mine. She knows there's not a damn thing you can say to a person about a time like that.

"Those fellows make out all right?" She's bent at the waist over her tackle box now, all dark legs and whispers.

"Guess so, fools that they are. They're alive."

"That's nice."

I stop wiping my face with a towel and focus on the woman again. She's standing straight, and her eyes are hard in a way I recognize. My daddy's eyes when he was rigid with angina. The eyes of a luckless yeoman crushed in a cargo bay.

She repeats herself. "That's nice. I'm glad." She wrestles every word until it comes out easy.

The world is night-watch black, and talk—even the sound of talk—is no good for either of us. I'm not going to save her from a damn thing. She's not going to ask anyone to try. I scrape into my corner, and she flips the bail on her reel and gets back to business. We stay that way a long while. It occurs to me that I'll probably never come out here without thinking of her, and knowing that is a strange sort of gift after the kind of night I've had. I'll be out here again, a hundred more times I hope, and somehow so will she, sketched darkly against land's end. Gone in body, held in memory, like we all might hope to be.

KATHLEEN HALME

(1986)

Diorama Notebook

1

The very I ants into the museum case of history—diorama, *tableau
    vivant*—
climbs the peasant girl's triple skirts and rests on the pale skin line
of her braided wedding crown, the white road of her head.
The stasis of faked history splayed in smudgeable terms.

2

North is pure delusion, snowblind and rapturous.
Peasant saints abuzz in the miasma,
the presences and outcomes of lexicons,
know how long a dog can bark.

3

Slashers and burners, escape artists, a family sick of the past,
with a name that translates: "burnt-over field sown with grain,"
"he hasn't been seen in these parts for some time."

I want to live in a commonwealth of heroes
where history hasn't lost its nerve.

4

Our matriarch never owned a pair of pants.
She won't speak English or use spoon sugar. She won't turn lights on
when the woods around her stitch up at night,
and now, she must finally leave the farm.

Whoever you are, you could buy this life-size diorama
of immigrant life for less than the price of a nice foreign car.

5

My father kept a clean-shaved face.
The week before he was to sail back home to find a wife,
he found my mother at a dance.

The accordion pleats a schodish. Lenin's portrait beams
—a new world saint behind the stage.
My father smiles as though taken by a universal spell.
My mother has saved herself for the wholly invisible.

I see them as a couple on a cake,
moving without moving
for their own sake.

6
Lard in two-pound coffee cans makes a sauna stove burn hard.
When the wooden door slams shut, blood boils in the thick of skin.
Corpuscles scream in heat that might make you think
of old-time words like god and sin.

7
I have been a bride, a wave motion of crinoline,
have seen the broken strand of pearls wash away in waves.
What does the partner want—to make a new wife out of gold?

I have watched men shave and taken them to bed.
Lovers with seams, have you stayed stitched?
Oh, the wholly naked sex. We lather in the new world mess.

8
Leave the homestead unlocked, unboarded,
and tell the flannel town the credenza's full of bric-a-brac.
Let them wake up spoons and pull the needle
through the lace. Let them strop the double blade
and shave the window frame. Let the townkids liquor up
and hump the metal beds. Let hunters fire through the floor.
When the table burns, let them burn the door.
Douse the husk with gas and let it finger flames.
Let the dead line up and laugh, still awkward in America.

SHARON DILWORTH

(1988)

The Cousin in the Backyard

My husband stands to inspect the bird feeder. He's wearing light blue Winnie-the-Pooh pajamas. He found them at Target, not what he had been looking for, but in his size, and the price, like everything else in that oversized, overstocked store, was right. On the breast pocket, Tigger and Pooh fight over the *hunny* jar.

Target, part of the new development that suddenly appeared on the bank of the Monongahela, is a place I refuse to frequent. To build it they tore down the Homestead Steel Mill and in doing so chipped away at Pittsburgh's greatest asset, its history.

I am often accused of having too many opinions, but I disagree. Rage is only one opinion.

Listen to how I see things.

Homestead was the site of the 1892 Steel Strike. That's when Henry Clay Frick hired Pinkerton Detectives to come in and end the stalemate. The Pinkertons (remember their motto, "We never sleep") floated downriver on coal barges, prepared to take on the steelworkers who were lined on the banks waiting for a solution to their misery. Like all unhappy workers, the men were fighting for a bit of respect, some dignity, better working conditions, more pay, and an opportunity to fill their days with something other than the dark mills. They never thought Frick would hire outsiders with guns.

The river ran red is not just a metaphorical phrase; the Pinkertons were ruthless—a real massacre, which is why Homestead should be remembered with something other than big-box stores, though I know it's being done all over the world. Why should Homestead, Pennsylvania, be any different?

Retribution for Frick's sins came later, when the anarchist Alexander Berkman attempted to assassinate him. Sentenced to fifteen years, Berkman served twelve before he and his lover Emma Goldman were exiled to the Soviet Union. Years later, when Frick died, Emma Goldman was adamant that Frick was a name history would forget. "He was only part of the passing hour," she claimed. "Generations after us will not idolize the rich. Instead our children will remember Alexander Berkman, a man who fought for what was right."

I laugh. Try getting fifteen people to name the anarchist. You can't. Frick's still famous. For eight dollars you can have a tour of his house. I've been twice. They still change the furniture wraps just like his maids did when he was alive—once every six months—white for summer, dark green for winter.

The gigantic steel mill has been replaced with a Dave & Busters, a T.G.I. Fridays, a Dick's Sporting Goods, a Bed Bath & Beyond, an Old Navy, a Giant Eagle, an Eat'n Park, and a Loew's megaplex. Another chain opens every few weeks. A plaque at the far end of the strip mall commemorates the strike, but the empty steel mill, a black idle mess of pipes, was a much stronger reminder of what happened. The complex is hugely successful, though I can't see how that's possible given the stagnant economic and demographic situations in Allegheny County.

I used to love history and once even considered getting a PhD. What could be more interesting than to read about what you love for several years? I took some classes at Pitt, but didn't see the point. The Civil War? The north won. Why sixteen weeks going over it? Knowing history is painful enough, analyzing it seems dangerous.

My husband, Sam, turns on the TV. Without cable, we get three channels. He watches public television, and this half hour is *Mr. Rogers' Neighborhood.* His bowl of Cheerios, too much milk, the big spoon, and I think, god we haven't come that far, when I see my cousin in the backyard.

"I am just not in the mood," I tell Sam.

Maggie is in her lawn chair, the big yellow tent in the far corner, a makeshift clothesline already filled with her socks and undies. Her shaggy dog Spot barks at the squirrels.

"Lock the door," Sam says. The Cheerio box is empty. He cuts out the coupons off the back and puts them with the others in the junk drawer.

My cousin sees us. She makes some sort of motion with her hands. I think it has to do with the bird feeder.

Sam interprets. "Coffee. That's what she wants."

The pot's almost done dripping.

My cousin is an outdoors freak. She doesn't like walls or roofs, or any kind of permanent structures, and has arranged her life so that she's not inside for very long. When employed, she's outdoors: bicycle messenger, hot-dog vendor, ticket taker at Exit 5 on the turnpike, because she believes being inside does funny things to a person's psyche. She's not antisocial, just messed up.

I bring out two mugs of coffee. Maggie thanks me, then peers in over the rim.

"I don't like cream," she says. The sweetness of her gratitude is fleeting.

"I can't take it out."

"Next time," she scolds.

"Next time, go to Uni-Mart."

She grunts and swallows her coffee in two gulps.

"Where have you been?" I ask. Last I heard Maggie was in Banff, working as a lunch lady at one of the ski resorts.

"The Appalachian Trail," she answers.

"Did you walk it?" I ask.

"I did."

"The whole thing?" The weeds in the driveway grow at an alarming rate. Someday they will probably take over the whole backyard.

"Do I look like I walked the whole thing?"

She looks tattered, and smells like campfires.

"It's not attractive to always say what's on your mind, especially if it's your mind," Maggie says.

I haven't said a word, but Maggie tells me she knows what I'm thinking.

"Since when is honesty considered a vice?" I ask.

"If you're going to be like that," she says, "then I need money." She gives me the empty coffee mug.

I don't think I look like anyone's maid. I hand it back.

"I want to go to France," Maggie says. She puts her feet up on the side of the tree. They are swollen, her toenails rimmed in black dirt. She probably did walk the whole Trail.

"Paris is where most of us want to end up," I say. I quote something I read somewhere once. "Twenty-two percent of Americans dream of dying in Paris." That doesn't sound right. Maybe I'm confusing it with another statistic—maybe it's 22 percent of the American people can't name the capital of France. They believe Paris to be its own country.

Maggie shakes her head. "I'll probably fly through Geneva and go to the Alps. I went to Paris once. I drank red wine there and my teeth stained blue for months."

Sam comes out with more coffee. He's changed out of his Pooh pajamas. They're hanging on the back of his bathroom door. He's afraid to wash them, that they'll lose that soft new feel. They were $7.99. I tell him to buy a dozen. If it makes him happy to have soft and cozy, cheap light blue pajamas with familiar animals in bright primary colors dancing about, why not just fill his drawers?

Maggie wants to know what her chances are that we'll let her camp out in the backyard all winter.

"Nil," Sam says. The bird feeder is empty. Sam refills it with a special blend of peanut butter and nuts—pricey items he gets at the Co-op.

"I won't be a problem," my cousin insists.

"You already are," Sam says.

Maggie studies him carefully, hissing a bit, a balloon losing air. "Watch yourself, Sammy," she warns.

Sam's not staying. "I won't be late," he says. He leans over and makes a noise near my ear, like he's kissing me good-bye. I pull away. Unless we have a good reason, we don't touch. He hurries away, as if he's late for an appointment.

I don't think Sam works anymore. It hasn't always been like this—he used to have a job. But his checks have stopped so I'm guessing he was fired. We don't discuss what he does when he leaves the house and I don't really care. For all I know he goes to the Fruit Loop in Schenley Park and picks up guys for anonymous sex. I let him have his charade.

Sam's got his own set of issues. I married him, knowing he wasn't exactly straight. His parents made their money in metal junkyards, something I approve of since no one was exploited. The security is nice. I like the house and the bank accounts that are replenished with the dividends from different stocks. I read the incident report in the *Post-Gazette;* Sam's never been arrested.

"Everything okay with Sammy?" Maggie asks.

I tell her she spends an enormous amount of time worrying about other people.

"Sam and I understand each other," she says. "We have a bond."

"That's what you say."

"Maybe because it's the truth."

"I don't want to talk about it."

"You never do," Maggie says. She gets up to check the clothesline. The sun is warm, but her things aren't dry.

Maggie thinks she and Sam are kindred spirits—they both suffered family problems and therefore share something the rest of us can only imagine. It's not a connection I would have made, but it gives Maggie some comfort to know she's not alone.

Sam's brother isn't right. Something went wrong years ago and now he's convinced they're out to kill him. It's a conspiracy theory aimed at him directly. They want to poison him. He carries around a stack of white handkerchiefs and wraps them around door handles and glasses, anything he has to touch. Convinced that the handkerchiefs are laced with the poison they've painted on everything around him, he discards them as soon as he's done with them. His thinking is inconsistent; he eats in restaurants, loves Taco Bell, and Pizza Hut. On good days he drives. He loves the new Waterfront Complex. Other days, he won't leave his house. He likes Sam, which would be a good thing, except when the two of them are together, all they ever talk about is death. He worries about an eternity spent in the ground and sometimes gets so frustrated with not knowing what will happen after he's dead that he throws up. I suggest cremation, but no one pays attention to what I say.

Maggie's never met him. She'd like to, but I don't see the point in bringing the two of them together. His brother's breakdown changed the family. Sam says it was like lightning going through the family. Nothing was ever the same.

Maggie relates.

"I am not alone," Maggie tells me.

I think she's talking about the dog. "The neighbors will complain about the barking," I tell her.

"Besides Spot," she says. "I brought a friend."

I walk over and open up the tent flaps. A head, blankets, the smell of someone in a deep sleep.

"She's Malaysian." Maggie says. "I met her in Tennessee."

"Is there something going on between the two of you?"

"I knew you'd ask that."

"Does the answer change because you had ESP?"

"She's just a friend. A nice person who needed help. You don't have to be all suspicious and weird just because I'm doing someone a favor."

"Where'd you find her," I ask.

"On the Trail."

"Did *she* walk the whole thing?"

"I don't know," Maggie says, drinking from my cup. "We never talked about it."

"Something seems to have tired her out." I take back my cup, but her lip marks are all over the rim. I let her finish it.

"She's a terrific sleeper," Maggie says. Turning the attention spotlight towards others is a developed trick with Maggie. She's more comfortable when she's talking about other people, so I hear all about the Malaysian's sleep patterns. The Malaysian, it seems, can sleep through everything, Spot's yaps, thunderstorms. Why once, she even slept while a group of drunk tourists from Muskegon came to their camp begging for food and drink.

"An incredible mettle," I comment.

"She speaks six languages. She's smart. Really smart."

"And you just found her in Tennessee? Just like that?"

"Including Mandarin. She helped out some tourists. They were from India, but somehow they had Mandarin in common and she helped them with their lost passports and credit cards."

The words rush out of Maggie like water overflowing from a wobbly spout. She's unsteady and I watch her carefully. Finally she stands and announces that she has to use the bathroom.

"I know exactly how much cash there is in my wallet," I tell her.

She's gone five minutes. I am just about to go in and check on her, when she walks out—one arm slung around her head.

"I swear to God, I saw a bat in your house," she says.

"Impossible," I lie.

The bat is not usually around in the daytime. The bat flew in last fall and though we've tried everything, we can't get rid of it. It hides from us, slips in, flies around at night. We shut the bedroom door, so we're not bothered, but I hear it moving about the house. It hit the mirror once; the impression of its body is outlined on the glass.

Maggie's made another pot of coffee. She fills her cup, doesn't offer me anything. Five minutes later, she's drunk the whole thing. We stare at the tent and I guess we're waiting for the Malaysian to wake.

Maggie's mother, my Aunt Velma, is slightly paralyzed from the stroke she suffered when the bullet hit her spine. When people ask why she limps, Aunt Velma tells them it was a boating accident.

Long before shooting your parents became a sort of *de rigueur* act of suburban malaise, Maggie's twin brother, Jack, shot their mother with a hunting rifle. It's not really fair to blame Maggie for being slightly off-kilter.

My mother is Aunt Velma's sister. They grew up together in Pittsburgh, took dance lessons from Gene Kelly, went to Margaret Morrison College for Women and majored in home economics. They had classes back then like Dinner for Two on a Shoestring Budget. You should see the way my mother can fold sheets, even 100 percent cotton. They married within six months of each other—my mother to a man so similar to her own father, they even shared first names. Uncle Max was different. As my mother used to say, he had a wider wallet than most of the men they dated.

Aunt Velma and Uncle Max lived on Northumberland Avenue in one of the grand old homes that were built when Pittsburgh was opulent. It was a magical place with secret passageways, hidden closets, back staircases, uneven floorboards, dark drapes, window seats, and panes of stained glass. The upstairs had views of the hills and houses beyond our neighborhood. It was dusty; the rooms were filled with stuffed furniture. I remember one piece that my aunt called a lover's nest. It had a triple seat that fanned out like flower petals. The walls were covered with paintings of dead family members, something Maggie never believed. "We don't know these people," she used to tell us younger cousins. "Ask her."

I did once. Aunt Velma stood in front of the old man in the white beard and answered without any hesitation. "That," she told me, "is somebody."

I loved the house. This was back before I understood that the steelworkers lived in the Southside flats along the riverbanks. The house wasn't anything like ours either. The place overflowed in an untidy way with things like pretzel bins, stacks of soda pop, glass containers for hard candies, stacks of newspapers. There were Russian boxes filled with cigarettes, safety matches, and postcards from around the world. Language tapes were stacked on the stairs, unfinished needlepoint pillowcases, abandoned jigsaw puzzles.

The family gathered at the Northumberland house for all holidays. I remember summer nights as one long continuous party, as something or another was always being celebrated.

I drive by the old house every once in awhile, the memories so fresh in my mind that I have to stop the car and wait until the dizziness in my head stops and my vision clears.

In Aunt Velma's words, Maggie and Jack were golden-haired children of God. "I'm so lucky," she said to my mother. "They're gorgeous, like movie stars. How can it be? What did I ever do to deserve them?"

Uncle Max and Aunt Velma were proud of the twins and didn't care who knew it. They bragged, way before bragging about your kids was what people did to fill the silences of the day. Maggie and Jack were perfect—not just stars—but starlight. They were playful, enthusiastic, always good-natured.

I was too infatuated to be jealous.

After the incident, I realized that a lot of their goldenness was manufactured. Like many spoiled children, they were no strangers to drugs and alcohol. I must have sensed that they were messed up, but I never connected it to anything other than their innate happiness. I might remember the smell of pot, the way the two of them spoke in code, the jokes they told, continuous laughter.

But if I knew, I ignored it.

Jack played guitar and I spent a lot of time at his feet, listening to him. His favorite song was "Puff the Magic Dragon," and he played it until one of the adults would finally wander over and ask him to lift the needle. "For Christ's sake, Jack. Turn it over. The record's skipping."

Jack found everything amusing and I guess I wanted to believe that that was his personality.

With Maggie, it was definitely pot. We had to have helped her perch on Uncle Doc's chair listening to him drone on about his failing dental practice. Later she said, "I would be so high, I'd stare at his nose hairs and wonder how anything on the human body could grow so thick without fertilizer." Jack burned, but he liked everything else as well. The few times Maggie and I have talked about, she explained his increasing addiction to harder drugs on his lack of imagination.

"A strong recommendation for creative and inspiring toys," I commented.

"Even as kids, he couldn't entertain himself. Mom would tell us to run out and play and Jackie would wander out to the middle of the street as if he expected to see a circus. He always complained of being bored. Couldn't stand the neighborhood kids, hated television. His own thoughts drove him crazy, but then he discovered hallucinogenics and life became tolerable. He only really liked life when he was tripping."

Maggie spent hours rummaging through the house challenging herself to find the most unlikely object to whittle into a smoking tool. A thick unpeeled carrot, maybe, a dreidel, some dried wood. She would sit on the far end of the diving board, toking on her homemade, ecologically friendly pipe. Then, high and happy, she'd bounce on the board. Up and down, twenty minutes, thirty minutes, up to an hour before she finally dove in.

Aunt Velma was a bossy woman, who spent a great deal of her days making comments on other people's business. Like an inherited heart problem, it was congenital gossip, she could not help herself. She must have realized at some point that something had happened to her

golden-haired, sun-kissed bundles of joy. They were lazy, sleepy creatures, who snacked too often, and sipped too much wine from the jugs
in the pantry. Their friends were an odd crew of long-haired, mumbling drug dealers. Money was always missing from purses and under-
wear drawers.

Aunt Velma eventually went on the warpath. She made it her mis-
sion to move her kids out of adolescence into adulthood. By summer's
end, they were going to be doing something besides sponging off their
parents. Maggie was too out of it to care, and by this time, Jack had lost
all traces of his good humor. He was paranoid and spent hours hiding
from his mother. As no one talks about it, no one actually knows what
Aunt Velma said to Jack that pushed him over the edge, but he went.
Luckily, Jack was too stoned at the time to do much damage. In court
he would claim that nothing was premeditated. He just did it. The bullet nicked Aunt Velma's spine, and ended her relationship with her
children. Maggie got thrown into the configuration of blame. Neither
twin was ever forgiven.

Jack served some kind of juvenile sentence in Bedford, Pennsylvania. When he came back, my father and I went to pick him up at the
downtown bus stop since he was estranged from most of the family.
My father didn't tell me where we were going—only that he had an
errand. We waited inside the car. The heater was broken and little
pieces of white paper flew out of the vents.

"I don't want you to tell your mother where we went."

"What should I say?"

He shrugged.

"I'll tell her we went to get a newspaper," I said.

"They never asked him where he got the gun," my father said. "It
was the one mystery the lawyers and police never answered. No one
knew where it came from."

"Did Uncle Max have one," I suggested.

"We're Jews," my father said. "We don't own guns."

Then I saw my cousin. He had changed; his goldenness was gone,
but I still recognized him. There were tears, mostly my father's. I stared
at the ground. My cousin thanked my father for coming to get him.

"Everyone makes mistakes," my father said.

"I think this overqualifies in that respect, sir."

We got back in the car. Jack turned to me in the backseat. "I forget your name," he said. I was embarrassed and sad, and only later
did it occur to me that maybe he had never known my name. I had

had fantasies of him, my first real sexual longings, but to him, I was just another one of the little girl cousins who sang along to "Puff the Magic Dragon."

My father laughed, but no one said my name. It seemed trivial under the circumstances.

We drove through the Fort Pitt Tunnel to the airport.

My father asked how he was.

"Fine," Jack said.

"In good health?"

"Very good," Jack said. "Except for the hiccups."

"Hiccups?" my father asked. "Now?"

"I had them last month," Jack said. "For eighteen days."

"My lord," my father said. "That's quite a long time."

All three of us laughed.

"It made me sick," Jack said. "I lost some weight."

"You look like you lost weight."

"I lost an awful lot of weight."

"You look different," my father commented.

"Do I?"

"Yes, you do," my father said.

"I wouldn't know, sir. They weren't any mirrors where I was," Jack explained.

"I didn't know that," my father answered.

"Not a one, sir," Jack said.

I wanted to tell him there was a mirror under the visor right near his head. If you slid it open, yellow makeup lights flashed on. My mother kept it down continually when we drove. She inspected her face and throat for new wrinkles. She did her lipstick, complained that the pallor of her skin made her look like a senior citizen.

We pulled up to the curbside check-in. I had assumed we were going to go in and walk Jack to his gate. Whenever relatives left, we always watched their planes take off. My father got out his side of the car and Jack got out his side. They were hugging again. There were more tears, mostly my father's.

Back in the car, my father smashed his fists against the steering wheel. "Maybe some of us have guns, but we don't point them at our mothers and pull the trigger."

The Malaysian wakes just as Maggie tells me she's exhausted. "All that coffee gets to me," she says.

"Can you entertain her?" Maggie asks.

"My juggling is a bit rusty."

Maggie gives me the thumbs-up. "You can do it," she coaches. She pulls the lawn chair over to the far corner of the yard and sleeps, the dog's head on her lap.

The Malaysian has a pack of Drum tobacco and rolls her own cigarettes. She flips out the paper, sprinkles a few strands of tobacco, then rolls it once and licks the ends to seal it. She hides the pouch into the folds of her sweatshirt as if she's afraid I'll ask to bum one. We don't speak, but she stares at the sky every time a plane flies overhead. She smokes one after another, furiously. The smell gives me a headache. I give her my coffee cup and tell her to use it as an ashtray.

She looks at me in confusion.

Evidently, English is not one of the six languages.

I pantomime putting out a cigarette and repeat the word "ashtray" several times. "For your ashes," I say. "Ashes."

The Malaysian shrugs, then strains to see a hospital helicopter fly by.

"You're doing a good job," my cousin shouts.

"I'm too old for babysitting," I tell Maggie.

The Malaysian brings out a bag full of lollipops. Unlike her precious cigarettes, she offers me one of these.

It says *cherry* on the wrapper, but it tastes of mothballs.

The Malaysian sucks on one too, juggling the cigarette and the lollipop. She says something that I don't understand, then suddenly we are talking about Kojak, the seventies television character. "My hero," she says. "Who loves you, baby?"

I go in the house and she follows. I turn on the television. Elmo and the gang are singing about bubbles in the bathtub. She flips channels, the same three over and over again as if we have one hundred. She sticks with Elmo.

Seen as a threat to the American way of life, Emma Goldman and Alexander Berkman were exiled to Russia in 1920, hailed as heroes by some radicals. The rest of the country just wanted to get rid of them. Carnegie and Frick are to blame for those lost lives. Why doesn't anyone do anything?

Sam is home.

He offers to make iced tea.

We don't have any mix. "That would be nice," I say.

He goes to the basement, and comes up with a container of powdered lemonade from a party we had some thirteen years ago.

He looks out at the yard. "A good thirty minutes and this place will be back to normal." He doesn't like the way the clothesline is wrapped around the sycamore tree. "The bark is shedding," he says.

He's introduced to the Malaysian, who asks if she can take a shower. They go upstairs and I hear him in the linen closet getting clean towels. He comes down and drinks what's left of the lemonade.

"We should talk," he says, but I shake my head.

"Not to worry," I say.

"Really?" he asks.

The groan of the water moves through the pipes overhead. I look to the ceiling. We need to paint.

"Maggie's leaving," I tell him. "She's found the money to get to France."

"Isn't she fortunate?" Sam says.

"I'm not sure I'd go that far."

I used to have a limit at the ATM machine. I'm not sure when it stopped, but I can transfer large sums from savings to checking with a tap of the keys. I grab the dog leash.

"I'll take Spot," I say.

"You don't solve anything when you throw money at her," Sam says. He knows I'm not just walking the dog.

I ask him if he wants to come along.

"I'm okay here," he says.

It's an offhand comment and will probably turn out to be true. But who's to say? Misfortune strikes in an instant. Ask Aunt Velma. According to the horticulturist who came to help me with the fall flowers, the sycamore tree in the backyard is two hundred years old. My cousin is not stable and that Malaysian smokes like a chimney.

It works like that. One minute, you're an abundantly loved child, with rays of light and warmth reaching down to you, the next, your brother's got a gun aimed at your mother's head. Then it's over. The passing hour. You sit in other people's backyards trying to be social so they'll give you money, but you don't really connect. It's not a life, but it looks like one.

I go quickly.

Givers and Takers

Father from afar,
where you have touched her,
you are not:

Almost a gush
as she opens up, famously loud,
inhaling the sky

and seminal dust
and man-made fly. Almost a gush
as you reel her out

and drop her on a pile.
One is a giver,
another a taker, life of fire.

Now your fingers,
quickly skillful, chop her up;
can't they tell her

from the captured,
lying stiffly on a platter,
torsos only,

grilled and blackened?
Wherever her mind is
(with the gutstuff, in the bucket,

floating homeward
without bonework), it's losing
focus, kindling inward,

winding down.
Trees ripple through her
severed fantail; aurora shadows

flail each eye.
Aren't you tickled, father, tackler,
to find her still alive,

find her bobbing,
like a fraction, top by bottom,
multiplied? Almost a gush

as partial daughter
loiters on the waist-high water,
flirting, gurgling,

words like tinsel,
Take me with you, I forgive you—
final shimmer, final bite.

The Evening Concert

There is a moment early in the evening
when everything seems possible.

An old man sits on a porch
eating,

telling you about sitting
on a porch eating.

Routine alone keeps an old man alive
on the first day of another spring.

Who knows what will happen next?
Then they hang the leaves back on the trees.

Everyone is on the edge of their seats
as the sun snuffs itself out

and the moment is over. It is night,
there are bats squeezed behind the shutters.

In the distance a car drives off the dock.
The cry of men running to help lifts up, a song.

My Government

The history of the world
is the history of rural malcontents
rising up against the capital.

The cat thinks something lives in the radiator and puts his mouth to
the vent—its breath.

No man is an island. Also, no one is interested in excessive
indeterminacy. The French will eat the horse right out from
under you. That, and so much more, have you taught me, World.

Your products will collapse after a short time and we will be forced into the streets for more.

It is possible to live only on what you grow yourself if you eat little and live very still.

SARAH MESSER

(1990)

Starting with that time

he shot a man in Mendota
for calling him pretty, *hey pretty, your hair's*
like spun sunshine, and then
the man fell down dead. Son of a
tin smith, he had inherited
those quick but delicate hands, and
always went for his revolver
as quick and absentmindedly as
an itch the same way he went
for those squirrel-boned
women even smaller than himself
with breasts like shallow tea-cups.

As an outlaw, he fell in love
with the wrong women—a seamstress
who sniffed glue, who sewed
her own sleeves to her arms
and flew off a bridge; a sad-faced
war nurse; a rich Northerner
who carried her father's
jawbone in her purse—
each one disappearing more
from herself, until he found
that he was mostly in love
with the shadow of a dress,
a wrist, or the outline of a mouth
pressed to the glass on the window
of the next train leaving town.

In the meantime, he killed:
any man who could ever be called
his friend. Ambushed the town
of Independence, killed 12
at Olathe, 20 at Shawnee, tied the scalps
of those he suspected most

to his horse's bridle, and rode
west. The mayor of Lawrence,
Kansas suffocated in a well beneath
his own house as the whole
town burned, the contents of every
train and wagon turned over.

In the end he came to me
because I was the timberline, way out
west, the last stand of trees.

Each night I told him about
the guns hidden in my house:
a .44 caliber in the chamber pot, a rifle
beneath the stairs, bird guns between
folded linen, revolvers hidden
in drawers, on shelves, the four boudoir
pistols plastered in walls, wrapped
in the hair of dolls.

He hid himself inside the sheen
of Smith and Wesson, the one breech
double-barreled Winchester,
my only Navy Colt. He hid because
I was the hideout, the inert
and sturdy home where he polished
his thoughts, the timber
of each trigger, the powder
in the coffee tin, the bullets
in the freezer.

In the end, I was
the safest place for him
to put his mouth.

WILLIAM LYCHACK
(1991)

The Old Woman and Her Thief

On her deathbed, as she drew what were to be her last breaths on God's green earth, the old woman made a confession so terrible to her husband that—even under circumstances as solemn and sorrowful as these—he could hardly take the secret as true, let alone forgive her for it. He listened by her side, as if struck dumb with a club, and when she pressed her lips tight against admitting anything more and a silence had passed, a long silence in which she could hear herself swallow away the brackish taste in her mouth, the taste like wet pennies off the street, just when she expected the final lifting of the veil to all her life's meaning, the old man hiccoughed.

It might have been the fever in her mind, but she could not accept this to be her life's reward, and she lay there and blinked her eyes and half expected her husband to cough up an olive pit. She watched for his lips to purse and spit an inky stone into her hand, but only the startle of his hiccoughs came, haphazard and loud in the room. She could feel each jump telegraphed through the bedsprings to her, and finally she asked him to go drink some seltzer water. She lay flat and let her eyes close to the dim room and tried to savor the slow lift and release of each breath in her chest, and on into the night she lay at rest and at peace.

But she did not die.

Contrary to all they had expected and provided for, in three days' time the old woman was sitting up in bed and answering her mail. Scattered about her lay books and dishes and flower arrangements, bowls of ripened fruit, her little radio and reading lamps. The curtains and windows were opened wide. And on the morning of the fourth day the doctor clocked his tongue and pronounced, almost begrudgingly, that she was quite recovered. The undertaker came and rolled the casket and wreaths out of the old couple's parlor, where she was to have been laid out, and the man's cologne lingered so long after him in the room that her husband lit matches to kill the scent.

Improbable as it became, in two more days the old woman's appetite for chocolate and red wine returned. And her husband knew she was truly well when she asked for a pot of coffee and a bundt cake. As he ventured to the bakery, he caught himself whistling—it was a brilliant

163

spring morning, after all, and he breathed in the cool air like water and stopped to look out over the hills in the distance, the clouds driven across the sky by the blue clear winds that never touched the ground, and all the trees in leaf and flower, and the traffic of people out walking and working, the report of hammers and whine of saws, the spring birds on the grass, the wet grass in the sun the color of old yellowed silver—and on he went walking for her cake, the thought dawning on him that soon she would be up and off to the market herself, lunching with friends and shopping for groceries, everything just like usual, her Tuesday bridge ladies, her Thursday museum committee, her Friday reading to the blind.

The old man's heart became divided after his wife's almost being carried off. On the one side, all his prayers had been answered in full: his wife alive, their world restored, and the warm sun of another spring upon them. What more could he ask for? And yet, in ways he couldn't help, her confession of the thief lay heavy on the other side of his heart. And this half grew increasingly heavy as the days passed. He began to fancy that he had somehow been tricked by life, a thing he had never before thought possible.

Perhaps as a consequence of this division in his heart, or as a result of the wear of his wife's illness put upon him, or even the peculiar strain of her growing wellness upon him, or the gout in his ankles when it rained, or the ceaseless passing of friends and family and whole ways of life, or perhaps it was the troubled rags of feeling old and dull to the world. . . . Whatever the reason, all the things in his life grew increasingly strange to the old man. He would glimpse—or would think he had glimpsed—fruit bats hanging folded with the coats in the closet, turtles in place of pillows on the couch. A pair of boots became muskrats under the bench in the hall, then they were dachshunds, and then, a step closer, they were boots again.

As the days passed, the old man went around braced against the world. He didn't know if he believed what he saw or saw what he believed. Was it what you saw or what you thought you saw? Or was it that what you believed in your mind was what you saw in the world? He didn't know the way he used to know, or thought he had known, and it exhausted him to chase his tail like this. He often had to lie down on the day bed and close his eyes for fear that the truth of the world would be revealed to him. He didn't trust his heart could take it.

On the face of it, of course, the man and his wife were destiny's darlings, not so much the envy of the little mountain town as its collective hope. You would have to be blind not to see the care and craft of the old man's silver shop. Not to allow that the woman's reprieve from death smacked of miracle and meant she had purposes unfinished in the town. And despite her years and her children all far-flung, wouldn't anyone say— among the many things people said—that the old woman appeared more radiant and unshakable than she had in months, if not years?

And when she walked into town, she looked less frail in her summer frock than anyone could recall, her basket on her arm as she went, her hard heels on the sidewalk. And everyone who stopped her on the street told her how impossibly glad they were when they heard there'd be no funeral.

Truth was, she said (and quickly touched wood), she'd never felt more, well, sprightly.

And they said, Yes, wasn't *sprightly* just how she looked? And they would hold her away at arm's length and say how they wept for joy. Then they would bend close and ask had she gained weight and snuck off to a spa? What, they whispered, are those new teeth?

The old woman would blush to the roots of her white hair and throw back her head, brim with the pleasure of a school girl really, and she would switch the basket of collard and turnip greens to her other arm and keep smiling. "Oh, now," she would say, "come sit-n-tell me how you've been."

And they would sit to lunch and gossip in the sleepy shade of the market's trees, a drift of carnival music turned from the blind organ grinder, to whom she read on Fridays, and whose swift little squirrel monkey tumbled through the square with his jingling pouch of dimes and nickels—everything really was like usual—the pranks of the monkey, the storm crabs for sale in the cages, the ice and fish and roasting nuts and seeds, the smell of burnt sugar and salt, and the warm coins in her one hand ready to give to the laughing monkey, her wallet clutched tight in the other, because she knew how the monkey too was a thief.

Home from the market she walked with her basket of greens and dinner sausage, a newspaper packet of sunflower seeds and a bottle of red wine, and the notion to tell her husband of all the household scandals she had heard and of how she had watched the monkey sneak his tail around a little boy and tip the boy's cap over his eyes. And as she went toward home she watched the sky for stray birds and for her old lost-to-the-world Romeo.

The sun settled behind the trees, and she stopped in a small garden park and set down her basket and rubbed the aches out of her hands. In the fountain a copper goose spit water up over its head onto its back. She waited and watched the sun-lit fingers of the highest tree branches. And softly she whistled his name, rustled his seeds against the newspaper, and again more boldly she called to him.

The air went powdery toward dusk, and she heard the slow ring of the vesper bell, and still there was no Romeo. She knew much better than to hope, but each stir of shadow in the damp air made her turn and call his name and see and know, despite her best hopes, that her thief was not there.

The old couple's history came back to them, if it returned at all, like a story they had heard about or read about somewhere long ago, the memories scarcely their own anymore, unspooling about them like rhymes for children. Once upon a time the old man—a young man then, still sticky with the things he touched in life—would go walking in the Lost Woods near his boyhood home. And this once he came upon a bird's nest in the path. In the leaves lay a crow, black and folded open, its feet cut off.

These days were days, back then, of great superstition and antique cruelty, days where local farmers poisoned whole cribs of corn to feed migrating birds, the birds thought to be omens of famine and death. For many years, you could pay your taxes with salted owl's eyes and crow's feet. Springtime brought festivals to the little towns, where cannons shot nets over fields of birds and children ran to club the struggling beasts with ribbon-tied broom handles. Many birds grew skittish over these years and learned not to sing. Some were thought to fly out to sea to become fish. And fewer and fewer returned each season, yet it was true that a-fowling parties still combed the woods every weekend and holiday and shook and chopped nests down from trees—no eagle, goose, or crane, no crow, or lark escaping unharmed. All that remains of some species—the Scarlet Hurry Hawk, for instance, or the tiny Skittlelink, who laid eggs smaller than jellybeans and sweeter than marzipan, or even the Passenger Pigeon, easily the most numerous bird on earth, so prolific its flocks hid the sun for hours on end, the cooing and the whirring of wings so loud that the firings of a gun could not be heard—these birds have only their names and the faded specimens behind the smudged-glass of the museum cabinets.

But once upon a time, when the old man—a young man—came

across the nest with the crow like an umbrella, the man couldn't take his eyes from the perfect circle of twigs and sticks, from the broken eggs and the glint of tinsel in the cup of grass. And whenever he thought back to this, the old man would see himself standing mesmerized by the milk-green egg in the hold of the nest, one egg as smooth as a moon opal, and as empty and marvelous.

He would remember not a speck of sound disturbing the woods, the quiet columns of trees, the pools of light falling on the path, falling as snow falls when there is no wind. And when, as from a dream, the man awoke and removed his sweater and stooped to wrap the nest, he heard leaves rustle above him. And as he carried the nest back through the woods, carried it like a boy carries a bowl full of soup, he hoped to high heaven that his young bride at home would know what to do with a thing such as this.

Hatch and raise him—was it ever a question?—into a silk-black crow, so perfectly black he moved like oil. Their orphan Romeo, they would keep him safe and teach him to speak and fly and to eat at the dinner table. And he learned to waltz and purr on the outstretched paws of the cat, and in the parlor at night the man would teach Romeo to sing like the nightingale, like the chaffinch, like the sparrow, like the gentle playing of the late-night radio, the piano and the soprano so like birds themselves. And with her knitting halted in her lap, the woman would watch Romeo on her husband's knee, the bird's knuckle-skinned feet grabbing the man's trousers, her husband's eyes closed and head tilted, the bird singing and looking back and forth to him and to her, as though they were tossing something between them.

And in the mornings, when the man arose and washed and readied himself, the silver shop—where day after day he hammered the town hallmark into the clattering piles of knives and forks and spoons, so many spoons you would have never imagined mouths for all the spoons—Romeo would fly alongside him as he walked the road to work. And when the bird hurried home to the woman, all the rest of the morning long she would tidy the house and chatter on to her Romeo in what would start out as gladness at his safe return to her and what would amount, in the end, to a steady pour of loneliness.

By the time their children arrived—two boys, two girls, each a year apart—and by the time the children were half grown and half out the door and married and moved away, many things had come to pass in the couple's life together, many things in what had seemed to the woman just a heap of idle days, days scarcely strung along together where not a thing appeared to happen or change or move and where time, if it existed at all, was the thinnest of strings suspended and invisible, with no end to hold the beads of days which slid clean off the skin of the world, as if they had never really been, or better still, as if they had always been, fleeting and eternal both.

She couldn't quite get her head around this paradox—of time's being something entirely different than her experience of it—nor did she try particularly hard. It struck her simply that the old man's silver shop had always put the tableware in homes this side of the mountain. And no one had ever before read to the blind until she was there to read on Fridays. It was all like asking when Romeo had become her thief exactly, or why it had been kept a secret. Romeo had not so much learned to steal as he had forever stolen.

Just as sure as the sun crossed the day, the old man would arise and wet his head and go to work each morning to heat and shape the sterling bowls and caldrons and the endless and loud piles of cutlery. And each morning Romeo would fly along with him and perch from tree to tree to sing the songs of the whippoorwill, the bullfinch, the forktail, the bluebird, the naked-throated robbybell—it was a long walk— the songs of the whiskey-jack, and the waxwing, the waxbill, and as the man unlocked the door of his shop, Romeo stood balanced atop the roof's peak, singing his catalogue of night lieder from the radio. Then, when he caught the first sweet whiffs of coal smoke from the chimney, Romeo would start home to the woman, who had already seen the children off to school and sat on the porch with her coffee and cake.

He knew she would scan the horizon of trees for his wind-tossed silhouette flying safely home. And always he would come to the porch and walk his nodding walk, his toes clicking on the wood; he would bow for her to come scratch the nape of his neck and to rub his feathers against the grain, as so he liked, and he would begin to purr. And when she reached out her hand to him, palm up, Romeo would open his beak and place into the cup of her open hand a child's jack, or a bullet shell, a long necklace of pearls with a gold hasp, an earring, a heavy brass plumb bob, a crucifix, a pair of golden mustache scissors. . . .

Each became a gift picked special for her, and the best of these prizes set to motion the scandals she brought home to her husband from the market each day. An eternity ring from the stable-boy, the young man disappearing with the ring, his employer's horses falling ill and nearly dying from, of all things, grief. A gypsy pendant said to be a nail from the Cross, the caravan leaving a bitter curse on the town that would scatter all the children to the winds far from home. There was a heart locket, which undid a promise and the lives of two young lovers. And there was the pair of platinum-rimmed eyeglasses taken from the jeweler, the man stumbling to his death out the open window of his studio, a scatter of uncut diamonds cast about his body in such a way that people said he must have become, through long practice and labor, the very stuff of his art. Even the holy priest requested that the undertaker eviscerate the jeweler for hidden gems. In the weeks that followed, children would throw stones at the glass blower to see him shatter, the banker would snip off his little finger with a cigar cutter, the aged silversmith—the old man's mentor—would be bound to trees in the woods, his veins opened so that his blood could be drawn and cast into coins. And the town would never rise out of its shame to breathe a word about the fate of the quiet vintner, Lord rest his soul.

Many years passed in this way—the town secrets tied to and tied by a crow and a thin old woman—and anonymously she parceled her hoard to the museum and library and church charities. She gave to the organ grinder and quietly stirred the silver brooches and rings into her husband's foundry pots, which cooked in the center of his shop. And though she wanted only to tell her husband the real secrets beneath the secrets she brought home from the market, she didn't know how to explain so he would understand.

Even when she confessed and she felt the weight of the world lifted, she couldn't dare tell how she held the picture in her mind of Romeo flying through the woods and town—a complete shadow—flying over the trees and streets for that glint of gold that he could bring home to her. She fell in love with that idea, fell in love so deeply that no matter how wrong and weak and terrible she knew it was, no matter that the longer she kept the secret the more highly-keyed it seemed to become, until even a lowly tin soldier or a bell off a cat's collar was enough to break her heart for an entire afternoon, she fell in love so deeply that nothing could bring her to deny herself her thief, nothing could bring her to deny herself the idea of him flying through town, a chain swinging in his beak.

And when all the years had passed, when even Romeo's feathers had gone lusterless and grayed, the old man still worked the spoons in his shop and Romeo still flew as her thief. And at night, as she tucked the bird into his cage to sleep, Romeo would purr and coo back to her the voices and soft words of each of her children, the sighs and coughs of her husband, the squawk of the kitchen door being opened and closed, her own voice saying, "Pretty bird."

And she would whisper, "Yesss, Romeo, pretty bird."

The old man no longer slept well, especially during his wife's illness, and he had taken to napping on the day bed. He could sleep during the short winter's days with the noises of the street to distract his mind from the bellows-like wheeze of her breathing and the pauses which he feared would not end.

When she had first taken seriously ill, their children all swarmed home with their caravans of spouses, pets, children, toys. And yet, as their old mother's illness dragged into the spring, they begged off and returned to jobs in scattered cities far away, each travelling with silver goblets and cutlery from the front hutch and sideboard. And as the nights passed, the old man sat in the room alone again with his sleeping wife, listening to her labored breaths, and he thought it funny how none of the children had mentioned Romeo's absence. He thought this showed how deeply they grieved the imminent loss of their mother; but later, in the smaller hours of night, he took it more as a measure of the distance and time between them. He didn't know what to do with the sadness he felt when, in the sober bright of the next days, he could see that not one of their children had become a friend to them, that he and his wife had passed all their years with his apprentice, with his wife's bridge ladies, with each other and work and Romeo, with the town market.

He didn't do anything with this sadness, unless allowing it to wash over him was doing something, unless traipse-wandering through the Lost Woods with packets of seeds counted for something. And though he feared him dead, the old man whistled up to the trees and looked for the bird's crushed bones amongst the ferns and the wood-roses, and all the woods held quiet around him, the clouds in the sky through the leaves far above like the breaking surface of the sea, the spears of light as though through water. And with a swell of sadness again and of sympathy—for the birds and his wife and Romeo and his friend the vintner and the numberless sufferings of the little town he felt sympathy, as he would for himself and his hunched-over life of silver and chasing tools—and there in the woods the weight of the crow seemed to rest on him, that unmistakable weight of Romeo on his leg, light as a bird is light yet isn't light, and the old man found himself singing the night songs until his throat was red.

No Romeo came to him, and with his boots wet-through from push-ing aside the morning ferns, the old man started home and a flash caught his eye, a baby's bracelet. He brushed the dirt from it and hur-ried home all full of pride—sticky as pine pitch again—smiling to hold the little prize out to his wife. She would fly to him, he thought, her eyes all alight for him. But instead she screamed so fiercely that he thought she was in pain and dying right there. She clutched at the bracelet, and he tried to cover her with blankets. "What have you done with him?" she cried, her face tight and scoured-looking. "What've you done? Where is he?"

Her words fell on him like mallets, and the old man stuttered back to her how, in the woods, by chance, he'd found the bracelet under a fern, with other ferns. He pointed to the toes of his boots, as if he needed more proofs, and took mushrooms from his coat pockets and cupped them in his hand. He held out a tiny pine cone from his breast pocket.

She looked at his feet, the brown boots dark with wet, and she lay back heavily and brought the gold metal to her face, touched it to her tongue, and tried to catch the humid smell of Romeo on the bracelet. She didn't look to her husband, even when he sat down beside her on the bed and took her hand and toward his weight she tipped slightly and poured—until she closed her lips again tight against anything more—her life's confession out to him.

The old man would go to his grave wondering what more he could have asked for: his wife recovered, their world spared, spring upon them. And yet, as the days passed, he found himself unable to be roused from bed, unable to venture far from the house, and many mornings he would lie in bed, staring at the window, trying to listen to his heart as he would the sound in a sea shell, and his mind would flit in and out of dreams and memories, the difference between the two no longer important for him.

What's more, the old woman had become well with a vengeance. Her appetites restored and habits renewed, she went out each day and bounced as she stepped down the sidewalk into town. The old man watched her go, her white hair shining in the sun. And he watched, and kept watching, the empty street. A little breeze came in the window, and the curtains waved up and bowed down slow before him. And when the old man stepped outside into the light, he thought diamond necklaces hung on the wet grass. Or had the house windows shattered? Could the dew be the tears of stars?

Stand up straight, old man, he said to himself. Enough.

And he would turn from where he stood and go back inside to lie down on the day bed and look at his dry spotted hands until he had chased himself inside out. He looked through the window and curtains and was back to watching as the sun—with all the patience and fortitude of the mountain and woods—did its work of turning the shadows of the lamp post and the tree up on their ends, of holding those shadows there, and then of gently laying the shadows out again opposite. And dusk brought the vesper bells and the approaching click of his wife's heels on the walk, the heavy creak of her basket filled with dinner greens and fruit, the old man's heart chanting that the trouble's no trouble, the trouble's no trouble. . . .

And over dinner and wine he listened as she chatted cards and told how, in the market, the monkey tipped the hat from the boy and how last week she read a pirate story to the organ grinder and could swear the monkey was weeping when the parrot in the story is captured by the mutineers and is made to stand trial against his captain.

In the living room, late into the night, they sat and listened to the radio. Sometimes they would remember the past for one another— their marriage trees as saplings, their trip to Barcelona—but mostly they just remained quiet together in the room, the man absently turning through a book of still life paintings, and the woman's knitting halted on her lap as she stared at the dark empty windows, the soprano on the radio rising onto her toes, her piano slowly falling to the floor—and coming to rest—like a leaf.

"You know who'd've liked that song?" he asked her.

The needles in her hands began to tick together again up and down, and she looked over at his finger running along the edge of a page, and when she raised her eyes to his, he winked. She dropped a stitch and pulled out lengths of yarn from the skein tumbling on the floor.

After the next song—a waltz that had been popular when they were courting—she said, "That wasn't so bad either, was it?"

"Incredible," said the man. He hummed just slightly and closed the book on his lap and watched as she knit. He lay aside the book. "Know what I'd most like to be in my next life?"

"What's that?"

"A musician and play like that."

"I'll see what I can do," she told him.

He sat down. It was a joke and he had been sitting right along, but he sat down even more, as though forcing air from his body to touch bottom. He sat heavy in his old bones and looked at her. He had been looking at her all along, all his life he had been looking, but he looked more—and she was a wolf with knitting in her lap, then she was a little girl frail and lost in gray hair and old lady clothes, knuckles swollen, and then again what, old man, who was she besides the only one you'd ever love in this life of clattersome spoons and singing crows?—and sudden and soft he had landed in this chair in this room in this night. A smile floated up to his face all by itself, he could feel it rising in his cheeks and eyes, this brightening, and he found a laugh starting out of him, and soon he was laughing in that big easy way some men have, men of the moment who can shake off their troubles by the door and let out that three-cheers-to-fiddle-player's laugh, which rattles bottles against barroom mirrors.

When she started to say something, to apologize, he rose to his feet and took her hand and led her out to the porch, where they stood together and watched the night, the black trees, the moon, the stars so close you could stir them with a finger, an animal in the leaves under the porch. And they closed up the house and went to bed, it being so late, but the man had a tickle in his throat and couldn't sleep in the quiet and began coughing. He got up and went to the kitchen for seltzer water and lemon. In the silvery moondark he sat at the kitchen table and cleaned his teeth with a toothpick.

That morning—the sunlight streaming into the house through the curtains, the birds outside singing—when she went to the room with the day bed, she carried a tray with their coffee and juice and muffins to him and found that, during the night, he had died.

There was consolation to be had in the busy details of the wake and funeral, in the playing of host to friends and family, in the attending to train schedules and sleeping arrangements. An odd, quiet solace also crept into the old woman's answering of sympathy cards and her writing of money orders to the churchyard and stonecarver and undertaker, that cologne of his carrying the memory of every death in town. And at every other corner someone waited to keep her distracted with lunch in the market, with gossip, with invitations to dinner. It struck her that everyone—in a fit of pity—conspired to let her never be alone again.

And as the old woman withdrew from them all, they would talk of how she carried her grief—so sad, they said, silently worrying over their own ends—and they would turn their leading questions to the organ grinder, for he was believed to have second sight. What with his accent and those cream-clotted eyes and the little-man monkey over his shoulder, who would not look twice at the man and feel the cool, root cellar air of an oracle about him?

Well the bridge ladies, for one, couldn't care less and complained mostly about forgetting their cards. And of what concern was it to the museum committee, their anonymous donors all but vanished, bankruptcy staring them in the face so close that by the middle of each month they had to rent out their halls to wedding and birthday parties. And nothing ever seemed to touch the organ grinder, either, to whom the old woman still read on Friday mornings, even though she wondered if he still cared to listen. It seemed to her that he would awaken only when she stopped reading or digressed from the story.

"Excuse me," he would say, "but it says that for real?"

And she would smile over to the monkey—who crouched so attentive in his little mustard-colored suit—and return to the page and clear her throat before she picked up from where she had broken off. The man wanted only ghost stories, of late, and the more avenging the justice, the more haunted the conscience, the better. And the monkey would snort at each turn, at each squeaking door and midnight romp he would somersault in his seat, and a dull guilt would tie up the old woman's neck, as if her reading held within it something mildly illicit. With the bright morning and the chirping birds, the stories of graverobbers or shipwrecks seemed to her like brandy at breakfast.

But to see the monkey squirm in his seat and begin to clap as she reached lunchtime and the end of the tale, where the ghosts all march onto the waves to their foggy ships, that was fine. And as the monkey clapped, the organ grinder opened his onion-white eyes, "Brav-o!" he said. "Brav-o!"

And she whiled away the afternoon with lunch and coffee and the organ music in the market, the crabs and roasting seeds and fruit stalls, and the water-cool shade of the trees by the benches where she sat and met the usual passersby, whose pity she despised more and more with each smile and new scandal that came her way. And closer to evening, the old woman sat out on the porch with her wine and chocolate and the sun behind the trees, the branches in strong tangled shadow. It was autumn but the light was warm and she waited for night to fall as birds flew home to their nests. She carried sunflower seeds out of habit, but she hardly ever watched for her Romeo and his soft return, which she had once seen in her mind so clearly, a smudge of black against the horizon, his raucous flying home at one time so fully imagined to her it seemed already fulfilled somewhere—the roll of his wings, the fanned spread of his tail, the silky hiss of his feathers, the tick of his feet upon the wood porch—to her.

"Hello, bird," she says to a grackle in the shrub, who tips his head and looks to the seeds she's holding out in her hand.

She says, "Take some," and the bird squeaks a rusty gate of a song and flits to a branch in a tree, slightly higher, and the old woman stands and comes forward with her hand out. When she is close enough to see how his eye shines yellow and how his black feathers gloss purple, he whets his beak and then twitters to a tree near the street and turns on his perch and watches her again. She is on the sidewalk and with him past the post office and fire station and market, her bird before her in the tree just distant, past houses and smells of dinner, past the cemetery and church she follows tree by tree until they are beyond even the railway station and he is gone from view.

The sky darkens left to right over the town, over which the moon also rises, nearly full, bright and clear enough to cast shadows. And into the gutter the old woman pitched the seeds in her hand. Beyond the shuttered market stalls, she could see the glow of lights against the museum façade. Every light must have been on—the whole place alive with light—but not a soul stood on the steps at the entrance, no guard or coat-check with his arm draped over the ancient lion in the foyer. Music, yes, and the muddled drone of voices and glassware from the ballroom, like some empty and haunted ship, the old woman feeling close to invisible as she turned at the suits of armor down the long side hall, draped ceiling to floor with royal tapestries, the music and voices fading behind her, only the occasional burst of girl's laughter flying after her, as though released.

At the end of the hall double doors with portal windows stood dark, and when she pushed them, all their heaviness swung easily and silently aside and opened onto her favorite of all rooms in the museum. The doors closed behind her and she let her eyes adjust to the dim light of the room. All was quiet. And slow and gradual, the sponged clouds came clear on the high-domed ceiling, and once more she was in the company of the gulls and kestrels suspended and the wandering albatross hanging there on wires above her.

She walked beneath them—the big wheeling birds under clouds—to the wall of bright cases, each holding a bird as posed and half-real as a painting of a bird, a painted bird under smudged glass and glare of lights. The last known Passenger Pigeon, who had been named

Martha, sat alone in her case and stared with her glass bead eyes at the room, at the woman, at the other birds. And next to her, as remote as the rest, the Bourbon Crested Starling sat on a branch, holding a cricket in his beak forever, accounts telling how this bird could be batted down with a yard stick, it being so trusting and tame. And the old woman came to the Great Auk and could practically hear him say his name as she stood before the antique specimen, his feathers soft as velvet, his wings spread, her hand on the glass as if he could be frightened away. She passed the Mysterious Starling and the Paradise Parrot and the Rodriguez Solitary, who looked so delicate and alert that she had to re-mind herself that these birds—the Spectacled Cormorant, the Chat-man Island Rail, the Bonin Wood Pigeon, the Society Parakeet—were all hollow inside, all staged, stuffed, and dead to the world.

And at the end of the room, and at the window, the old woman watched herself in the glass and reached up and turned the metal lock on the window sash and lifted open the window, the weights in the walls banging, the night dark outside, the air cool, the sounds again of a party, the stars, the streetlamp moon. And what was so wrong with ad-mitting it, admitting that she would love to fly home right now like a bird? That she would have given anything to go dark through the black air, instead of having to walk past the tuxedoed thickwits splashing in the fountain after the gold fish, the bare-shouldered women giggling as they held the men's shoes dry in their arms. That the insolent look of the night guard with his feet up on the desk, that look enough to crush her, those eyes enough to make her feel more small and lonely—if this made any sense at all—lonely for her life when it was as yet undimin-ished, for the vanishing of her life behind her.

She walked home cold under the moon—which had two blue rings around it, meaning frost—and she was home again, her red wine where she had left it on the porch, next to the chocolate and fruit. She took everything inside and sat in her chair and hugged herself with a heavy shawl wrap until her teeth stopped chattering. She stared tiredly at the room, the fireplace, the radio, the rug, her husband's empty chair, her basket of yarn. And she didn't know, in the end, how to sit without hope, how to sit without wishing for his return, for her Romeo to open his beak and place a necklace in her palm and return to her all the many voices she had grown so lonely for.

She heard the rumble of a train running through town, and then all was quiet again. She raised her palm to her mouth to taste the salt, and she heard mice in the walls. Far away a dog barked. And she must have fallen asleep, for she was awakened by the scratching in the kitchen. She feared the mice had become rats, their clawings so persistent that she took the iron poker from the fireplace with her. She turned on the light, and the noise stopped. At the counter she checked that the flour and sugar jars were closed, and when she turned to leave, the scratching like tapping began again.

Then at the back door, his hand on the screen, she caught the little gray face in the bottom corner of the screen; it was the organ grinder's monkey in his mustard-colored suit, and she smiled and let him in. "My, my," she said, "what a surprise!"

And the monkey climbed up on the counter and held out his hand to shake.

"And what brings you here, you little rascal?"

The monkey's smile widened as he went across to the table and sat down, his tail coiled around the chair back. He crossed his legs like a gentleman.

"Well then," she said, "may I offer something to eat?"

She set the table and began putting out cheese and crackers and nuts, a tiny bowl of olives, some fruit and wine, and the monkey nibbled at a pretzel and never took his eyes from her. And when she sat down, she offered him chocolate and began her talking. She told what amounted to a long pour of days and once upon a time memories, the monkey listening rapt, her voice stopping only long enough to refill a glass or crack a nut for her little friend.

Then, in the distance, they heard the voice of the organ grinder up the street. "Don't do this, Archie," he called, his voice breaking and raw, "come home, please."

Neither the monkey nor the woman moved. They stared at one another, and the man passed the front of the house. "Arch-ie, please," he called, and neither the monkey nor the woman seemed to breathe, they held so still.

"Bad Archie," said the man, "you're a bad, mean monkey."

And when the man's voice had passed the door, the old woman stood and looked out on the street to see the organ grinder, blind and bareheaded, stumble like a drunk along the gutter in the cool moonlight. The old woman turned to Archie and watched him sleeve a butter knife, his thin brown hand taking up his glass by the stem and placing it back down in the ring of wine on the table cloth.

"Now, Archie," she said and sat again, "where were we?"

Lie Big

One time Mitey-Mike tripped a silent alarm in a jewelry store. It was three-thirty in the morning. The cops came.

He told me about this the next day.

Mitey-Mike saw the cops at the front window. He didn't try to run or hide. He walked right up to them. "Hey," he shouted through the glass. "You have to go around back. Through the alley. The back door. I don't have the key to this one." He met them at the back door—the door he'd jimmied—and invited them in. "I'll get some coffee going," he said. "Caf or de-caf?"

The cops wanted to know who he was. There were four of them. They said they were responding to an alarm.

"I'm Jerry's nephew," Mitey-Mike told them. "Come on in. Give yourselves a break. We've got chairs in here. There's coffee if you want. I'm going to have coffee. Actually, I'm going to have a beer. You know what I mean? A late-night beer. There's beer in the basement. Here, let me get some lights on."

He roamed around the store looking for the light switches. Three of the cops sat down in chairs; the fourth remained standing and watched him. Mitey-Mike found the lights. He turned them on. He walked back over to the cops. "Listen here," he said to the cop who was standing, "have a seat. Mi casa, su casa." He brought a chair over. These were the chairs customers sat in to peer into the jewelry cases and try on rings and bracelets and talk to the jewelers. It was that kind of store. The cop finally sat down. "Now what can I get for you guys?" said Mitey-Mike. "How 'bout a beer?"

One of the cops said, "We'd like to see some I.D., please."

Mitey-Mike stared at him, then stared at each of them, and laughed. "You mean Jerry didn't tell you about the boat?" He paused. He looked them in the eye. "The boat. You know about the boat, right?" He laughed again. "You guys don't know about the boat. You probably have no idea why I'm here."

He pulled a chair up for himself. "This was the big weekend," he said. "Jerry decided it was time. Well, goddamn, he's been dating the girl the better part of three years. It was more than time. You know her? Nika? The surgeon? No? Okay. Anyway, he's taking her up to Drummond Island for the weekend. He's got the place there. The beach house. Comfy but there's spiders. He gets me to come along. Anne, too. He wants us to video-tape it when he pops the question. The idea is, we've got the camera out and we're just messing with it. On the beach. Filming the sunset. Then he'll get down on one knee."

The cops looked on with a mixture of bafflement, boredom, and lingering suspicion.

"The ring," Mitey-Mike continued. "Now Jerry's got some nice rings right here in the shop. In fact, if you'd like, you're welcome to try some on. Look around. Let me know what catches your eye. But the point is, Nika used to work here. Before med school. She knows the goddamn inventory. Jerry's not going to just pluck something out of the case. It's got to be special. It *was* special. Listen.

"They went to Morocco in February. Sure, just leave me here alone, Jerry, just leave me here all alone to run things during Valentine's Day rush. Thanks a *lot,* Jerry. So. They're in Marrakech. The market-place. Crazy narrow streets. Thousands of twists and turns. I saw pictures. Well, what happens is, they get separated from each other in there. Jerry's not worried—Nika's a big girl, she can take care of herself, she can find her way back to the hotel. This is perfect, though. Jerry can look for a ring in secret. He finds this old man jeweler, a nomad—they call them Blue Men—they're tribal peoples, desert folk. This old guy makes these rings, okay? You know what a quarter-cusp is?" Mitey-Mike leaned in toward the cop nearest him. "Here, let me see your hand."

"We can't stay long," said the cop. His walkie-talkie buzzed with radio traffic.

"Okay. Fast forward, fast forward. Listen," said Mitey-Mike, "Jerry's all ready to give her the ring. This was the big weekend. Today we get out in the boat, me and Jerry, and yeah, you guessed it. *The boat fucking flips.* Now this is the weird part. We'd hit something underwater. That's what flipped us. But guess what it was. I'll tell you. It was a *car,* an *automobile,* for example, what you'd drive to the market in or pile full of kids for their Saturday morning soccer game. We hit a car with his boat. Jerry had the ring in his coat pocket. Well, that's gone. My wallet's gone, too, but that stuff's easy to replace.

The cop who was last to sit down now stood. "What'd he do," the cop chuckled, "send you all the way back down here to get another ring?"

"Yes, sir. And his Scuba gear."

The cop looked at him. "I thought the guy who owned this place was named Maynard."

"Maynard?" said Mitey-Mike. "Maynard's just the manager. He's a moron. No, he's a nice guy. But he's terrible with the books. You know what, though. He saved Jerry's life once." He raised his eyebrows. "Australia. Sharks."

At this point in his recounting, Mitey-Mike fell silent. We were shooting baskets at Wheeler Park, down by the old train station. "Well, what happened?" I asked him

"What do you mean?"

"What do you mean, 'what do you mean?' What happened next?"

"Nothing. They left. I told them I'd close up. I told them to stop by during business hours and take a look at our fine selection." Mitey-Mike reached into his jeans with both hands and pulled a long gold chain from each pocket. "Here," he said. "Take your pick."

I looked at him.

"There's a lesson in this," he said.

"What's that?"

He bounced the basketball and shot from thirty feet, an airball that rolled all the way to the grass. "*Swish!*" he said. He grinned at me. "Lie big."

Mitey-Mike always lied big. He told marvelous lies, outlandish lies, terrible and astounding lies, sad and dangerous lies, silly lies, beautiful, exquisite and thunderous lies. He lied, mostly, to get out of trouble, but often he lied for no reason at all. Times when truth would have sufficed, when a small lie would have done the job, he still lied big. Preposterous lies, he said, had more style. He lied to teachers and cops, to employers, to girlfriends, and even to me, his best friend. Once, twenty minutes late to pick me up from Bell's Pizza, where we both worked, he arrived with a story of taking his cousin's ferret on an emergency trip to the vet.

"Look, don't worry about it," I said.

"I *am* worried," he said, "I'm worried about little Smokey. I don't know if the poor rascal's gonna make it through the night. They think he was poisoned. What kind of creep would poison a little kid's ferret?"

Nothing was too sacred to use for material. In high school, I'd heard him explain to a math teacher after class why he hadn't brought his homework in. His brother in Rhode Island, Mitey-Mike said, had called him the night before, suicidal. Mitey-Mike spoke very softly and slowly and stared at his hands. "I could hear that his voice was funny," he said. "Not funny like upset, just weird-sounding, and I asked him why, and he told me, well, the gun was in his mouth."

Mitey-Mike sometimes said that as an authority on lying it was important to pass his knowledge on to others, and by others he meant me. He said that the best lies didn't have to make sense and didn't have to relate directly to what you were lying about—if something disastrous had really just happened to you, it's unlikely you'd be able to explain yourself clearly. One of his favorite strategies was to appear badly shaken and cry out in deep, inexpressible sorrow, "The *dogs*. They were shitting *everywhere*. They just kept shitting and shitting!" He believed there were other can't-miss lines, like any that involved spilling a steaming-hot drink into your own lap and burning your penis. No one in history had ever been asked to supply a doctor's note for a burnt penis.

Mitey-Mike always cautioned me not to say too much, not to overexplain. People who are telling the truth, he said, never feel the need to go into too much detail, though there were also times, he acknowledged, when an incredible story was necessary, like when he'd been caught inside the jewelry store.

Never back down from a lie, Mitey-Mike instructed me. Whenever someone challenged him, he'd respond with wounded ferocity, with such blazing and forceful conviction that people either believed him or gave in to the lie rather than continue the argument. He was a bully in that way. On the basketball court, if his team scored the first point of the game, he'd call out the score, "Four nothing."

Someone on the other team would protest. "Four? That's the first bucket."

Mitey-Mike's eyes would go wide and he'd howl, "No fucking *way*— I scored twice myself,"—he'd point at me—"and my man right here scored one. That's three nothing. Check it up."

Sometimes the lies turned ugly. Mitey-Mike lied to his girlfriends. He usually had two or three girlfriends at the same time. I saw the hurt in their faces when he lied to them—they knew he was lying but pretended to themselves and to him that they didn't. Mitey-Mike found ways to make me complicit in his lies. He'd leave one girl's house and pick me up at my grandma's, and together we'd drive over to another one of his girlfriend's houses. She'd be upset that he was an hour and a half late, and he'd explain that we'd been giving my grandma a bath. The girl would look at me and I'd nod gravely and explain, "She gets

sores if we don't get her out of bed and into the tub every few days."
Then Mitey-Mike would drop me off back at my house and speed
away with the girl.

You might think I'd get tired of all the lies but I never did. Each sad
and damaging lie he told was followed by thirty wild, joyous, sprawl-
ing, magical lies. It was a glorious feeling to be in cahoots with him, to
be backstage, behind the curtain, on the side of *knowing,* and watch
him weave his brilliant tapestries. People delighted in him and his
power over them was mesmerizing.

From fifth grade on, Mitey-Mike was my best friend and really my
only friend—when I hung out with other people he got jealous and
brooded around town until I abandoned my new friends and came
back to him. In me he had a sidekick, someone to witness all of his impossible feats; in turn, he provided me with adventure and a way to
meet girls. We were a pretty good team for about fourteen years. But
you know how it is. Things fall apart.

First, Katy appeared. She came into Bell's Pizza one night after we'd already closed, a shy, beautiful, pale-skinned girl with green hair, wearing big jeans and a Joe Dumars jersey. I was up front counting out the
register; Mitey-Mike was in back mopping out the walk-in cooler—if
we'd been reversed, things might have unfolded differently. I gave Katy
two free slices of pizza and asked for her phone number; within a
couple of weeks we were a couple.

My love for Katy was sharp and aching. When she wasn't right next
to me I was miserable. Even when we were laying close together or, you
know, making with the love, I still couldn't seem to get close enough.
I'd always imagined that Mitey-Mike would disapprove when I finally
found a girl to be with because I'd be less available to him, but he was
cool about Katy. He said it made him feel good to see me so wrapped
up in someone. He seemed genuinely happy for me. A couple of week-
ends in a row he covered my shifts so Katy and I could go camping up
north.

One night in August I got off work early, before midnight, and went
looking for Mitey-Mike to see if he wanted to play some basketball.
Through the front window of his house, in the glow from the TV, I saw
him making out with a girl on the living room floor. I'd actually happened upon this type of scene at his house a couple of times before and
had jetted, but this time I stayed for a moment because the Tigers game
was on the TV and I could see that Detroit had runners at second and

third with nobody out. I must have gotten caught up in the game be-cause a couple of minutes later I realized all of a sudden that Mitey-Mike and the girl were sitting up and staring at me. You know how you can look at something and not really see it for what it is, and then there's this tremor and things flip into place? For about a second and oh, maybe another third of a second, it was just Mitey-Mike and a girl—then things popped into focus, and it was Mitey-Mike and Katy.

A great, deafening roaring sound filled my ears; blood banged its way through my neck and my arms; my entire body buzzed like I'd grabbed hold of a downed power line. The world came to me in a se-ries of fade-ins and fade-outs. I remember running as hard as I could, chased by Mitey-Mike. The next thing I knew I was sitting on the front porch of a house somewhere, Mitey-Mike standing over me, his face a foot away. I was yelling at him and he was yelling back. At some point the porch light turned on and an old man appeared in the doorway. "The fuck you looking at!" Mitey-Mike screamed at the guy. Next we were running again, all the way through downtown, and then we were standing on the basketball court at Wheeler Park, heaving for breath and drenched in sweat.

Mitey-Mike shook me by the shoulders. "Look at me," he said. "Look at me! You think you know what you saw—but you don't! You don't!"

I pushed him away from me and screeched for him to fuck off.

He shook me again. "You need to chill the fuck out! I was giving her a back-rub! Do you understand? A silly fucking back-rub!"

Maybe I was crying, I don't know. I sagged away. "Can you tell me the truth," I said. My head pounded. "It's me, okay? Come on, now. It's me. Just tell me what's happening. I just want to know what's happening."

"Nothing's happening," he said. "We're here at the park. We're talk-ing. Katy's probably wondering where the hell we are."

I tore at my forehead and my cheeks. "Mike, I saw, okay? I saw it all. You don't have to make anything up. I saw what I saw. I saw you guys."

Mitey-Mike was quiet for a bit. The night pulsed. Finally he said, "Okay, listen. You want to hear everything, I'll tell you. I asked Katy to come over for a reason. I asked her to bring me something specific over, some medicine, some hydro-cortisone cream. Listen to me! She was helping me put it on. Earlier today—listen to me! Earlier today, I spilled bleach on myself. Listen! I burnt my penis."

Memory is strange. I don't remember punching him, I just remem-ber him saying that last thing, then looking up at me with his face covered in blood. "You're bleeding," I said, surprised by it. Then I turned and ran.

For about six months my dad had been in my ear, asking me to come out to Sacramento and help him with his business. He sold trampolines to rich people. A week later I was out there learning the ropes.

In late December, two days before the new year, Mitey-Mike was killed in an accident. It was the kind of spectacular tale he might have come up with himself after missing a week of work. What happened was he was walking his neighbor's dog in a field near his house and he got hit by an airplane. A little two-man Cessna. Both pilots died and so did Mitey-Mike but the dog lived. Hassan, my old boss at Bell's Pizza, explained everything. I'd never heard him so upset. "Will you come back for the funeral?" he asked me. I told him I didn't know.

Katy called the next day, New Year's Eve. She was crying. We talked for a long time. She told me she'd loved Mitey-Mike; I told her I'd loved him, too. She said they'd found an apartment together in Ypsilanti and they were supposed to move in on the first of February. They'd bought some furnishings already—drapes and a furry toilet-seat cover.

"What are you gonna do?" I asked her.

"I don't know," she said. "I was thinking of moving out there to California."

"Here?"

"Well, to L.A. You remember Jenna? She lives there."

"It'd be nice to have you out here. L.A.'s not too far from here."

"Yeah. That would be nice." She began to cry again.

"You know what I'm wearing," I said, "I'm wearing that gold necklace he gave me. Remember the long gold chain he gave me? From when he broke into that jewelry store? He had one that matched it. Remember?"

Katy said, "I know which necklace you're talking about."

"Yeah, I wear it every day. I guess I have since he gave it to me." I wrapped the long end of it around my fingers and through them. "Katy, you know the jewelry store story, right? How he broke in and there was a silent alarm and the cops came?"

"I know that story," she said. "That's your favorite Mitey-Mike story. You love that story. You always tell that story. You told me that story before I even met him."

"Yeah. It's a good story."

"Well, he made it up. Last week he told me. No, two weeks ago. He got that necklace at Bunky's on Michigan Avenue. His necklace, too, the one that matched. He traded his old Nintendo for them. And a bunch of games." She took a long, staggered breath. Someone else was saying something to her in the background. "Listen," she said. "I got to go. Let's talk later. Can we talk some more? Can we talk tomorrow? I think we should keep talking."

My head and my hands felt light. "Call me tomorrow," I said.

"Okay. Bye then. Happy New Year's."

"Okay," I said. "Okay. Okay. Happy New Year."

MICHAEL BYERS

(1996)

A Lovely Night

Beth's family had money, Don's did not, and it was occasionally a problem one way and another, so when they married they decided, in common agreement, to pay for the wedding themselves. Beth and Don didn't have much money as a couple, but they themselves rented the white tents and hired the single trumpeter to stand in the meadow, and together they drove an uncle's borrowed pick-up to the island's best farm and bought basketfuls of vegetables that could be grilled, and visited the island's friendliest fisherman, Henry Fine, and bought from him arm-length filets of tuna that had been caught offshore. Dark, oily, slippery, the filets seemed individual creatures themselves; in their two deep coolers they lay wrapped in plastic, smelling of the deep, clean ocean. Don counted out the cash into Henry's palm, feeling a swell of sexual pride that the tall blonde dark-eyed woman beside him was about to become his wife. "Good choice," Henry told him, seemingly not only about the fish, and gave him a look of complicit congratulations. The tuna, enough to serve their forty guests, cost them two hundred dollars.

The wedding went just perfectly. Everyone cried, and afterward laughed at how much they had cried. His homemade dance floor, made of plywood and two-by-fours, was a flop, but their friends danced in the grass instead. It was Beth's family's summer house; the house stared west into the Pacific from its gently rising lawn, and the meadow climbed the gradual hill behind into a creaking stand of ash trees. The food was cooked by two caterers they'd hired from a nearby town at fourteen dollars an hour, and dinner was served at the rented round tables set up in the orchard. Beth's family did not do weddings this way, to say the least. But they were good-natured people, and nobody complained, and after dinner everyone got drunk and smoked a lot of cigarettes, and when the older people were hustled off to their various rented cabins around the island the newlyweds and their friends smoked pot and lit fireworks on the rocky, driftwood-strewn beach, and stayed up very late watching the supertankers sliding past across the darkened water. All in all it was a success. They were happy to have done it this way. Don in particular felt, as he did not always feel, that they had managed to pull something off without being too frugal (they had once hosted an embarrassing party where there wasn't enough food), or, through Beth's family's money, too lavish (for six months they had owned a new Honda Passport that was a gift from her father until a festering self-disgust propelled them back to the dealership). Their wedding certificate was signed by a friend who was a certified Minister of Reasoned Light in the Temple of the Living Earth; he had received his investiture over the Internet.

Don himself, the child of a Lutheran minister, had been conceived in a dark back flat in Cleveland. He felt this fact as the first of a series of autobiographical impoverishments, followed by his father's early death by stroke, his mother's remarriage to an elementary-school principal, his brother's descent into the world of muscle cars, and his own unhappy college days, in payment for which he still carried seventeen thousand dollars in loans at eight-point-two-five percent. He had survived by virtue of a lucky intelligence and skepticism, and maybe even more than this, his own good looks. He was handsome— dark-eyed like his wife—and he suspected his looks had helped him get his first job after college, taking tourists around a minor-league ballpark. Certainly it had helped him in countless ways since then, not least in his marriage to the beautiful Beth. He did not think of himself as particularly distinguished or promising. At thirty he was a marketer for an advertising firm called Hartman + Culligan, where he invented tag lines: *The solution is everywhere. Style for the rest of us. Excellence comes standard.* He'd also named a few companies: *Fieldwork. Mandrake.com. Blossomania.* The money wasn't great, and to be sure the work was anything but noble. But he liked coming up with fitting words, words which filled all the necessary spaces in the brain, the way an answer in a crossword lays itself down letter by letter. He had a facility for the language, he supposed, and recoiled when his supposedly literate co-workers mistook *their* for *there* or *it's* for *its.* Beth worked down the street in a flower shop; their apartment was constantly filled with flowers on the soft, nearly odorless brink of wilting. His dead father's impoverished congregations had had the same sad smell, of donated flowers.

Italy, where they honeymooned, surprised him. He had never been overseas before; Beth had, in college and after. After a week Don was tanned and looked good in his white shirt and dark pants among the old sooty porticos. Not Italian exactly, he didn't flatter himself that much, and Beth looked very American in her flat white shoes and crumpled sundresses. And they were always looking at a map or walking the wrong way, or reading the *Herald Tribune.* But they were a handsome couple, and it was especially good to be with Beth here because she knew how to negotiate the trains, and knew a little more about art than he did. In the Uffizi he found himself drawn to the Fillippo Lippis: the angels, the cardinals and petitioners all realer-than-real, as though their supernatural fourth dimension had imparted to them an extra measure of roundness. Beth liked the expressionless Giottos, which he thought looked mostly dumb. How could you be considered a serious painter if you couldn't even paint hands? "But this," she said, standing before an enormous gold-shining panel, "is what it felt like to *be* Giotto. This is what the world *looked like* to him. *Stacked-up.*" Well, he didn't buy it. He couldn't draw either, but he knew what a hand looked like. But the guides, when he eavesdropped, said more or less the same thing. She was better, it occurred to him, at seeing things. And she was better with the language than he was, too. Even the primitive Italian coming from her had a nice tilt, an implied admission of happy incompetence that was expected to be overlooked, assuming, as she flipped up the brim of her sun-hat, that people would mostly get the gist. Usually they did. Whereas when he talked he was hopelessly ministerial, and received looks of pained pity in return. It was a little worrying. He was supposed to be the one with the facility for language, and here he was struggling. He put it down to nervousness.

But really they did fine in Italy. They saw Florence, Rome, Venice. He relaxed as the weeks went on. They traveled west on the train through Tuscany, then out to the high warm tourist coast of the Cinque Terre, which was full of Germans, and where no one really expected anyone to speak Italian. They swam naked off the rocks below Cordelia, full of lunchtime wine, and Don even in his postprandial fullness felt himself buoyed by the salt water, the blue air, the hot brown rocks that formed the walls of their isolated lagoon. He scraped himself on coral climbing out. Bright blood pulsed over the bones of his ankle. Below him Beth's breasts were brilliantly pale in the bright water; her short white fur swam between her legs as she kicked, kicked, kicked away from him, wearing sunglasses. In their rented apartment afterward he knelt and peeled down her dress and fastened his mouth to her, his knees cold on the hard stone floor. Their set of rooms was cool, shaded, and had been cheaply rented at the last minute from a man named Alberto. Their kitchen window looked down on a shadowed courtyard full of fluttering laundry, and beyond the bedroom the cobblestone street tipped down to the Mediterranean. From the windows they could hear the echoing calls of boys playing soccer before dinner. From the courtyard came the sound of water trickling ceaselessly from a broken faucet into a stone saucer. Beth, on the broad flat bed, with her legs open, was content to do nothing forever but lie and shift her hips, and caress his hair as he worked between her legs, while around them, despite its freight of sounds, the air seemed very clear and weightless, full of nothing. On the nightstand, left behind by another renter, was a paperback by Lawrence Kurtz; Don's eye kept drifting to its bright orange cover. *Brush-Off* it was titled, one silver word above the other.

Afterward they showered and walked out into the evening in their white, sink-washed clothes. Don's ankle was beginning to throb, but it was a beautiful evening. He was proud to walk with his beautiful wife through the narrow streets of Cordelia. Far below them the coastal train ran clicking from town to town, a long green serpent, and far out on the water ran gray ships he could not tell the shape of. Down a side street they passed a pair of old ladies on a bench, who called out to them in Italian, "What a lovely night it is!" and he, feeling a masterful, sublime mood rising in him, cried, "Yes, yes, yes it is!" as he and Beth walked by. Only a minute later did it occur to him—did he belatedly decipher in his own head—what the old women had been saying. They had been crying, "What a beautiful couple this is!"

Bright-faced with shame, he confessed his mistake to Beth. "I know what they said," she told him. "But that's awful," he moaned, "that's terrible! How embarrassing!" "But we *are* a beautiful couple," she told him, with a great unshakeable serenity. "They were happy for us, sweetheart."

His ankle took weeks to heal, and was itchy for months afterward. He scratched it through his sock while sitting in his glassed-in office, remembering that evening with a violent inner cringe. He could not decide which bothered him most: that he had embarrassed himself so completely in front of two old women he would never see again; that he had ended up with a wife who was capable of such marvelous satisfaction with things, while he was not; or that he could not keep himself from thinking of the incident over and over again—twirling and twirling it in his brain—while outwardly he appeared to be going about the decent, blameless business of living a normal, admirable, and husbandly life, free from that kind of prideful concern.

TUNG-HUI HU
(1999)

Balance

Soon after I moved to California
I felt tremors everywhere: it made for
headaches and a vivid idea of how
delicately each thing was balanced,
bird upon sky, sky upon roof, roof
upon post & lintel. What trees I saw
had shifted in their sockets towards the
sky, some hanging loose and some
undressed by fire until black, wire-tipped,
and deaf. The heat loosened from
the ruptured earth was the same heat
I felt once leaving the surgery room:
with one eye out I saw things as a
fish does. A flat world, pulled
in all directions by this tremendous
current that sets down the world's
balance, aligns people with doors
and throws me off the sidewalk,
a tremor of mind: in less than a small
touch I crumple down, and the tea
I am holding is immersed in the
puddles, and my body turns
the waters fragrant.

A rock a fish

Here there is breath.
There are rocks, but only
as an abdomen pulled
apart, that red color of
correction marks, cracked
lips, and swellings.
The people who live here,

stringy men, wispy
women, as if spun from
clouds, they are capable
of greater passions than
us: one man, infuriated
at his car, the lemon
that had cost him a life's
savings, drove it to the
canyon edge and cut away
the metal cord that coupled
the car, the rocks. Sliding
through the waters,
it breathed, and its gills
began to whiten with air—
how small the car must
have looked from above,
but to the fish it was as if
a continent had shifted,
stretched, and birthed
a new mountain range.

RATTAWUT LAPCHAROENSAP

(2003)

Priscilla the Cambodian

The only thing I ever learned about wealth was Priscilla the Cambodian's beautiful teeth. All her teeth were lovely ingots, each one crowned in a cap of pure gold. When she smiled it sometimes looked like that little girl had swallowed the sun. Dong and I would often ask to look and Priscilla would open her mouth wide. We'd move in close, stare into its recesses until her jaw got sore. "You're rich," Dong and I would say, and Priscilla the Cambodian would smile and giggle like we'd just told her she was beautiful.

Her father was a dentist. When things started looking bad in Cambodia, he hired somebody to smelt the family's gold. He put all that gold in Priscilla's mouth. And then they took him away. Priscilla remembered sitting on his dentist's chair in the empty hospital while bombs fell on Phnom Penh. Over the next three years, as Priscilla and her mother moved from camp to camp, she sometimes went for days without opening her mouth—her mother was afraid the guards might get ideas. She made Priscilla nibble on gruel and salted fish in the relative secrecy of the warehouse they shared with hundreds of other refugees. "Awesome," we'd say. "They should make a movie about your life, girlie."

This was the summer Dong and I wasted in the empty community pool the development company never got around to finishing. Priscilla and her mother had recently arrived in Bangkok with two other Cambodian families. They all squatted in a tin shack compound by the train tracks bordering the development. Before we met Priscilla, Dong and I in our unflappable boredom would sometimes stand on the rails and throw rocks just to hear the satisfying clang on the Cambodians' corrugated roofs. Priscilla's short, flat-faced mother would run out and bark at us in a language we didn't understand, but it wasn't too hard to understand the rusted shovel she waved threateningly in our direction, so we'd run and laugh like delighted hyenas.

Mother said the refugees were a bad sign. "God's trying to tell us something," she said. "God's probably saying, 'Hey, sorry, but there won't be a health club or a community garden or a playground or a pool or any of those other things you suckers thought you were getting when you first came to the development. I'm gonna give you some Cambodian refugees instead. They're not as fun, but hey, life isn't a store, sometimes you don't get what you pay for.'" Father nodded and said refugees meant one thing and one thing only. It meant we'd be living in the middle of a slum soon. "Those fuckers move in packs," he said. Their little refugee camp would get so big we'd probably start thinking we were refugees too.

By that time the prognosis was already bad. The factories had moved to the Philippines and Malaysia. Mother was reduced to sewing panty hose out of a Chinese woman's house. Father carried concrete beams at a construction site for minimum wage. Some of the families in the development had already moved on, leaving their pets and potted plants and empty duplexes behind. Early in the summer, Father and Mother tried to sell like the others. But the market had turned; it was already too late. When the development company realtor came to appraise, Father's face turned so pale I was afraid he'd pass out. "That's a goddamn crime," Father said, after the realtor offered little more than half the duplex's original price. "No crime here," the realtor replied, fingering the knot of his tie. "Just old-fashioned economics." So Father said, "Get out of my house. Get out or I'm gonna show you something else that's old-fashioned." But the realtor just kept smiling and said, "Fine. Suit yourself. Have fun living like savages."

One April afternoon, Dong and I were breaking our asses attempting stupid bike tricks in the unfinished pool. I sat in the shallow end wiping a stain on my pants while Dong prepared to ride off the diving board. It was going to be a good trick, we thought. A girl-seducing trick. We were sure that once all the girls saw us soar off that diving board and land in the deep end they'd swoon, fall on their knees, and trip over each other in the hopes of doing some delightfully nasty dancing with us. Dong and I had decided that our access to dancing of any kind would not easily be granted on our good looks alone. For one, we were both too dark. For another, my dogged asthma had earned me the moniker of Black Wheezy from the Thicknecks at school. And, for yet another, Dong was knock-kneed and kind of fat. The Thicknecks called him the Pregnant Duck. When girls were around, all they'd have to say was "Hey look, guys, there goes Black Wheezy and the Pregnant Duck" or "Quack-Quack! Hack-hack!" and suddenly it was like the word HANDSOME had just been emblazoned on their foreheads. Needless to say, this was not funny to us at all—not even a little bit—but apparently very funny to Dong's parents and my own, because they laughed so long and hard when we went crying to them that we believed we'd become the most psychotically depressed eleven-year-old boys in the history of the planet. So we needed a talent. Aerial acrobatics seemed like a good idea. Unfortunately, none of our attempts thus far had been very acrobatic or even very aerial.

That afternoon, just as Dong got halfway down the diving board, Priscilla the Cambodian appeared poolside out of nowhere. "Wheeeeee!" she squealed like a happy little succubus. Dong hesitated, turned to look at Priscilla, lost crucial velocity, and tumbled off the edge of the diving board. It made a bad sound. It sounded like a dog getting hit by a car because even with all the bike's clanging and screeching I could still hear Dong yelp when he hit the pool's hard bottom. Priscilla pointed and laughed, and that's when I glimpsed her gold fangs glinting for the very first time.

"Refugee fuckass," Dong muttered, getting up off the mildewed tiles. "What do you think you're doing?" He collected his bike, teetered on his feet. But Priscilla the Cambodian just laughed and laughed some more. "Hey," I said, walking down toward Dong in the deep end. "The pool's ours. Get out of here." She looked at me curiously. She was younger than us. She wore an old Kasikon Bank T-shirt that came down to her knees. Short black hair sprouted in matted tufts all over her head. And she had that mouthful of gold.

She stopped laughing, frowned, pointed an accusing finger at us both. "Leave my mother alone," she said sternly in Thai, her tiny voice echoing around the pool. "No more rocks." Dong and I exchanged glances. We didn't know she could speak Thai. We'd seen her around the housing development with the other Cambodians, but they'd always spoken to each other in that gibberish.

"I don't know what you're talking about," Dong said, rubbing his head with the heel of his palm.

"Don't lie," she answered. I glimpsed her teeth again. I thought about pirates. "I'll kill you next time. I'm not kidding, guys."

"Okay," Dong said, shrugging, getting on his bike. He started riding in large swooping circles, the chain creaking noisily, the wheels singing beneath him. "Sure. Whatever, girlie." She stared at us impassively, watched Dong gliding along the bottom of the pool. "You speak pretty good Thai," I said after a while. "What's your name?"

Dong shot me an incredulous look from his bike.

"Priscilla," she said almost sheepishly, fingering the hem of her T-shirt.

"Some name for a refugee," I replied, laughing, "That's not a Cambodian name. That's a farang name."

She opened her mouth as if she might explain. But then she turned around and started walking away. "Just don't do it again," she said as she went through the unpainted gate. "No more rocks. My mama doesn't like it."

She'd been gone for all of ten minutes when Dong and I climbed up the pool ladder, fished the bike out, and started making our way toward the railroad tracks.

"Did you see her teeth?"

"Yeah," Dong said. "She's a freak."

A thin strand of smoke curled out of Priscilla's shack. Somebody was cooking inside. We stood on the railroad ties, grabbed a few choice rocks, felt their cold, lovely heft in our hands. "Bombs away," Dong said, winking.

The first rock elicited no response. But as soon as the second one rang the corrugated roof, Priscilla emerged from the house like an angry little boar, fists at her sides, nostrils flared, bushwhacking her way through the knoll separating the train tracks from the Cambodians' shanty. I saw her contorted face, started laughing, started sprinting. But halfway back to the road, I noticed Dong wasn't running beside me.

I turned around. That tiny Cambodian girl had Dong pinned facedown to the railroad ties. She sat on his back while he bucked and thrashed beneath her like a rodeo horse. She yelled at him, pummeled the back of his head repeatedly with her hands. I thought about leaving him there. But then I remembered that the girl had said she was going to kill us, and I suddenly didn't know how serious Cambodians were when they said something like that, even if the Cambodian was just a little girl. She could've been Khmer Rouge—a term Mother and Father always mentioned in stern voices when they complained about the refugees—although I only understood at the time that Khmer Rouge was a bad thing like cancer was a bad thing. Khmer Rouge probably made you bald and pale and impossibly skinny, and Khmer Rouge probably made you cough up vile gray-green globs of shit like Uncle Sutichai when we visited him at the hospital every Sunday. If that little girl had Khmer Rouge, I certainly didn't want Dong to get it too.

Dong looked at me helplessly when I arrived. Priscilla had both his arms pinned to the earth with her feet. "Dude," he pleaded. "Do something."

"Say you're sorry!" Priscilla screamed. Dong grunted, struggled some more in vain. She didn't notice I was there. "Say you're sorry!" she screamed again, hitting Dong's head a few more times, the sound flat and dull.

I touched her shoulder. Priscilla turned around and hit me so quick in the face that I fell back stunned. She got off Dong, leapt toward me like a little panther. She bared her golden teeth and for a second I was afraid she might bite me. But she just started hitting my head with her palms. I raised my arms for protection, her blows short and stinging, but I also found myself laughing the whole time, taken aback by the intensity of the little girl's rage.

"Apologize!" she screamed again and again and again.

"Okay, okay," I managed to say after a while. "Sorry. You win. Mercy already."

"God, girlie," Dong said, getting up, wiping the dirt from his pants with both hands. "Give peace a chance."

She stopped. She looked at us both. "I told you I'd kill you," she said proudly, crossing her arms. And then she reached out and punched Dong in the shoulder. "Fuck," Dong said, flinching. "All right already. You know, it's a good thing you're a girl because—"

"You didn't say sorry," she interrupted him sternly. Dong rubbed his shoulder with a hand. She raised her fists again.

"Okay," he grunted. "Sorry. Happy now?"

"No," she said. "Now I want you to say sorry to my mama."

"No way," I said.

"Fuck no," said Dong, shaking his head, but Priscilla had already yelled something in Cambodian toward the shack and her mother was already walking slowly across the knoll, wiping her hands on a greasy apron.

Priscilla's mother was the shortest woman I'd ever seen, barely a head taller than us, with a face as flat as an omelet, wide black unreflective eyes, and a man's broad shoulders. Her teeth weren't gold like her daughter's. They were just slightly crooked, a bit yellow, boring and regular. Priscilla said something else to her in Cambodian. Her mother nodded, scowling at us silently the whole time. "Say you're sorry," Priscilla said in Thai.

Dong looked at me. I looked at Dong.

"Do it," she said, her face creasing into a severe frown. "Or I'll beat you again."

"Sorry," we finally said in unison, staring at each other's feet.

Priscilla's mother kept on scowling at us. I though she'd start barking in Cambodian. I thought we might even discover what ungodly thing she'd meant to do with that rusted shovel. She'd probably bury us alive, I thought. I got ready to run. But instead Priscilla's mother just reached out and slapped us lightly on the back of our heads. And then, to our surprise, she smiled at us broadly—a genuine smile—before saying something to Priscilla. And then she walked back down to the shack.

Priscilla eyed us curiously, picked at her golden teeth with a pinky nail, as if deciding what to do with us.

"Can we go now?" Dong asked.

"If you want," Priscilla said, shrugging. "Unless you guys want something to eat."

That was the beginning of a nice thing. We never threw rocks at her house again. Although Dong continued to insist that we hadn't fought back because Priscilla was just a little girl, I think we both knew there was little we could've done that afternoon to beat back her angry advances. She was so pissed off it was the purest expression of fury I'd ever witnessed aside from the night Mother took a broomstick to a gigantic rat that had been raiding our trash.

So we didn't mind when Priscilla showed up at the pool the next morning. We gladly took her in. The three of us would horse around aimlessly down there, wasting those bright summer days. That's when Priscilla told us about her father and her teeth. That's when Dong and I would look into her mouth and tell her she was rich.

We initiated Priscilla to the simple pleasures of a normal, non-refugee-camp summer. We introduced her to ice cream. We bought a kite and flew it from the bottom of the pool. We took her to a movie at the cheap theater in Onnut—a horror movie about some witch living by a canal—and Priscilla gripped me so hard during the frightening parts that I discovered tiny bruises on my forearms when we got out. We even taught her how to ride a bike. The first time she got going on her own, zoomed down the slope to the deep end, she screamed so loud you could almost feel the pool's porcelain walls vibrate.

For our part, Dong and I got better with the bike. We managed to pop a couple of wheelies, though the diving board trick was still far out of reach. "You guys are so stupid," Priscilla would say, watching us work up the courage to try again. "That's the dumbest thing I've ever seen." But then she'd laugh so hard after we fell that it was almost worth risking our necks just to hear her guffaw.

When it got too hot we'd go to Priscilla's shack. Her mother cleaned houses in the nicer development down the road from ours—where the Thicknecks frolicked in their Olympic-sized community pool—but on days off Priscilla's mother would often make sticky rice for us. There was never more than that, no fish or pork or anything, but the rice felt good and substantial to have in the stomach. Priscilla's mother watched us eat impassively and the three of us would teach her a few Thai phrases. Dong and I taught her how to swear in Thai. We'd laugh because there was nothing funnier than hearing a flat-faced Cambodian refugee woman saying "Dickwad" and "Fuckface" and "Hairy beaver."

That's when we learned about Priscilla's name. She was named after Elvis Presley's wife. One of the few possessions her mother brought with her was an LP showing Elvis's fat farang mug framed by those thick bushy chops. The record sat on top of a milk crate, propped against the dirty tin wall like a centerpiece to a shrine, and although Priscilla said she'd never heard the record—they didn't own a player— her mother had done renditions during nights at the camps to get her to sleep. Dong and I looked at the LP cover and said we didn't understand how anybody could think the guy was handsome. If he grew up in Bangkok he wouldn't be king of anything. The Thicknecks would probably call him names. He'd be no better than the rest of us plebes. "Look at the guy," we said. "He's wearing a cape."

Aside from the Elvis record, there was also a small picture of Priscilla's father taped above the moth-eaten pallet she shared with her mother every night. In the picture, Priscilla's father stood before a massive concrete building wearing light green hospital scrubs. He had large, clunky glasses, stared intently at something outside the frame. "Now that guy there," we told Priscilla. "That guy's handsome. Elvis is puke compared to that guy." Priscilla believed her father was still alive. We weren't about to suggest otherwise.

The Cambodian shanty grew just as Father predicted. They really did move in packs. There were four, then six, than eight shacks and near the end of the summer there must have been thirty Cambodians living across the railroad tracks bordering our housing development. Their tiny houses leaned haphazardly against one another; from afar their shanty looked like a single delicate structure made of crinkled tin cards. Like Priscilla and her mother, they were mostly women and children, though a few dark, gaunt men appeared as well. The Cambodians never seemed to say much to each other, and when they did they spoke in hushed tones, as if being refugees also meant being quiet.

They might turn blue with laughter or gesticulate wildly or get angry at each other, but they always seemed to do so at half the normal human volume. During the evenings they chatted, kicked around a takraw ball, sewed blankets and pillows, tended to the herb garden they'd started planting in the knoll. Dong and I never spoke to any of them, but we thought it was nice the way they nodded or waved or smiled when we came by on our bikes.

Every morning a white pickup truck would arrive to take some of the Cambodians to work at a road construction site. They'd pile in back, bunched together so close there wasn't any room to sit. Once, Dong and I got up early enough to see this, and there was something about the faces of those Cambodians going to work that nearly broke our hearts in half. Their quiet anxious expressions said they weren't sure they were coming back. They looked at their dilapidated little world by the railroad tracks as if for the very last time. The truck would drop them off in the early evening and they would all be there, of course—nothing to worry about at all—and it was almost understandable to me how they could look relieved to be back at such shitty little shacks. Surviving each day seemed a victory and a wonder to them.

Two of Priscilla's teeth came out that summer. The first was a lateral incisor, close to her front teeth. She cried all day when she discovered it loosening from her gums. "I don't know what to do," she said, a finger holding the tooth in place. By that time Dong and I were already veterans of the ordeal. We told her not to worry. We told her it was natural. "I don't care if it's natural," she said, and then she cried and cried some more. We spent most of the morning consoling her. We told her to imagine the things she and her mother would be able to buy with the gold. A television. A record player. A refrigerator. But she said she didn't want anything. "It's my tooth," she said. "It's mine." Then I told her it had probably been her father's plan all along—he probably thought Priscilla and her mother would need the gold to find their way home to him—and the idea seemed to console her momentarily.

A week later, the tooth came out at last. We were sharing a bag of fishballs at the pool when Priscilla suddenly spat the tooth into her hand. We stared for a while at that ingot sitting in a small pool of spittle and blood and masticated fish, then Priscilla wiped it off and passed it around. The tooth didn't seem so brilliant outside of her mouth. It just looked like a shiny little pebble, impossibly light in my hand. We took the tooth back to Priscilla's mother and she put it away in a teakwood box next to Elvis Presley's portrait.

The housing development's decline became painfully visible, just as my parents had predicted. For the first time the development company didn't bother to fill the gaping potholes created by the wet-season floods. There were so many craters in the roads Mother said she was beginning to think we lived on the moon. She said, "Dear God, I really don't care about the health club or the pool or the community garden anymore, I just want to ride my bike to the bus stop without breaking my goddamn neck."

More rats started appearing as well. There were so many of them by the end of the summer that Mother could not have prevented them from getting to our trash even at her angriest. I watched in horror one evening as a mangy, mean-looking stray nosed a sewer grate outside our house only to scurry away frightened when three rats came lumbering out to greet her. "It's an invasion out there," Mother said. "It's a goddamn rat apocalypse." Father set poisoned rat-paper in the outdoor kitchen every night. In the morning, there'd always be two or three rats, large as small kittens, squealing and moaning, struggling against the glutinous surface like demonic little dinosaurs dying in some tar pit.

Dong said rats were super-horny. He'd seen some documentary about it on television. One rat, he said, can make up to fifteen thousand little rats in a single year. Priscilla laughed and said that was nothing. "This is easy," she said. She told us that at one of the camps things got so bad people went to sleep hugging a stick just in case.

We discovered a rat in the pool one day. It had fallen in and couldn't find a way out. We stood at the edge of the pool staring at the hideous red-eyed thing prancing around. We didn't know what to do. So we wandered aimlessly for the rest of the morning. Dong seemed so upset about the rat I thought he'd start crying. But when we went back later that afternoon it was gone. We never saw a rat in there again. But the pool was different for us after that.

Father blamed the rats on the refugees. He said they always brought vermin with them. "It's no wonder about the rats," he said one night when some of the men in the development came over for drinks. "Those people shit and piss wherever they please. You can't have people shitting and pissing wherever they please and not expect to have rats."

The men nodded along, passed around a flask of rye. Dong's father was there as well. I brought over a tray full of Heinekens and a pail of fresh ice for the men while Mother sat in the kitchen getting angry at the checkbook.

"They're probably raising them," one of the men said. "Cambodians probably think rats are a delicacy."

"Cambodians," somebody else scoffed. "They're the real rats, if you ask me."

I poured the men their beer, emptied the ashtray into a plastic bag. Father put his hand on my shoulder. "This is my boy," Father said, shaking my shoulder vigorously. "This here's our future. This is who we're fighting for."

The men nodded drunkenly along. A chill passed through my body right then. I wanted to tell the men that the refugees had built a proper outhouse hidden discreetly behind a hedge. I wanted to tell them that they didn't shit and piss indiscriminately like Father had said. I wanted to tell them about Priscilla and her mother. But I didn't think the men would appreciate these revelations.

I woke up late that night to the sound of their high, excited voices. I got out of bed and watched them standing around my father in the yard, nodding their heads in unison. Somebody arrived with a pickup truck and the men climbed in, their deep, drunken voices murmuring up to my window. They left their empty bottles on the straw mat in our yard, and for some reason I thought about how Mother and I would have to pick up the mess in the morning. The truck puttered down the street, the men chanting now, as if working up the courage to do something valiant. I walked down the stairs with my heart in my mouth. I threw on my rubber slippers, started running into the night, down the street and out toward the railroad tracks.

Halfway there, winded from running, I saw all I needed to see. The men were torching the Cambodian shantytown. A light red glow bloomed at the end of the development's main street, like a second sun rising in the night. I heard gruff, exasperated voices, the high-pitched screams of women. Something exploded. Glass shattered. Somebody yelled profanities. I stopped walking then and sat cross-legged in the middle of the street. I watched a rat scuttle into a sewer grate, appear once more to forage for food. Watching that awful red flickering in the distance, I felt so weak and dizzy that if the rats had emerged to eat me alive I couldn't have done a thing to stop them.

I don't remember walking home. But I must have, because I woke up in my own bed the next morning, head throbbing with pain. I thought I was losing my mind. I tried to convince myself that I had dreamt the previous night's events, but when I embraced Father that morning he reeked of smoke and gasoline.

I went to Dong's house immediately after breakfast. I tried to tell him about it, but Dong stopped me halfway and said he already knew. He told me his father had also smelled like gasoline. He said all the fathers in our development smelled like gasoline this morning.

"It happens," Dong said. "What can you do? They had it coming. It was only a matter of time. My pa said it wasn't even their land. He said you can't live for free like that, it's really not fair to the rest of us."

"What about Priscilla?"

"What about Priscilla?" Dong repeated. "She'll be fine. She's a survivor."

"I can't believe this," I said. "I can't believe I'm best friends with a fat, knock-kneed asshole."

"Hey," Dong said. "Watch it, fucker."

Then he turned around and went back inside the house. I stood there gaping at his front door, shaking with fury. I didn't know what to do. I wanted to hurt him. So I went over and took his bike from the yard. Dong screamed at me from his window but I was already pumping away at the pedals, racing toward what was left of the shantytown to find Priscilla and her mother.

Bits of ash swirled around the railroad tracks. A thin veil of smoke hung in the air, stinging my eyes. When I arrived, it was as if the Cambodians' shanty had never existed. There wasn't a shack left standing. The ground smoldered with blackened sheets of tin. Their herb garden, too, had been razed. All the Cambodians stood around picking through the rubble, muttering to one another quietly in the early morning sun. Fortunately, some of their possessions had been saved; they piled bags and belongings together on a small patch of clean ground. Nobody looked particularly panicked. Nobody seemed particularly sad. It was as if they'd expected the fire. But nobody acknowledged me when I arrived.

Priscilla stood with her mother next to the Cambodians' stuff. The other women milled around them waving smoke from their faces. Her mother sat on a knapsack and stared at the rubble, a bored look on her face. She seemed to look right through me at first, but then she nodded seriously. Priscilla smiled when I arrived. She had dark rings around her eyes and her face was blackened from the fire, like somebody had smeared it with charcoal. "Hey," she said. "Hey," I said, panting, throwing Dong's bike to the ground. "This really sucks, girlie."

She told me that nobody had been particularly hurt. She and her mother hadn't lost too much. The golden tooth, the Presley album, the picture of Priscilla's father—all had survived the fire, though they'd have to find a new pallet to sleep on. Priscilla said the men had come banging on their houses with sticks last night, told them to get out before they burned them alive in their shacks. I listened, nodded along, tried to look like she was telling me something I didn't already know. I told her I was glad she and her mother weren't hurt, but I could barely look at her. Priscilla shook her head and said the same thing had happened at the last place they'd squatted. Just like Dong, she told me it was only a matter of time. She said it could've been a lot worse.

"We're leaving," she said finally. "We're going. I'm gonna miss you guys."

She looked at Dong's bike and asked me where he was. I told her he was sleeping. I invited Priscilla to the half-finished pool one last time. She asked her mother if she could go and her mother nodded silently, told Priscilla to be back in an hour. Before we left, I went up to Priscilla's mother and apologized. It seemed I was always apologizing to that short, flat-faced woman. It seemed, too, that I'd never be able to apologize enough. "I'm very sorry about your house," I said in Thai, and once more Priscilla's mother slapped me on the back of the head, smiled widely out of that omelet face. "Hairy Beaver," she answered in Thai. "Dickwad. Fuckface."

We didn't do much at the pool that morning. We just sat around with our feet dangling off the edge chatting about this and that, the weather getting hotter and hotter. If we lived in a better world, I would've ridden that bike off the diving board and landed perfectly in the deep end for Priscilla. She could've remembered me by that. But it didn't feel like a morning for bike tricks; it didn't feel like a morning for clowning around. Priscilla was tired, uncharacteristically quiet. She hadn't slept all night. Another incisor was coming out. She showed me, nudged it lightly with a finger, the golden tooth wobbling to and fro on her short pink gums. I stared at it transfixed because I knew that this would be the last time I'd peer into Priscilla's golden mouth.

We made our way back to the smoldering shanty. To my surprise, Dong was there when we arrived, chatting with Priscilla's mother. We didn't acknowledge one another. The Cambodians were gathering their belongings, getting ready to leave. I went with Priscilla to her mother, listened to them talk for a while, tried to ignore Dong standing beside me. It suddenly made me nauseated being around the Cambodians.

Priscilla was asking for something in a pleading voice. Her mother nodded, looked at her sternly, looked over at Dong and me every so often. They were arguing about something. But then, after her mother nodded once more, Priscilla skipped excitedly to their knapsack and dug out the teakwood box.

"This is for you," she said, putting the tooth in one of Dong's hands. Dong looked at me for the first time. "I can't take this, girlie," he said, shaking his head, extending his open palm back to her.

"It's for you and your mama," Priscilla said, closing his fingers around the tooth. "Take it or I'll beat you again." Dong shrugged. "Okay," he said, shoving the tooth into a pocket. "Thanks a lot, girlie."

She looked at me. I was next. I wanted to tell her no. I wanted to stop her. But Priscilla was already working away at that incisor, wobbling it back and forth with a thumb and a forefinger, her face contorted in pain and concentration. All the Cambodians stopped, looked over at Priscilla and me. She seemed to work at that incisor for an unbearably long time. I could hardly look at her do it. And then with a strong, vigorous gesture she got the tooth free at last, and there was a small gap now where there should've been gold, a smidgen of light red blood on her gums.

"And this is for you," she said, wiping the tooth clean on her pants, handing me the thing. I took it, put it in my back pocket. I thanked her. And then she went over and helped maneuver the large knapsack onto her mother's back.

We never heard from Priscilla the Cambodian again. Those, too, were the last days Dong and I spent together. Soon after, Dong's parents sold their duplex back to the development company for half the original price. My parents eventually did the same for even less money.

That day, however, Dong and I stood by their ruined shantytown and watched them walk away, their figures getting smaller and smaller by the minute. But then, wordlessly, I decided I couldn't watch them leave. I walked over to Dong's bike and picked it off the ground.

"Hey," he said. "Give me my bike, you asshole."

"You fat fuck," I said, scrambling onto the seat. "Come get it yourself."

I started pumping away at the pedals again, standing upright, the wind blowing quickly through my hair, Dong's exasperated voice trailing off behind me. I don't know how long I biked that morning. In my mind, I'd decided to bike to the ends of the earth. The development flew by. I biked past its limits, out onto Pattanakan Road, past the Thicknecks' pristine development. I crossed through the fresh market. The streets and the people became stranger by the minute. I biked through thick traffic, smoke and exhaust whipping around me, cars honking every so often as I maneuvered haphazardly between them. I climbed over the bridge spanning some wide black canal. I went farther from my house that morning than I'd ever been on my own. I kept biking until the sun rose high in the sky and my body quivered from exhaustion and my thighs burned as they'd never burned before.

I stopped at an intersection; men and women in business suits looked at me sternly as they walked by. I didn't know where the hell I was. I didn't know how long I'd been biking. I needed to get to a bathroom. I needed to piss; I needed to vomit as well. I left Dong's bike by a telephone booth and went into a noodle shop. The owner eyed me curiously over steaming vats of broth. He asked me what I wanted. I could tell that he thought I was some street urchin. I didn't say anything. I just marched to the back of the shop and slipped into the bathroom before the owner could stop me. In the bathroom, as I was urinating, I remembered the tooth Priscilla gave me. I threw that keepsake into the toilet bowl. I flushed. I decided I couldn't keep a thing like that.

When I emerged from the bathroom, the owner was waiting for me, frowning severely. "What the hell are you doing, kid?" he asked me.

"I was taking a piss," I said. "What did you think I was doing?"

He reached out and tried to grab me by the collar. I slipped from his grasp just in time. I tried to punch him in the stomach. But he'd reached out to grab my wrists—one, then the other. His hands were strong. He gripped me hard and pulled me toward him. All the strength left my body, and my eyes suddenly felt hot with tears. I was crying, though I hadn't realized it until then.

The owner of the noodle shop knelt down to look me in the eyes.

"I'm not one to thrash another man's child," he whispered through gritted teeth. I felt my hands getting numb from his grip. I tried to writhe away but the more I struggled, the harder his hands held me in place, his thick fingernails digging into my skin.

"So this is what we're gonna do," he said. "We're gonna pretend that you didn't just try to punch me. I'm gonna let you go and I'm gonna count to three. By the time I get to three, you're gonna be gone. You're gonna go back to wherever the hell you just came from. You understand me, boy?"

I started crying in earnest then, the tears streaming freely down my face, mucus salty on my lips.

"Let me go," I whimpered. "Please."

"I'm not running a goddamn orphanage here, kid," he continued, still gripping me. "I'm not running a public rest room, either. I'm running a business, you understand me?"

He stared at me for a while, his face contorted with exasperation.

"You understand me?" he asked again.

"Yes, sir," I stammered. "I understand you, sir."

"Good," he said, letting go of my wrists. "One. Two. Three."

Hopwood Winners, 1931–2005

Robert Jefferey Aamoth
1976, 1978
Darrel Abel 1941
Katherine Ann Abend 1998
Heather Abner 2000
Dawne Adam 1987
Amy Adams 1946
Ellen Adams 1956
Stephen J. Adams 1988, 1989,
1990, 1991
Michael S. Adelman 1962
Peggy Adler 2000
Val Agostino 1996
Stephen W. Ajay 1965
Fay Ajzenberg 1944
Patricia O. Akhimie 2002
Van V. Alderman 1933
Frank C. Aldrich, Jr. 1934
Tess Aldrich 1996, 1998
Arthur W. Allen 1936
David Allen 1996
Deborah Jean Allen 1976
Elizabeth Allen 1933, 1936
James B. Allen 1972, 1973
John L. Allen 1972
Kelly Elizabeth Allen 1998
Robert Leslie Allman 1974
James Allyn 1971
Henry Alpert 1991
Halimah Ali Al-Qadi 1987
William M. Altman 1941
Lilia P. Amansec 1955
Albert J. Ammerman 1961,
1964
Dargie Anderson 2005
David M. Anderson 2000,
2001
Joan Patricia Anderson 1974
John C. Anderson 1983, 1984,
1986

Laura Anderson 1996
Peter C. Anderson 1969, 1971
T. J. Anderson III 1987
Robyn Anspach 2001, 2002,
2003, 2004, 2005
Jimmy Jess Anthony 1976
Tasha Antonello 1997
Thomas M. Antrim, Jr. 1967
David W. Appel 1965
Jessica Pearl Apple 1995
Max I. Apple 1963, 1970
Philip Barry Ardell 1970
James Richard Arden 1973
Ethel B. Arehart 1940
Eseohe Arhebamen 2000
Allan J. Arlow 1966
Brent Armendinger 2002
Jan Armon 1985
Dorothy Arms 1939
Katherine Marguerite
Armstrong 2001
Robert Manning Armstrong
1947
Linda A. Arndt 1968
Evelyn R. Aronson 1949
Lisa Arsuaga 1986
Michael Asciutto 1988
Marie Nikol Ashley 1992
Jane E. Ashton 1986
Ruth L. Asness 1941
Laurence Aufderheide 1969
Henry Root Austin 1974,
1976
Marjorie Avalon 1938, 1941
Alvin K. Averbach 1963
Margaret Avery 1940

John U. Bacon 1988
Wallace A. Bacon 1936
Jerome A. Badanes 1962

James A. Baffico 1972
William Fairfax Bahr 1981
Margaret E. Bailey 1960, 1961
Leslie Carol Bailian 1975
Brooke Baker 2001
James Volant Baker 1946
Jennifer Baker 1994
Laverne Baker 1933
Sanna Anderson Baker 1974
Dean Bakopoulos 1997
Natalie Bakopoulos 2005
Aime M. Ballard 1988
Jason Baluyut 1992
George E. Bamber 1955
Sylvia Bandyke 1970
Geoffrey Bankowski 1995
Frank Graham Banta 1939
Mary Beth Barber 1990
Rowland O. Barber 1940
Amber Jewell Bard 2005
Barbara Baril 1957
Erik S. Barmack 1994
Juliet K. Barnes 1989, 1991
Regina Barnes 1998
Sharon Barnes 1962
Phillip Barnhart 1986
Mary Kelley Baron 1971
Michael Barrett 1988
Paul Barron 1998
James A. Barry 1960
Susan Barry 1978
Linda Baskey 1985
Elaine Baumann 1943
Leslie Prescott Bayern 1979,
1980
Donald Beagle 1977
Scott Beal 1994, 1996
Edmund Beard 1966
Vicki Jean Beauchamp 1982
Frank E. Beaver 1969

Alexis Maye Beck 1973
Ronald Beck 1957
Art Becker 1977, 1978
Jody K. Becker 1983, 1984
Michele Becker 1975
Bernard Alan Bedell 1975
Arthur James Beer, Jr. 1957
Burton K. Beerman 1956
Sarah Beldo 1997, 1998
Howard Belkin 1973
Kate Bell 1999, 2000
Marilyn Bell 1941
Barbara Bell-Chabot 1978
Hilda Beltran 1989
Deborah D. Bennett 1975,
  1976
Elesia K. Bennett 2004
Ruth Ann Bennett 1970, 1971
Nelson G. Bentley 1940, 1942
Robert R. Berger 1967
Mary Brita Bergland 1973
David Elliot Berkman 1979
Rogers W. Bermond 1950
Debra Bernhardt 1973
Julie Bernstein 1984
Carole Rose Bernstein 1984
Laura Janis Bernstein 1987
Betty B. Berris 1942
Stephen Berry 1986
Steven Best 2002
Harry R. Bethke 1936
Meredith Bethune 1970
Andrea Bewick 1989
Ronica Bhattacharya 1997
Donn Joseph Bialik 1998
Thayer B. Bice 1960
Megan Biesele 1967
Scott Burdett Billings 1976
Amy L. Bingaman 1993
Otto Bird 1935
Sven Peter Birkerts 1973
John Bishop 2003
Trim Bissell 1963, 1964
Marc A. Bittner 2002
Barbara Bizek 1987, 1988
Hunter Blair 2002
Elaine M. Blandino 1963

Mary Jean Blessington 1981
Brett-Ellen Block 1995
Erika Block 1985
Leanore Ann Block 1968
David Wels Blomquist 1974
Stephen E. Bluestone 1971,
  1973
Sheila Marie Bluhm 1973
Katherine K. Blunt 1962
Alan Boatman 1968
Sydney Bobb 1936
Anne Louise Bobroff 1983
Toby Leah Bochan 1993, 1995
Joanna Ruth Bock 2005
Nancy D. Bock 1977
Malcolm D. Boesky 1948
Donald A. J. Bohlen 1965
Jordan Bohy 2004
Dorothy Boillotat 1931
Patrick Boland 1949
Angela Bommarito 1990
Nora Jean Bonner 2002
Sue Grundy Bonner 1931
David Bornstein 1979
Beatrice Borst 1941
Barbara Van Noord Bosma
  1968, 1969
Malcolm J. Bosse 1956
Diane Elizabeth Bosworth
  1978, 1987
Edward H. Botts 1956, 1957
Everett Warner Bovard, Jr.
  1947, 1948
Kent Thomas Bowden 1972
Renee A. Bowles 1985
Sister Mary Antonia
  Bowman 1955
John Boyd 1958
Jonathan A. Boyd 1985
Richard B. Bracken 1952
Isabel Bradburn 1978
Anne Holden Braden 1950
Catharine Bradner 1957
Gillian Bradshaw 1977
Jillian Bransdorfer 1987
Mark Bransdorfer 1984
Ronald D. Brasch 1968, 1971

William R. Brashear 1953,
  1955
William Brashler 1969
Lorie Brau 1979
Richard Emil Braun 1955
Jason Bredle 2000
Eric Leigh Breedon 1994,
  1998
Jonathan Brenner 2000,
  2001, 2002
Elizabeth Brent 1998
Peter D. Brett 1970
Eugene S. Brewer 1935
Mike Breymann 1999
Howard Brick 1975
Floy Brigstock 1934
John Malcolm Brinnin 1938,
  1939, 1940
Brett Briskin 1974
Casey Briskin 1979
Gloria G. Briskin 1970
Laura Britton 1979
Michael Joseph Brochue
  1974
Joanna Brod 1990
Lee C. Bromberg 1963
Richard J. Brooks 1974
Miriam Brous 1936
Paula Brower 1944
Carrie Lee Brown 1988
Florence Maple Brown 1944
Kenyon Brown 1982
Laura Brown 1996
Robert B. Brown 1934
Robert G. Brown, Jr. 1956
Russell A. Brown 1953, 1955
Devin Browne 2005
Anne-Marie Brumm 1970,
  1973
Matthew Brune 1986
Carl Brunsting 1953
Mary Brush 1947
Neal H. Bruss 1966
Larry Bublick 1992
Claudia W. Buckholts 1965,
  1967
David Buckley 1952

Anthony C. Buesser 1953
Carmen Bugan 1993
Uyen Bui 2004
Evelyn L. Bull 1931
Carol Jane Bundy 1940
Lesly J. Burgamy 2000
Linda L. Burk 1973
Gerald Burns 1941
Gabriel Burnstein 2000,
　2001
Anne E. Burr 1965
Elaine P. Burr 1957
Suzanne Burr 1983
Edwin G. Burrows 1940
Phyllis S. Burrows 1961
Robert E. Burt 1963
Brenda Butka 1972
Charles E. Butler 1949, 1950
Michael Byers 1996

Beth Anne Cahape 1975
Matthew B. Cain 1973
Jennifer Call 1993
Bruce D. Callender 1946,
　1947
Peter A. R. Calvert 1961
Leslie G. Cameron 1942
James Camp 1953, 1955
Charles Marsh Campbell
　1950
Daniel R. Campbell 1965
Elizabeth Ainsley Campbell
　1973
Robert C. B. Campbell 1936,
　1937
Sylvia Camu 1956
Mary Cann 1939
Beverly Canning 1955
Patricia Cannon 1959
Dennis John Caplis 1974
Donna Caputo de Benitez
　1982
Lesley Kristin Carlin 1996
Margaret J. Carlson 1961
Todd Carmody 1999, 2001
Chris C. Carpenter 1965
Wilhelmine F. Carr 1934

Barbara Carter 1946
Anita Carvalho 1938
Jean F. Casale 1971
Christopher Case 1983
Franklin D. Case 1959
David William Caspar 1981
Marie Louise Caspe 1956
Sally Ann Cassidy 1949
Thomas Richard Cassidy
　1950
Erica V. Cassill 1981
Sarah Eden Cassill 1974
Michael Z. Castleman 1972
Anna M. Prineas Catanese
　1990
Sean C. Cavazos-Kottke 1993
Martin Joseph Cerjan 1975
Alys B. Chabot 1965, 1966
Jeremiah Chamberlin 1997,
　2003, 2004
Lorna D. Chambers 1931
Barbara Ferris Champion
　1975
Gayle Chan 2000
Charles Chang 2002
Diane Chang 1999, 2000
Neil S. Chang 1998
Victoria M. Chang 1992
Celia Hwaguen Chao 1942
John Dwyer Chapman 1974
Louis Charbonneau 1988
Stephanie A. Chardoul 1990
Joshua L. Charlson 1988
Cara Chase 1999
Herman Chasin 1939
Beatrice Chauvenet 1940
Ivan Joel Chaves 1982
Timothy Joseph Chester 1975
Charles Alan Chiavarini
　1977, 1979
Albert Paul Chiscavage 1999
Stephen Chonoles 1983
Peter Christenson 1999
George S. Chu 1968
Philip D. Church 1957, 1962
John Ciardi 1939
Louis Cicciarelli 1998

Alex Cigale 1985
William Jay Citrin 1995, 1997
Gabrielle Civil 1992
Carin Claar 1957
Anna Clark 2001
Anne Clark 1948
D. Philip Clark 1936, 1939
James H. Clark 1951
Martha Taliaferro Clark 1979
Thomas W. Clark 1963
Virgil G. Clark 1947
Deborah Clarke 1979
Brigitta Cleland 1990
Kathleen A. Cleveland 1966
Arthur Clifford 1932, 1933,
　1934, 1935
Robert E. Clifford 1977
James F. Coats 1963
Carolyn Coffin 1962, 1965,
　1975, 1977
Steven D. Coffman 1965,
　1966
Dov Cohen 1987
Richard L. Cohen 1973
Theodore Kane Cohen 1932,
　1933, 1934, 1935
Annie Coleman 1957
Gregory Coleman 1983
James Coleman 1968
Janet N. Coleman 1962
Durward B. Collins, Jr. 1959
Sister Mary Alice Collins
　1943
Susan Collins 1983
David C. Colson 1962
John G. Conley 1962
Barnes Connable 1953, 1955
John Conron 1968
Richard Constantinoff 1954
Cory Graham Converse 1993
Frank M. Conway 1937
David Cook 1959
Diane Marie Cook 1997
John R. Cook 1947, 1949
Kristin Cooke 2003
William Cooke 1945
Mary Elizabeth Cooley 1941

Nancy Coons 1973
Kevin Douglas Cooper 1974
Theodosia Coplas 1955
Sidney Corman 1947
Art Corriveau 1993
Kristi Coulter 1994
Kevin Jerome Counihan 1975
Harold Courlander 1931, 1932
Barbara Couture 1977
Carrol Byron Cox, Jr. 1959
Clinton H. Cox, Jr. 1955
Keith Cox 1946
Robert Sayre Cox 1989
John R. Coxeter 1957
Marion Cranmore 1936, 1937
Frank Crantz 1968
Jeffrey Cravens 2004
Kathryn Elizabeth Crawley 1984
James W. Creaser 1947
Frances M. Crowley 1954
David M. Crumm 1975, 1977
Victor A. Cruz 1980, 1981
Phillip Crymble 2002
Sue Cumberworth 1959
Kellan B. Cummings 2003
Scott Thomas Cummings 1974
Nancy Cummins 2003
Laura Elizabeth Curl 1981
William Curl 1992
Stuart A. Curran 1959
Bruce F. Currie 1970, 1971
Jayson Curry 1991
Nelle A. Curry 1951
Christopher P. Curtis 1993
Jerry Czarnecki 1992

Steven A. Dabrowski 2003, 2004
Heather Hayes Damp 1979, 1980
Frederick J. Danaher 1976
Miriam Bruce Dancy 1948
Thomas E. Danelli 1950

Melissa Danforth 1991
Stephen A. Daniels 1966, 1967
Thomas M. Danko 1974, 1975
Carlin Danz 2004
Jim C. Danziger 1975
John Joseph Darago 1975
Anna Elizabeth Darsky 1979
Maureen Anne Darmanin 1981
Miriam Darmstadter 1983
Melinda Dart 1974, 1975, 1977
Anita Dascola 1971
Joseph I. Dassin 1958
Tina Michelle Datsko 1978, 1979, 1980, 1981, 1982, 1983, 1984, 1985
Steven Joel Dauer 1976
Allison Daugherty 2005
Mary Rachel Daunt 2002
Elizabeth Davenport 1954
Jane Davey 1977
David M. Davidsen 1956
Gerald E. Davidson 1940
Jessica Davidson 1991
Katherine Davidson 1969
Blair Davies 1973
Adam Brooke Davis 1982, 1984
Mary Ann Davis 2003
Robert C. Davis 1959
Charles R. Dawe 1971
William F. Dawson 1957
Saire Wiltse de Quincy 1978
Alice Marie de Stigter 1977
Larry Dean 1982, 1983
Margaret Lazarus Dean 2001
Maury Dean 1972
C. Ryan Deardorff 1994
Tiziana Dearing 1992
Michelle M. Regalado Deatrick 2004
Jim M. Deem, Jr. 1975
Tom DeKornfeld 1977
Francesca Delbanco 1999, 2000
Carolyn Delevitt 1968, 1969

Roger A. DeLiso 1972
Judith A. Delk 1963
Michael George Deloro 1976
Paul DeLucco 1970
Susan Michele DeMaria 1974
Laura Deneau 2003
Richard Deres 1954
Frank DeSanto 1994
Helga E. DeShazo 1976
Sharon P. Deskins 1979
Laynie Tzena Deutsch 1984
Kevin S. Devine 1983
Tiffany DeVos 1999
Daniel DeVries 1980
A. Keewatin Dewdney 1967
Margaret Avery Dewey 1942
Daniel DeWitt 1988
Lawrence Dick 1982
Marcia E. Dickman 1965
Suzanne Dieckman 1971
Martha Ann Dieffenbacher 1947
Amy Diehl 2001
Sharon Dilworth 1988
Lisa D'Innocenzo 1982
Michelle Dinsmore 1981, 1982
Della DiPietro 1973
Barbara Dittman 1938
Ruth Lininger Dobson 1936
Laura Wells Dodd 2003
Leah L. Dodd 2000
Alonzo Rollo Dodge 1974
Jane Pike Dodge 1950
W. Matthew Dodge 1993
James V. Doll 1936
Walter P. Domanowski 1935
Patricia Dombrowski 1973
Ann F. Doniger 1957, 1959, 1960
John Donovan 1980
Eleanor L. Dorn 1954
Nigel Douglas 1986, 1987
Amy L. Downey 1945
Gregory Marshall Downing 1975
Matthew Drake 1998

Sarah Drasin 1956, 1958
William J. Dressler 1957
Ellen Ruth Dreyer 1980, 1983
Cecilia Dreyfuss 1969, 1973
Kevin R. Dreyfuss 1992
Elaine Duberstein 1958
Jason Dubow 1992
Linnea Dudley 1972
Gay E. Duerson 1953
Ruth Duhme 1931, 1932
James Dulzo 1969
Cora Duncan 1951, 1952, 1953
Will Dunlap 2004
Shawn M. Durrett 1999
Kathryn Duthler 2002
Nick Dybek 2002
Gloria J. Dyc 1982
George Orest Dzule 1981

Raymond R. Early 1942
David W. Eaton 1970
Edward C. Echols 1948
Mary V. H. Echols 1946
Josephine Eckert 1943, 1946
Kathy Edelman 1969
David Edwards 1990
Melodie S. Edwards 2002
Sharon Edwards 1958
Betty L. Ehlers 1953
Elizabeth Ehrle 2000
Allan M. Eisenberg 1964
Randy Eisenberg 1993
Sarah K. Eisenberg 2004
Nicole Eisenmann 2001
Ira N. Eisenstadt 1970
Jehan El-bayoumi 1976
Donald B. Elder 1932, 1933, 1935
Donald M. Eldridge 1959
William Curtiss Elkington 1974
Brownlee W. Elliott 1962
N. Katherine Elliott 1955
William D. Elliott 1959, 1961, 1962
Ernest E. Ellis 1960
Joanne V. Ellis 1954

Jane E. Ellzey 1950
Mahynoor El Tahry 2003
Ema Adam Ema 1976
Judith S. Engel 1961
Donald Epstein 1943
Elizabeth Erbaugh 1945
Christopher Erickson 2002
Marilee J. Erickson 1966
Peter Ernst 1978
David B. Espey 1970, 1971
Robert Evans 1945
Roberta J. Evans 1970
William H. Evenhouse 1964
Scott Edwin Ewing 1978, 1981
Richard H. Eyster 1972
Joshua Ezekiel 1978
Tish O'Dowd Ezekiel 1978, 1979

Ann Fagan 1944
Susan Fair 1988
Ruthie Fajardo 1982
Joseph R. Fargnoli 1968
William Lee Farmer 1975
Dorothy J. Farnan 1938, 1941
Jack D. Farris 1950
Lisa Farris 1985
Barbara C. Faulkner 1953
Chris R. B. Fay 1990
Craig Feigen 1979
Robert E. Feinstein 1973
Gabriel Feldberg 1993
Lynda S. Felder 1976
Joseph D. Feldman 1963
Nelson Feldman 1970
Richard Feldman 1984, 1985, 1986, 1987
Stephanie A. Feldstein 1999
Alan Ferrari 1969
James Robert Ferry 1972
Rania Fetouh 2001
Brian Fichtner 1997
Lawrence J. Field 1965
Liza Todd Field 1986, 1987
Gerald J. Fife 1965
Kenneth Fifer 1971

Esther L. Fine 1968
Sheldon Finkelstein 1941
Marianne S. Finton 1943, 1944
Rudy Fischmann 1992
Peggy Fisher 1944
Jack Aaron Fishstrom 1994
Fynette Fiske 1934
Jennie Fitch 1943
James M. Fitzmaurice 1964
J. Brandon Fizer 1997
Frances Flaherty 1938
Mary Jo Flaherty 1977
Ryan Flaherty 2002
Brenda Flanagan 1978, 1984, 1985
Dennis Flanagan 1937
Elaine Ruth Fletcher 1975, 1978
Joe Fletcher 1999
Stanley Fletcher 1932
Richard Flewell 1946
Scott A. Florence 1959
Kasha Fluegge 1989
Stephanie Fody 1987
Charles J. Fogel 1989
Don E. Folkman, Jr. 1941
Kristin Fontichiaro 1988
Dennis Foon 1972
Christopher Reid Ford 1975
Stephanie L. Ford 2001, 2002
Erica Forman 1972
Helen Fortune 1931
Alyson Foster 2001
John L. Foster 1959
Helen L. Fox 1966
Jane Fox 2000
Joan Fox 1952, 1955
John P. Fox 1959, 1963
Scott Howard Frank 1976, 1977
Nik Frank-Lehrer 2003, 2005
Arnie Frantz 1977
Celeste Fraser 1985, 1988
Eva Frazee 2001
John Frazier 1962
Jon B. Frazier 1992

John J. Frederick 1935, 1937
Edward E. Freed 1934
Erica R. Freeman 1999
Robert L. French 1934
Virginia French 1941
Kimon Friar 1939
Robert H. Frick 1943
Alec E. Friedman 1976
Devin Lowell Friedman 1994
Elizabeth Friedman 1963
Joseph Friedman 1971, 1972
Steven J. Friedman 1962
Victor Friedman 2003
Alvin E. Fritz 1963, 1965
Amanda Frost 2002, 2003
Gordon Jay Frost 1984
Katherine Diane Fry 1974
Murry Frymer 1955
David Neal Fulk 1974
Michael Joseph Fuller 1975
Vivian Fung 1975
James W. Furlong 1973
Timothy E. Furstnau 2000

Marie Lucille Fucci
  Gaenslen 1973
Edwin Gage III 1967
Pauline Doris Gagnon 1985
Mary Lawrence Gaitskill
  1981
Bernice Galansky 1944
Duane Gall 1974
Rich Gallagher 1994, 1995
Juanita M. Galle 1972
Michael A. Galle 1965, 1966
John H. Gallion 1975
Helen Gammie 1979
Gary Bruce Garcia 1988
Anne Gardner 1949
Barry Garelick 1971
David M. Garelick 1967
Mary L. Garland 1943
James Edward Garner 1981
Gary Wayne Garrison 1983
James Garvey 1968
Suzanne Gary 1960, 1961,
  1967

Thomas Gaughan 1983
Burton S. Gavitt 1942
Nigel Trevor Gearing 1972
Audrey Joan Gebber 1987
Eric H. Geffner 2001
John B. Geisel 1936
Katharine Gell 2002
Jack Gellman 1949
Andrea K. George 2002
Emery E. George 1960
Margaret Gergely 1976
Lee F. Gerlach 1954
Edward B. Germain 1969
Christine Gesell 1936
David Seth Gewanter 1980
John S. Ghose 1998
Vanessa Giancamilli 1995
Oliver J. Giancola 1994
Linda Marie Giasson 1985
Kathleen Maria Gibbs 1932
Laureen V. Gibson 1978
Marion Giddings 1933
Dorothy S. Gies 1933, 1934,
  1935, 1936
Thomas Gies 1940
Merrill D. Gilfillan 1967
Gail Gilliland 1985, 1988
Jean A. Gilman 1931
Susan Jane Gilman 1992,
  1993
Andrina Iverson Gilmartin
  1945
Naomi Gilpatrick 1943
Raymond S. Ginger 1947
Beverly Gingold 1959, 1960
Paul L. Gingras 1967, 1973
Colin Gipson 1995
Laura Gladhill 1987, 1988
Kathryn Glasgow 1986
Connie Glaze 1988
Gretchen Glazier 1968
George H. Glover, Jr. 1961
Mary Glover 1988
John Eugene Glowney 1975,
  1976
Carol A. Godfrey 1968
Archolose Godoshian 1941

Louis Goldberg 1984
Tracey-Lynn Goldblum 1975
Barbara Faith Goldoftas 1975
Ann Goldschmidt 1960
Raphael K. Goldsmith 1965
Kenneth Goldstein 1951
David Alan Goldstick 1982
Ian Gonzalez 1989
Ruth Good 1953
Richard B. Goode 1953
Peggy Goodin 1942, 1943,
  1945
Richard C. Goodman 1966
Iola L. Fuller Goodspeed
  1939
Peter E. Goodstein 1964
Leonard Goodwin 1953
Alethea Baleri Gordon 1992
Kathryn Gordon 1980
Max Gordon 1990, 1992
Melvin I. Gordon 1967, 1968
Nancy J. Gordon 1967
Neil S. Gordon 1980, 1981
William J. Gorman 1931
Katherine Gotham 1997
Saul Gottlieb 1950, 1951, 1952
Mary C. Gough 1961
Rae Gouirand 2001
Paula Kay Gover 1986
Richard D. Graddis 1966
Paul Graham 2000
William Parker Gram 1939,
  1940, 1942, 1945
Paul Mueller Grams 1974,
  1984
Evelyn Grantham 1941
Frances Ann Gray 1941
Derek Green 1987, 1988, 1991
Dorothy Green 1968
H. Gordon Green 1937, 1939,
  1941, 1948
James Green 1940
Jeremy Green 1992
Marianna McDevitt Green
  2003
Martin Green 1954
Leonard Greenbaum 1955

Joel Greenberg 1961
Gabriel Greene 1998
Joseph A. Greene 1953
Susan Greene 1987
Joshua J. Greenfeld 1948, 1949
Morris Greenhut 1934
Dorothy Greenwald 1933
Jean Grey 1954
Jessica Grieser 2002
Tery Aine Griffin 1995
Patricia A. Griffith 1967, 1970
Peter F. Griffith 1969, 1971
Edward Joseph Grinnan 1975
Nancy J. Groberg 1944, 1945
Joseph R. Groenke 1996,
    1998, 2000
James Patrick Grondin 1975
Frederick Gropper 1932
Harvey S. Gross 1953
Joshua Gross 2003
Aaron D. Grossman 1963
Frederick D. Grossman 1993
Damon Darrell Grosz 1998
David W. Grove 1986
Julia Cesar Guerrero 1994
Karen Kay Gulliver 1975
Myron Anthony Gunsaulus
    1978
Elaine Leslie Guregian 1975
Maizie Gusakoff 1947
Dan J. Guthrie 1962
James R. Guthrie 1971, 1973
Robert B. Gutterman 1972
Hazel S. Guyol 1965

Gertrude Haan 1945
Elizabeth A. Haas 1991, 1993
Rosamond Edwards Haas
    1943
Janet Mackie Hackel 1985
Josephine Hadley 1933
Karla Hafner 1978
Suzanne Hague 1997
Alyson Carol Hagy 1984
Irene J. Hahn 2004
Jeannette M. Haien 1943,
    1944, 1945

Theodore Hailperin 1936
Diane Rollins Haithman
    1976, 1979
Mitchell Halberstadt 1970
Harriet Hale 1939
Marjory A. Hall 1962, 1964
Theodore D. Hall 1963
E. Milton Halliday 1937
Kathleen Halme 1986
Jay G. Hamburg 1958, 1959
Shirley Hamburg 1944
Gilbert S. Hamilton 1966
Robert M. Hamilton 1967
Steve Robert Hamilton 1983
Natalie Hamm 2002
Harriett B. Hamme 1956
Ruth C. Hammeter 1957
Laia Hanau 1942
Suzanne Hancock 2003
Anita Handleman 1971
John Hanley 1992
Allan Hanna 1952
Willard A. Hanna 1939
Polly E. Hanson 1946
Sally Hanson 1958
Walter L. Hanson 1947
Roberta K. Hard 1955
Dale Harger 1968
Laura Harger 1990
Nicholas Allen Harp 2001
Rosemary Harp 1993
Philip Brian Harper 1979
Angela P. Harris 1979, 1980,
    1981
Jerome W. Harris 1937
Jonathan Hart Harrison
    1992, 1994
Kristen Harrison 1991
Kara Hartig 1990
Susan Beth Hartman 1967
Suzanne Hartman 1964
Dennis John Harvey 1981,
    1983, 1984
Howard J. Harvey 1953
Janet B. Harvey 1964
Hitoshi Hasegawa 1988
Shirley Hastings 1943

James E. Hatch 1968
Kristin M. Hatch 2001
Baxter Hathaway 1936
James Hervie Haufler 1938,
    1941
Robert F. Haugh 1947
Jane H. Hawes 1969
William K. Hawes 1957
Robert C. Hay 1968
Robert E. Hayden 1938, 1942
Amy D. Hayes 1998
James Healy 1999
Mark Heasley 1997
Christopher J. Hebert 2001
Heidi Hedstrom 1990
Anneliese D. Heiner 1987
E. K. Heitmann 1935
Margaret Heizmann 1957
Padma Hejmadi 1958
Robert J. Hejna 1978
Melissa Heller 2003
David Hellman 1992
Elaine Catherine Henderson
    1976
Helene Henderson 1988
Burley L. Hendricks 1957,
    1958, 1960
June Ferrill Hendricks 1975
Vanessa Mae-Chern Heng
    1999, 2000
Joshua Herbert Henkin
    1992, 1993
Michael Henry, Jr. 1992
Claudia Rogers Herman
    1988
Jeffry Herman 1995
Joshua Aaron Herman 2000
John T. Herrick 1962
David John Herring 1978
Ruth Herschberger 1941
Carol Hershey 1952, 1955
James C. Hestand 1963
Mary Patricia Heyn 1975,
    1976
Natasha Higgins 2000
Richard Higinbotham 1968
Erik Stahl Hildinger 1979

Cynthia Leigh Hill 1976, 1977
Heather Hill 1990, 1993
Ruth Hinz 1979
Andris M. Hirss 1960
Matthew Hittinger 2004
Charles A. Hix 1963
Gerald J. Hoag 1947
Eugene J. Hochman 1953
Dolores Hodge 1970, 1971
Jean Hoffman 1934
Lillian M. Hoffman 1964
Rebecca B. Hoggan 1996,
   1998
Donovan Hohn 2003, 2004
Karen A. Holcomb 1953
Travis Holland 2003, 2004
John A. Holm 1965
David Marion Holman 1981
John H. Holmes 1978
William V. Holtz 1952, 1953,
   1954
Hannah Holtzman 2005
Janet Homer 1977
Clinton Hone 1972
Garrett Hongo 1975
Gwenyth Elise Hood 1979
Patricia A. Hooper 1960,
   1961, 1962, 1963
John Hill Hopkin 1961
Vivian Hopkins 1931
Alexandra Irene Horevitz
   2002
Theodore Hornberger 1933
Lewis B. Horne 1960
Andrew D. Horowitz 2002,
   2003
Loralee Ann Horton 1976
Harold H. Horwitz 1953
Douglas R. Hotch 1961
Paul Lawrence Hough 1974
Sara Houghteling 2002, 2003
Charles A. Houghton, Jr.
   1948
Donald Ray Howard 1957,
   1958, 1960
John W. Howard 1947
Murray Howe 1978

Grant W. Howell 1933
Jonathan Howland 1988
Susan Hruska 1977
Michael I. Hsu 1994, 1995,
   1996
Mabelle Hsueh 1953
Tung-Hui Hu 1999
William Hubert 1969
Rachael Hudak 2004
Rollie Hudson 1989
Sara Hudson 1999
William R. Hughes 1985
J. Richard A. Humphreys
   1939
Richard Noble Humphreys
   1931
Adam Hunault 2001
John Dixon Hunt 1960
Robert M. Hunt 1965
Maureen A. Hunter 1969
Raymond T. Hunter 1964
Mick Hurbis-Cherrier 1986
Aaron Hurst 1993
Phyllis L. Huston 1939, 1942
Scott Hutchins 2001
Lizzie Hutton 1999
Virgil G. Hutton 1960
James Glendon Hynes 1976
Simon Hyoun 1999

Alessandra P. Iaderosa 1980
Steward David Ikeda 1991,
   1992
Ellen Ilfeld 1980
J. Peter Ingalls 1988
Ray W. Ingham 1941
John A. Ingwersen, Jr. 1946,
   1947
James S. Irwin 1947
Morris Isaacs 1932
Bernice Kavinosky Isaacson
   1937
Betty J. Isaacson 1963
Stephanie Ivanoff 1987, 1989,
   1990, 1995
William J. Ivey 1966
Josh Izenberg 2001, 2003

James Jackson 1941
James Richard Jackson 1981
John Barnett Jackson 1980,
   1982
Sharon Jackson 1988
Nick Charles Jacobs 1985
Kristoffer Olaf Jacobson
   1977, 1980
Daniel Freeman Jaffe 1958
David Jaffin 1956
Eric Jager 1987
Irene Jakimcius 1983
Kenneth Thomas
   Jakubowski 1984
Rana M. Jaleel 1996, 1998,
   1999
Frank D. James 1978, 1979
Mildred June Janusch 1941
Gregory M. Jarboe 1969
Amy K. Jarvis 1992
Badria Jazairi 1983
Ransom Simon Jeffery 1970
Frances Jennings 1931
Michael Jennings 1992
Ted Charles Jennings 1976
Margot Poritsky Jerrard 1955
William Jestat 1969
Robert Jillson 1955
Gordon R. Jimison 2000
Chandy C. John 1985, 1986
C. Charles Johnson 1991
Edith Luella Johnson 1939
Emmy Lou Johnson 1970,
   1971
Isabel S. Johnson 1962
Jerry A. Johnson 1977
Lemuel A. Johnson 1967
Marian Johnson 1943
Meryl Johnson 1964
Nels S. Johnson 1976
Shelton Arnel Johnson 1981
Timothy Clayton Johnson
   1982
Faith M. Johnston 1943
Nora B. Johnston 1943
Paul Keith Johnston 1981
Thomas E. Johnston 1963

F. Randall Jones 1935, 1936, 1937, 1938
John Richard Jones 1972
Leisha J. Jones 1990
Melissa L. Jones 1997, 1999, 2000
Nathan S. Jones 2002
Susan Laurie Jones 1984
Wayne Allen Jones 1968, 1969
Anne W. Jordan 1968
Lawrence Martin Joseph 1970
Richard Alain Josey 1983
Louise E. Juckett 1934
Thomas Charles Juster 1977
Jeffrey Arthur Justin 1970, 1971

Judith Kafka 1994
Kimberly Kafka 1984
Lori Stefanna Kagan 1976
Carol Lee Kageff 1955
Steven E. Kagle 1964
Daniel Kahn 1999, 2001
Howie Kahn 2000
Catherine E. Kalbacher 1966
H. Mark Kandel 1977
Michael Kania 1992
Greg Kanter 1991
Doris J. Kaplan 1937
Carol Diane Kaplan 1965
John W. Kaplin 1966
Michael J. Karpinski 1993
Anna C. Karvellas 1992
Karl Gary Kasberg 1954, 1955
Lawrence Edward Kasdan 1968, 1969, 1970
Laura Kay Kasischke 1981, 1982, 1983, 1984
Karen Kasmauski 1973
Elias Kass 2000
Edith Katz 1944
Jamie L. Katz 1998
Stephen Hunter Katz 1974
Patricia Kaufman 1949
Stacey M. Kaufman 1987

Kelli Elizabeth Kaufmann 1990, 1993
Donald William Kaul 1959
Ingeborg Kayko 1941
Josephine Anna Kearns 1981, 1982, 1983
Marilyn J. Keck 1949
Joseph J. W. Keckler 2003
Nancy Keefer 1963
William John Kehoe 1941, 1942, 1943, 1944
Sybil Kein 1975
Marilyn L. Keith 1953, 1958
Lara Kelingos 1990
Jean Keller 1934
Elizabeth Kelley 2003
Sarah Margaret Kellogg 1979
Ariya Kelly 2003
Eileen Kelly 1990
Jay Martin Kendall 1966
Kimberly Ann Kendall 1967
Kent Kennan 1932
Joseph Charles Kennedy 1959
Melanie Kenny 1996, 1998
James T. Kent 1958
Charles Moir Kenyon 1941
Jane Jennifer Kenyon 1970
Ronald Warner Kenyon 1961, 1962
Jane Kernicky 1984
Harriet K. Kesselman 1935
Jascha Kessler 1952
John M. Keyes 1960
Katherine A. Kibbey 1991
Gary Kikuchi 1979
Daniel Kilpela 1989
Caroline Kim 1995
Daniel Y. Kim 1986
Howard Kim 1995
Jennifer Kim 1992
Daniel P. Kimble 1957
Thomas E. Kimble 1980
William A. Kincaid 1976
Frederick A. Kinch 1991
Kathryn King 1979
Shannon P. King 1960

Lauren Kingsley 1995
Arthur F. Kinney, Jr. 1961
Jason Kirk 1998, 2000
Martha Jean Kirkpatrick 1944
Leo Kirschbaum 1937
Gayle Kirschenbaum 1987
Judith Kenyon Kirscht 1974, 1984
Dave Kissinger 1954
Mitchell Kiven 2003
Louis Kivi 1941
Lois H. Klausner 1953
Beth Kleber 1991
Margaret A. Klee 1962, 1963
Rachel Klein 1972, 1977
Don William Kleine 1959
Diane Gail Klempner 1981
Samuel Kliger 1936
Andrew Henry Kline 2003
Renee Kluger 1954
Lynne Knight 1962, 1964
David Harmon Knoke 1966
Elizabeth T. Knowles 1948
Joe H. Knox 1947
Wallace John Knox III 1988, 1990
Aric D. Knuth 1998, 1999, 2001, 2002
Cecilia J. F. Kochanowski 1982
Preston Stephen Koehl 1973
John Archibald Koenig 1972, 1973, 1974
Richard A. Koenigsberg 1963
Gary Kolar 1977
Laura Kopchick 1998
Matthew Hans Kopka 1978
Richard James Koppitch 1942
Suzanne Koprince 1961
Mary Louise Koral 1975
Alexander David Korn 1981, 1982
Karen Elaine Kornblum 1976
Donald Korobkin 1978
David Kosky 1990

Mitchell Herman Koss 1975
LaVerne Anne Kostelnik 1955
Elizabeth Kostova 2003,
    2004
Madeline Kotowicz 2004
J. David Kotre 1989
Hillary Kover 2002
Cathryn Ann Kowaleski 1976
Kathleen Kozachenko 1974
Robert C. Kraft 1992
Karl Krahnke 1960
Robert Krajeski 1973
Carolyn Wells Kraus 1996,
    1999
Richard Kraus 1947, 1948,
    1952
Belinda Kremer 1997
Barry Kriger 1962
Steven Thomas Kronovet
    1973
Donald John Kubit 1968,
    1975
Ruth E. Kuchel 1963
William Kueser 1992
Rene Leilani Kuhn 1943, 1944
Elinor Chamberlain Kuhns
    1951
Karen Kelly Kukla 1977
Andrew Kula 2005
Abhishek Kumar 2001
Moran Kuntze 2003
Andrew Kurtzman 1977,
    1978, 1979, 1980
Thomas Kush 1971
Anne Kwok 1974
Jennifer Kwon 1983

Mary Ellen Laberteaux 1967
Roy Ernest Lachman 1971
Dorace E. LaCore 1938
Russell M. LaDue, Jr. 1944,
    1946
Christine S. Lahey 1968
Martin Bruce Lahr 1969
Clara Margaretta Laidlaw
    1941, 1942, 1946
Judith Laikin 1946, 1948

Richard Laing 1953
A. K. Lake 1935
Valerie Laken 2000, 2001
Rita Lakin 1955
Sangeetha
    Lakshminarayanan 2002
Jessica Hawkes Lamb 1985
Josh Lambert 2005
James Fulton Land 1946
Nelson Prentis Lande 1965
Susan Landers 1993
Catherine Landis 1981
Winifred Leona Landy 1944
David J. Lane 1964
Roger A. Lane 1982
Maaza M. Langdon 1991
Karen Langner 1997
Judith Lantz 1984
Rattawut Lapcharoensap
    2003
Konstantinos Nick Lardas
    1961
Ted Lardner 1984
John Larkin 1961
Kathryn Larrabee 1994
Pamela Larratt 1988
Grace Larson 1957
Robert F. Larson 1964
Anna Virginia LaRue 1939
Scott Lasser 1988
Hope Latimer 1998
Sister Janice Marie Lauer
    1963
Kenneth A. Lauter 1966
Jerold D. E. Lax 1960
Jack D. LaZebnik 1953
George Lea III 1956
Edward C. Leach 1982
Janice Yvonne Schofield
    Leach 1984
Lisa Ann Leafstrand 1978
Charles A. Leavay 1940, 1944
Charles F. LeBaron, Jr. 1971
Alison S. Lebwohl 1993
Margaret LeDuc 2004
Derek Lee 2005
George Henry Lee 1983

Martin A. Lee 1972, 1974,
    1975
Marshall W. Lee 2005
Susan R. Lee 1976
Richard L. Lees 1970
Joshua Lefkowitz 2001
Erica Lehrer 2001
Anne Susan Leiman 1974
John Michael Leimer 1968
Zachary Leland 2002
Kristin Lems 1969
Gail Diane Lenhoff 1968,
    1969, 1970
Gabrielle Lensch 2004
Craig Kimball Leon 1979
Frank Lepkowski 1982
Igor Levin 1984
Jenifer M. Levin 1973, 1975,
    1977
Mark Levin 1987
Joanne Levine 1952
Lee Daniel Levine 1983
Miriam Tova Levine 2004
David Elliot Levy 1954, 1957
Catherine N. Levy 2001
Scott D. Lew 1990
Barbara J. Lewis 1956
Man Kuei Li 1936
Jardine Raven Libaire 1997
Elisa Lichtenbaum 1990
Richard Wald Lid 1955
Laurence James Lieberman
    1955, 1958
Tyler Lieberman 2003
Dana Elizabeth Liebert 1988
Bradley Joseph Liening 2002
Jon Daniel Ligon 1986, 1987
Daniel Liimatta 1980
Mary Ellen Liles 1980
Jason Lindner 1998, 1999
Demian Linn 1996
Norman Dale Linville 1961,
    1962
Daniel Rehr Lipman 1972
Lori Beth Lippitz 1978
Kalian Douglas Liston 1969,
    1970, 1973

Karen Anne Liston 1983
Erica Littler 1981
Yue John Liu 2000
Mark I. Lloyd 1977
Benjamin T. Lo 1990
Brian Lobel 2004
Joan E. Lochner 1944
Thomas V. LoCicero 1963
Dorothy Mae Lockhorn 1952
Mariama J. Lockington 2004
June Elizabeth Loeffler 1978
John Hoult Logie, Jr. 1985
Michael Lombardo 2000
Mary Ruth Lomer 1955
Michael Lommel 1989
Berton Lee London 1948, 1950
Margaret Mary Long 1974, 1975, 1976
Hanna LoPatin 2000
Steven Lopez 1995
Richard Earl Loranger 1979, 1980, 1982
Fay Lorden 1944
Gregory Joseph Loselle 1989, 1990
Adrienne Losh 1993
Rachel Losh 2004
Susan Carol Losh 1965
Alice Louie 1955
Alfred H. Lovell, Jr. 1935, 1936
Courtney Loveman 1992
David Garrard Lowe 1957
Henrietta Lubke 1952
David M. Lubliner 1988
Earl B. Luby 1937
Richard M. Ludwig 1939
Thomas Yuntong Luk 1976
Deanne Lundin 1996, 1997
John William Lungerhausen 1975
Jon Reed Luoma 1971, 1973
Z. N. Lupetin 2005
Carol Ann Luse 1956, 1959
Gail Kathleen Lutey 1973
Jennifer Lutman 1999

Ralph Richard Luttermoser 1977
William Lychack 1991
Mary Lynch 1986
Frederic N. Lyon 1966, 1967, 1968
Daniel J. Lyons 1991, 1992

Robert Macadaeg 1995
Russell MacCracken 1932
Dorothea MacGregor 1935
Patricia MacGregor 1942
Gabriel T. Machynia, Jr. 1973
Donovan Mack 1983
Jean MacKaye 1943
Nancy MacKaye 1945
Beryl MacLachlan 1983
Susan E. MacLaren 1988
Martha Havens MacNeal 1964, 1965
Charles F. Madden 1947
Michael J. Madigan 1967
Corey Michael Madsen 2002
Laura Magnus 1983
Michael B. Maher 1983
Helen Major 1955, 1957
Nadine Major 1971
Lila Mae Makima 1944
Jennifer Lynn Malik 1973
Dorothy Anne Malloy 1976, 1977
Patricia Malloy 1955
Marcia Maureen Malvern 1961
Teri Lynn Malwitz 1972
Paul David Mandel 1968
Rosalee June Mandell 1955
Patricia Mandley 1958
Courtney Mandryk 2004
Robert Ethan Manis 1974
Frances E. Mannard 1960
Edward P. Manning 1950
Sister Frances Manor 1976
Laura Mansnerus 1970
Paul Manwiller 1982
Louise-Annette Marcotty 1975

William C. Marcoux 1978
Chad Markert 1991
Edward T. Marquardt 1965, 1966
Tilney Marsh 1995
John P. Marshall 1989
John E. Martell, Jr. 1980
Caroline Martin 2004
Daniel P. Martin 1970
Jo Nobuko Martin 1972
Maureen Sue Martin 1975
Wendy Martin 1984, 1985
Laurence E. Mascott 1946
David A. Masello 1976
Graham Mason 2005
Kelly Murphy Mason 1995
Larry Gordon Mason 1957, 1959
Gloria Ann Masterson 1945
Ann Mathisson 1958
Rosemary Matson 1978
Joan Lord Matthews 1973
Richard H. Mattox 1935
Joseph Matuzak 1982, 1984
Amous J. Maue 1986, 1987, 1988, 1989
Barbara Louise Mary Maurer 1969
Carey H. May 1952
David Nicholas Mayer 1973, 1974, 1977
James R. Mayes 1992
Charles E. Mays 1951
Peter Zaragoza Mayshle 2005
Susan Arlene McCarthy 1973
Peter McCarus 1980
Richard McCaughey 1951
Mark McClelland 1992
Jay W. McCormick 1938, 1940, 1941, 1942
Nancy R. McCortney 1961
Eleanor McCoy 1939
Dana L. McCrossin 1984
Theresa McDermitt 1991
Mary Catherine McDonough 1977
Anna Maria McEwen 1987

Evan McGarvey 2005
Bryan Joseph McGee 1977
Cammie McGovern 1990
Matthew McGregor 1951
Kristi A. McGuire 2000, 2001
Carmelita McGurk 1987
Ann Lowe McIntosh 1962
Dennis F. McIntyre 1964,
   1966
Donna McIvor 1957
Richard L. McKelvey 1938
Victoria McKenzie 1995
Thomas S. McKeown 1968
Todd McKinney 1994
Nora McLaughlin 1991
Mary Anne McLean 1950
John Breese McManis 1949
Eileen McManus 1933
Peter McPartlin 1989
Angelina E. McPhail 1938
Sandra Ann McPherson
   1960
Bernard F. McPhillips 1958
Ursula Yvette McPike 1980
Anthony Joseph
   McReynolds 1980, 1982,
   1983
Jenifer McVaugh 1962
Gia Krystine Medeiros 1993
Alice Katherine Meech 1956
Elizabeth A. Meese 1965
Maureen Megerian 1984
Louis Geza Megyesi 1958,
   1959
Victoria Mehl 1986
Martha Mehta 1971
Hendrik George Meijer 1973
Seth Reuben Meisels 1995
Rose Anne Melikan 1983
Charlotte Ann Melin 1978
Emmanuel P.
   Menatsaganian 1937
Steven Richard Mendelson
   1974
James Mercurio 1990
Russell Edward Meredith
   1980

John Armstrong Merewether
   1945, 1946
Beth Merizon 1942
Dena Mermelstein 1986
Ada Mertz 1974
Sarah Messer 1990
Jennifer Metsker 2003, 2005
Peter Meyerhoff 1990
Gerald Wayne Meyers 1966
Lewis Arthur Meyers 1962
Helen Michaelson 1985
David Michael Michalak
   1982, 1983
Sarah Shaw Middleton 1993,
   1995, 1996
John Philip Milhous 1938,
   1939, 1940
Amy J. Miller 1961
Arthur A. Miller 1936, 1937
Charles H. Miller 1939, 1940,
   1941
Deborah Miller 1973
Ella Judith Miller 1936
Harry Miller 1951, 1952
Jacob Miller 1978
Jane Trimble Miller 1958
Janet E. Miller 1958
Kenneth Edd Miller 1982
Linda Miller 1987
Nolan Miller 1943
Robert James Miller 1945,
   1946
Ross Lincoln Miller 1968
Susan Beth Miller 1970, 1973
Teresa Gayle Miller 1974
Michael Henry Millgate 1957
Alexander Mirsky 1991
Suzanne Misencik 1986, 1987
Ruth R. Misheloff 1952
Ann Elizabeth Mitchell 1932
Jack D. A. Mitchell 1942
Elena Mitcoff 1938
Peter Mognetti 1935
Diane J. A. Monach 1978,
   1980
John O. Monaghan 1959
Nancy Joan Moncrieff 1974

Derek Mong 2005
Barbara Louise Monier 1976
Cherisse E. Montgomery
   1999, 2000
Deborah Jane Montwori
   1983, 1984, 1985
Samuel Moon 1941, 1942,
   1943
Charles Michael Moore 1974
Gerian Steve Moore 1972
John E. Moore 1936
Kathryn Doris Moore 1982
Ethel H. Moorman 1940
Harold C. Moran 1966
Erin Aileen Morris 2004,
   2005
Rosemary Morris 1951
Sandra Morris 1988
Walter Morris 1933, 1934
Victoria Morrow 1998
David Morse 2002, 2003
Stuart Dean Morton 1960
Howard Moss 1940
Rebecca Mostov 2004
Michelle Mounts 2003
Michael Mueller 1980
Katie Mulcrone 2001
Marjorie Mullin 1940
William V. Mulroney 1931
Peter Muñoz 1998
Carol A. Murchie 1978
James Murdock 1950
Kathleen Murphy 1933
Terrence Murphy 1951
Michael Charles Murray
   1994, 1995
Florence Musser 1931
Kathleen Musser 1951
Deborah Mutnick 1975

Barbara Irene Nagler 1965
Suzanne H. Naiburg 1965
Betty Nancarrow 1945
Martha Cook Nash 1970
Pamela M. Nash 1995
Reid H. Nation 1933, 1934
Karen P. Nauta 1964

Julia Neal 1945
Janet Lee Near 1966
Charlotte Nekola 1979
David Erik Nelson 1996, 1999
Lyle Emerson Nelson 1950
Rachel Nelson 2003
John Nerber 1940
Greg Netzer 1994
Adi Neuman 2001
Marie Neumeister 1945
Andrew Livingston Newberg 1994
David Newman 1957, 1958
William H. Newton 1938
Bich Minh Nguyen 1994, 1996, 1997, 1998
Nathan G. Nichols 1989
Bradley R. Nielson 1957
Priscilla R. Nirdlinger 1964
Anna Nissen 1978, 1979, 1980, 1981
Randon Billings Noble 1994
Elizabeth Noll 1984
David Derbin Nolta 1980, 1981, 1982
Julie Nord 1978
Suzette Normolle 1987
Jack E. Noyes 1960
Ron Nyren 1997

Beth Ann Oberfelder 1973
Rosemary J. Obermeyer 1942
John George O'Brien 1962
John Harrington O'Brien 1934
Marcia Ochoa 1991
Laurie Ochsner 1984
Sister Mary Edwardine O'Connor 1941, 1946
Richard A. Ogar 1960
Carl Preston Oglesby 1961
Douglas John O'Hara, Jr. 1996
Francis Russell O'Hara 1951
Patrick O'Keeffe 1999
Julia Older 1963

Joan Valerie Oleck 1968, 1969
David S. Oleshansky 1975, 1978
Colleen M. Olle 1991
Stacey Olster 1979
Thomas O'Malley 1964
Sharon Marie Omell 1963, 1964
Judith Oppenheim 1960
Myrna Oppenheim 1960
Roberta Ormandy 1959
Arthur K. Orrmont 1943, 1944, 1945
George Joseph Orupabo 1976
Esohe Osai 2004
Hadley Osborn 1953
Francie Lynn Oscherwitz 1979
Anthony J. Ostroff 1948, 1949
Barbara Lee Otto 1963
Diane Ouding 1965
Karen E. Outen 2003, 2004
Mack Owen 1968
Mary E. Owen 1937, 1939, 1957, 1958
Carolyn Hicks Owens 1968

Jon Stephen Pack 1973
James Robert Packard 1957
Thomas Greg Page 1975
Allan George Palmer 1965
Mary S. Palmer 1943
Benjamin Paloff 2001
Kit Pancoast 1988
Tom Panzenhagen 1982
Caroline Diane Parker 1990
Douglass Scott Parker 1949
Gregory Parker 1996
John Leonard Parker 1994
Sharon Parker 1987
Bradford Scott Parks 1981, 1984
Nan Parrish 1984, 1985, 1986
Deborah Parry 1942
Vivian La Jeunesse Parsons 1938

Veronica Pasfield 2001
Kenneth James Passage 1975
Barbara Paton 1932
Arthur Joslyn Patten 1971, 1972
Amy Pattulo 1977
James Allen Paul 1973, 1977
David Pava 1992
John George Paval 1974
Ava Justine Pawlak 2002
Nicholas Pawlowski 1994
Benjamin B. Peacock 1960
Carol Pearce 1962
Allan R. Pearlman 1977, 1980
Sheryl Sherman Pearson 1972
Susan Coolidge Peck 1966
Mary Sponberg Pedley 1972
Mary Jo Peer 1976
Victor Haim Perera 1961
David Perkins 1964
Virginia Chase Perkins 1940
Ellis Edward Perraut 1976
Jacqueline C. Perret 1977
Marcia Ann Perry 1973, 1975
Annemarie Persov 1932
James Paul Peters 1967, 1968, 1973
Jeffrey Peters 1986
Richard L. Peters 1958
JoAnn Peterson 1942, 1943
Paula Peterson 1986
Sister Ingrid Peterson 1969
Nick Petrie 1991
Helen E. Pfeifer 1939, 1940
Robert L. Pham 1997
Nora Phend 1984, 1986
Raymond Yao Phillips 1997
Robin Pick 1992
Joseph P. Pickett 1980
Arte Ira Pierce 1974, 1975, 1976, 1980
Clarence M. Pierce 1932
Suzanne Pierce 1993
Marge Piercy 1954, 1956, 1957
Michael Pifer 2004
Kevin Thomas Pilon 1971, 1972

Diane Pinkley 1970
Craig D. Piper 1979
Daniel J. Pipski 1999
Phillip J. Pirages 1973, 1974
Bart Plantenga 1977
David Stanley Plastrik 2004
Daniel G. Plice 1989
Ardath Ploegstra 1952
Erin Podolsky 2000
Sue L. Pohl 1963
Eve Polk 1935
Carl H. Pollmar 1935
Sharon Pomerantz 2001, 2002
Katherine A. Pond 1986
Lisa Douglas Poneck 1989
Jim Poniewozik 1990
John Ponyicsanyi 1998
Laurie W. Porter 1981
Martin Alan Porter 1975
Arthur S. Postle 1947
Grace A. Potter 1940
Russell Potterfield 1993
Gilda Povolo 1987
Earl Jean Prahl 1957
V. Prasad 1997
Clifford H. Prator, Jr. 1934
Brenda Pratt 1985
Peter Phillip Pratt 1985
Tim Prentiss 1977
Christopher Prescott 1990
Grace Ann Preston 1953, 1954
Margaret Price 1996
Jeffrey Cress Pridgeon 1972
Margaret Anne Prine 1947
Herbert Propper 1963
Ellen Mary Prosser 1975
Christos Pulos 1938
John Purdue 1940
Jason G. Putnam 1991
Elizabeth Amelia Pypa 1975

Richard Arthur
    Quackenbush 1967
Patrick S. Queen 1980
Duane Quiatt 1959
Genevieve Quigley 1964

George Stites Quin, Jr. 1981, 1983

Paula Rabinowitz 1983
Stanley Gregory Radhuber 1962
Ramya Raghavan 2004
John Ragsdale 1939, 1940
Christian Raisner 1959
Elaine Raiss 1944
Alexander Ralph 1999, 2000
Helen Ranck 1970
Theodore Joseph Rancont, Jr. 1962, 1965
James A. Randall, Jr. 1933, 1960
Christopher Schmidt Ranney 1977
Matthew Ransford 1996
Marjorie S. Rapaport 1963, 1966
Ellen Raphaeli 1964
Dana Rapisardi 1991, 1993
Linda Loretto Rapp 1970
Lisa Jane Rapport 1980
Kenneth A. Ratliff 1934
Helen Mary Ratner 1961
Dennis J. Reardon 1971
Donald C. Reaser 1950
E. Paul Rebillot 1954
Della Rebish 1940
Ann Margaret Redisch 1974
Jeanne Funkhouser Reeder 1961
George S. Reeves 1949
Margaret Reges 2005
Matt Reichl 1997
Richard Morris Reichman 1966, 1967
Elwood Reid 1996
John David Reiff 1974
Ann Reinach 1960
John Reinhard 1989
Roberta Reisig 1964
Paisley Rekdal 1996
Rebekah Marie Remington 1991

Susanna Remold 1986
Joelle Lynn Renstrom 1998
Tatiana Retivov 1980
Charles Christopher Reynolds 1975
Rebecca Reynolds 1990
Precina Denise Rhodes-Tolon 1978
Darlene Rhodus 1952
Patricia Rose Rice 1961
William Craig Rice 1987
Shannon Emily Richards 1981
Jack Richardson 1952
Rachel B. J. Richardson 2003
Keith Bernard Richburg 1976
Michael Richman 1989
Robert Richman 1944, 1945
Emily Riddering 1973
Constance Opal Rinehart 1948
Katherine Ripman 1933
Daniel Rivas 2004
Aida Rivera 1954
Harriet Robbe 1944
Jill Robbins 1989
John N. Roberts 1967
Joseph Roberts 1952
Margaret Roberts 1941
Michael George Roberts 1969, 1970
J. Gardner Robertson 1964
Jack Robertson 1977
Shirley Rita Robin 1944, 1946
James Stephen Robins 1976
Eugene Harold Robinson 1971
Thomas J. Robinson 1980
Matthew Rochkind 1997
Leo Rockas 1956
Jeffrey W. Rodamar 1969
Maxine E. Rodburg 1987, 1988
Wendy Patricia Roe 1966
James Veblen Roelofs 1969
Amanda Leigh Rogers 1991

Charles Rogers 1977
Kathryn A. Rogers 1970
Rachel S. Rohde 1991
Michael David Rohrback 1977
Matthew Rohrer 1989
Jake Rollow 2001
Bruce David Rooke 1982
Laura Jane Roop 1981, 1985
Susan Ruth Rosegrant 1974
Steven R. Rosen 1972
Carolyn Hope Rosenberg 1975
David W. Rosenberg 1964
Jordan Rosenberg 2002
Ralph Rosenberg, Jr. 1936
Richard W. Rosenberg 1986
Robert Rosenberg 1951
Doris Rosenshine 1944, 1945
Lucy G. Rosenthal 1951
Marilynn M. Rosenthal 1970
Sydney Lewis Rosenthal 1932
Jean McRae Ross 1960, 1963
Norman Rosten 1938
Sebastian Ramon Rotella 1982, 1983, 1984
Ari Roth 1981, 1982
David I. Rothbart 1993, 1994, 1995, 1996
Ellen Flexner Rothblatt 1937
Donald Lewis Rothman 1966
Alec Rothrock 1978
Jess Row 2000
Donald Daniel Rowe 1963
Jonathan Dale Rowe 1975, 1976
Sallyann Rubin 1961
Sarah Rubin 2004
Tasha Rubinow 1993
David Ruderman 2003
Mary G. Rudolph 1952
Lawrence Irving Russ 1970, 1971, 1975, 1976
Kerry Russell 2003
Peggy Russo 1979
David Rutkowski 1971

Sister Mary Phillip Ryan 1944
Sara Ryan 1990
Christine Carol Ryba 1976
Dan Rydholm 1978
John Henry Ryskamp 1974
J. D. Ryznar 2000
Martha Jean Rzasa 1965

Laura Saaf 1984
Naomi Saferstein 1986, 1987
Laura A. Sagolla 1988
Suzanne Sahakian 1977, 1978
Jane René Sajewski 1976
Richard Barksdale Sale III 1973
Joseph Salerno 1970
Robert Salkin 1985
Tali Saltzman 2000
Darwin Sampson 1947, 1949
Nalini Samuel 1974
Anna Sophia Sandberg 1947
John Raymond Sanecki 1959, 1960
Clarissa Sansone 1993
Marilyn Beth Saulles 1971
David Arthur Saunders 1959, 1961
Florence G. Saunders 1964
Barbara Saunier 1981
Edwin C. S. Sauter, Jr. 1958
Marc Whitney Savage 1967
Sue Ann Savas 1978
John R. Savoie 1980, 1981
Patricia Sawyer 1955
Paul L. Sawyer 1967
Kurt Edgar Sayenga 1982
Incigul Sayman 1995, 1999
Marion S. Scanlon 1943
Patricia Ann Schaefer 1981, 1990
Frederic Warren Schaen 1959
Randolph Wolfe Schein 1974
Mildred Walker Schemm 1933
Monica Scherer 1988
Marilyn R. Schiffman 1965

Carolyn Tourner Schilling 2004
Anna Schlossberg 1989
Mia Schmiedeskamp 1985
Beatrice Schmitt 1933
Matthew Schmitt 1998
Elizabeth Ann Schmuhl 2005
Renée Eleanor Schneider 1945, 1947, 1948
Patrice M. Schoder 1977
Adina Schoem 2004
Martin E. Scholten 1935
Howard Schott 1987
J. Penelope Schott 1960, 1961, 1962, 1963
Michal Schover 1964, 1965
Lawrence E. Schreib 1953
Joseph Schreiber 1989
Robert Peter Schreiner 1973
Barbara Ellen Schroeder 1977, 1978, 1979
Dee Anne Schroeder 1961
Susan Wells Schroeder 1970
Charles L. Schulman 1984, 1985, 1987
Elizabeth Avery Schultz 1962
David L. Schwab 2001
Erin Diane Schwartz 1995
Lois Carol Schwartz 1954
Michael J. Schwartz 1996
Steven G. Schwartz 1974
Tony Schwartz 1974
Christopher Schweda 1993
Cydney Scott 1983
William Walter Scott III 1969, 1971
Laura Seager-Baddeley 1983
Marybeth Sears 1938
Mary Lou Seaver 1970
Dorothy L. Sedlmayr 1954
Anne Davidow Seeger 1948
Edna Seewald 1952, 1954
Jerome M. Segal 1966
Carole Anne Seidelman 1975
Barbara Francine Seiden 1965

Linnea Seifert 1977

Jeffrey Paul Selbst 1975

Daniel Aryeh Seligmann 1994

Peter Robert Serchuk 1974

Timothy D. Sergay 1983, 1985

Beth Serlin 1986

Corinne Alison Serra 1977

John Armson Sessions 1945

L. William Sessions 1938

Catherine Li-Ming Seto 1993, 1994, 1996

Gretchen Downing Settle 1963

Emily Severance 1987

Janet Durrie Shaforth 1940

Ralph Shahrigian 1965

Carol M. Shapiro 1957

Nancy Ellen Shaw 1968

Patricia Shaw 1952

Susan June Shaw 1969, 1971

William J. Shaw 1951

Gregory Shaya 1988

Joseph Shea 1984

Robert Gordon Shedd 1948

Marc J. Sheehan 1985

Anne Sheffield 1972, 1974

Elouise Kathryn Sheffield 1938

Stephen M. Sheffrey 1951

Sue Shekut 1985

Julie Shell 1996

Laurie Beth Shell 1974

Dorothy Sherba 1944

Erin Sherman 1998

Wendy Sherrill 1988

Deborah Gail Shields 1981

Bette Ellen Shifman 1976

Catherine W. Shilson 1943

Nina Shishkoff 1978

Bruce Kevin Shlain 1972

Abigail Elizabeth Short 2002

Spencer Ryun Short 1997

Porter Shreve 1998

John Alexander Shtogren, Jr. 1970

Allison Dean Shumsky 1949, 1950, 1951, 1952

William T. Sickrey 1954, 1963

Netta Siegal 1942

Rochelle Ann Siegel 1970 1971

Audra Leigh Sielaff 1997

Helen Jungell Sikkens 1950, 1951

Sherman Jay Silber 1965

Alan Lee Silverman 1966

Linda Silverman 1972

Aliyah Ariana Silverstein 1992

Philip Simmons 1989

Helene M. Simon 1951

Richard K. Simon 1967

William Simon 1951

Vance Charles Simonds 1943, 1947, 1948

Helen Frances Simpson 1942

Jeffrey Simpson 1969

Stephen G. Sinclair 1975

Beth Rita Singer 1948

Emily Singer 1995

Ian Singleton 2004

Madison Singleton 1980

Susan Siris 1950

Albert Sjoerdsma, Jr. 1980

Cindy Skandis 1978

David L. Skelly 1992

Hobert D. Skidmore 1932, 1933

Hubert S. Skidmore 1935

Davida Skurnick 1965, 1966

John Currie Slade 1967, 1968

Jennifer Slajus 1993

Ann Tashi Slater 1990

Hilda Jane Slautterback 1942, 1944

Timothy Slavin 1982

W. W. Sleator, Jr. 1935

Curtis Slepian 1972

Karen Ann Slezak 1972

Alfred H. Slote 1949

Bernice Slote 1944, 1945

Henrietta Howell Slote 1952

John Elias Slote 1975, 1977

Timothy Wood Slover 1981

Harold Geoffrey Slovic 1965, 1966

Albert Smallman 1954

Freya Figas Smallwood 1964

Janet Anne Smereck 1976, 1977

Carrie F. Smith 1977, 1979

Deborah E. Smith 1999

Elizabeth W. Smith 1931

Erika M. Smith 1998

Gordon L. Smith 1995, 1997

Ingrid Hokanson Smith 1973

Jennifer A. Smith 1990

Jessica Belle Smith 2000

Maggie Smith 2000

Marjorie Reins Smith 1965

Matthew Smith 2000

Philip Stanley Smith 1985

Stephanie Smith 2004

Thomas Allen Snapp 1967, 1968

Judith Larue Snider 1963, 1965

Anthony So 1980

Stanford Sobel 1941

Neal A. Sobol 1975

Richard Randolph Sogn 1983, 1990

Alisa Gail Solomon 1978

Don Solosan 1986, 1987, 1988

Theodore H. Solotaroff 1949, 1952

James C. Somers 1982

Nancy J. Somers 1953

Satinger Singh Sood 1976

Daniel Parley Sorensen 1976

Donet Meynell Sorensen 1941

Erik Sorenson 1993

Ronald Peter Sossi 1961

Stephen Southard 1978

Jerry Soverinsky 1987

Nadya Spassenko 1954

Holly Wren Spaulding 1994, 1995, 1997

Richard W. Speckhard 1947
Kean Spencer 1978
Lyssa Sperlich 2003
Kaylyn Spezzano 1963
Ferne Spielman 1945
Cara Spindler 1997, 1999
David C. Spink 1978
Brian Spitulnik 2005
Glenn W. Sprague 1954
Jane L. Sprague 1969
Douglas Sprigg 1962
Ronald Fleming Sproat 1955
Paula A. Spurlin 1960, 1965
Angela Ssengoba 1984
Robert Jay Staal 1957
Karl Stampfl 2005
Anthony Stampolis 1942
Jack R. Stanley 1972, 1973
Peter James Stanlis 1948
Therese Stanton 1997
Lara M. Stapleton 1989, 1990
Guy Stark 1977
Katherine Stasewich 1945
Elizabeth Ames Staudt 2005
Elijah Stearns 1932
Samuel Stearns 1933
Paul Stebleton 1992
Katherine Stecko 1996
Diana Katherine Steer 1967
Katie Stein 1994
Kevin D. Stein 1991
Maida Ruth Steinberg 1944
David M. Steingold 1984, 1985
Sandra K. Steingraber 1983
Bobette J. Stern 1962
Darlene Ellen Stern 1973
Josephine Stern 1931
Michael Stern 1999
Janet Scovie Stevens 1977
Jennifer Noel Stevens 1947
Mary A. Stevens 1954
Warren David Stevens 1932
Anne Katherine Stevenson 1951, 1952, 1954
Brett L. Stevenson 1989

David Harry Stevenson 1939, 1943
Charles G. Stewart, Jr. 1963
Leah Stewart 1996
John R. Stiles 1940
Martha Bennett Stiles 1956, 1958
Miriam Manafield Stimson 1944
Milan W. Stitt 1961, 1963
Sharon Lee Stiver 1968
Margaret Stoddard 1952
Barbara Stoler 1959
Harriet Ragir Stolorow 1968
Richard N. Stolorow 1967
Helen M. Stone 1965
Sarah Stone 1997, 1998
Charles Joseph Stoneburner 1965
Ursula Storbeck 1983
Carrie Strand 2003
Anne Marie Strass 1980
Joan Elizabeth Strassmann 1973
Albert Neil Stratton 1972, 1974
Jennifer Strausz 2002, 2003
Richard Daniel Streicker 1974
Joan Claire Striefling 1949, 1951, 1952
Herthe Striker 1956
David H. Stringer 1984
Barbara Stroebel 1937
Anna Stubblefield 1991
Karl Sturk 2004
Frances Eve Suffness 1947
Brian Ward Sutton 1970, 1972
Herman Suyemoto 1983
Harvey Swados 1937
Frances Swain 1933
John R. Swain 1932
Fritz Garner Swanson 1997, 1999
Glendon F. Swarthout 1948
Martin Sweeney 1990, 1991

Stanley Mitchell Swinton 1937
James Swiontek 1973
Larissa Szporluk 1988, 1989
Michael Andrei Szporluk 1991
John Robert Szucs 1958

Constance Anne Taber 1941
Deborah Tall 1972
Sara Kathleen Talpos 1997
Ju Kok Tan 1996
Alan B. Tate 1977
Maureen T. Taylor 1964
Tim Tebeau 2005
Mohezin Tejani 1974
Cheryl Teplinsky 1978
Roland George Tharp 1961
Patricia Theisen 1957
Jim Therkalsen 1998
Leona Eugenia Thoma 1939, 1942, 1950
Ann-Marie Thomas 1998
Harry Brandon Thomas 1979
Jennice Thomas 1959
Kerry Randall Thomas 1975
Laurence W. Thomas 1956
Lisa Kay Thomas 1978
Mary H. Thomas 1966
Richard K. Thomas 1956
Thomas Andrew Thomas 1974, 1976
Helena S. Thomassen 1946
John Ira Thompson 1974, 1975
Rick D. Thompson 1977
Melanie Rae Thon 1980
Matthew Q. Thorburn 1994, 1995
Michael John Thornton 1951
Oliver Thornton 1999
Kathleen Hughes Thumin 1944, 1945, 1946
Brie Nicol Tiderington 1997, 1999
Stacy J. Tiderington 2001

Amy Tikkanen 1990
Jeannine Timm 1973
Patricia A. Tingle 1987
Barbara W. Tinker 1939
Rebecca-Beth Topol 1987
Nathaniel Topping 2004
Carolyn Marie Torma 1972,
   1973
James Sullivan Torrens 1965
Priscilla E. Torsleff 1955,
   1956, 1957
John Loftus Tottenham 1969
Bonnie L. Towne 1973
Carol Trager 1973
Mary Trombley 1997, 1998
William Brown Trousdale
   1949, 1950, 1952
Jennifer Trudeau 1992
Robert G. True 1946
Alissa Tsukakoshi 2003
David McKinley Tucker 1973
David Turner 2003
John Mills Turner 1933
Tori Turner 1999
David R. Tuttle 1964
Ian Reed Twiss 1997
Dorothy Tyler 1932

Robert M. Uchitelle 1948
Jon Udell 1979
Leonard M. Uhr 1954
Carol Ullmann 2000
Kate Umans 2002
J. Harlan Underhill 1958
Donald N. Unger 1990
Steven Peter Unger 1967,
   1969
Lorraine Ura 1945
Alvin L. Ureles 1940, 1942
N. Renuka Uthappa 1988
Reba Uthappa 1989
Josephine Laurel Utley 1986,
   1988

Roger Michael Valade III
   1991, 1992
Eugene L. Van Buren 1946

Lois Van der Meulen 1942
Katherine E. Van Dis 2000
Henry L. Van Dyke, Jr. 1954
Philip W. Van Eyck 1989
Carol Marie Vanderkloot
   1946
Randall J. VanderMey 1972
Benson Varghese 2003
Robert F. Vaughn 1952
Arthur Versluis 1984
David Allen Victor 1976,
   1978, 1981
Joe Villella 2004
Leigh Vinocur 1977
Virginia L. Voss 1951

Karen E. Wagner 1969
Robert O. Wagner, Jr. 1947,
   1950
Jan B. Wahl 1955
Elliot J. Wait 1966
Kathleen Wakefield 1982
Victor Walbridge 2004, 2005
Virginia M. Walcott 1942
Charles Child Walcutt 1937
Margery Wald 1947
Daniel G. Waldron 1948,
   1949
Keith Waldrop 1958
Rosmarie S. Waldrop 1963
Peter Denbo Waldstein 1976
Augusta Walker 1942, 1944
George Lee Walker 1950
Robert G. Walker 1938
Sam Walker 1993
Vincent C. Wall 1933
Ronald Wallace 1970
Stephen Wallen 1994
Blake Walmsley 1987
Chad Walsh 1939
Frank W. Walsh 1959
DeForest P. Walton 1949
Mary Catherine Wank 1948
Beverly Waram 1965
David A. Ward 1964
Jesmyn Ward 2005
Patricia A. Ward 1995

Michael Stuart Warren 1992
Robert S. Warshaw 1934
Douglas Warshow 1983
Jennifer Lee Waterbury 2001
Leah Watkins 1980
Nancy K. Watkins 1949
Craig Watson 1978
Susan Watson 1981
Lindi Watts 2000
Robert J. Wayne 1938
Benjamin Webber 1978
Bruce Jay Weber 1975
Mark Webster 1976
Sara Weeks 1961
Matthew S. Weiler 1997
Odelia Weinberg 1987
Rebecca Weiner 1956
Jeffrey Lee Weinfeld 1974
Martin Mark Weingart 1956
Daniel Weingarten 1985,
   1986
Alisa Weinreich 1967
David S. Weintraub 1971
Jeffrey Lee Weisberg 1974
Bridget A. Weise 1993
Karen B. Weiss 1989, 1991
Michael Weiss 1990, 1991
Burton H. Welcher 1954
Stephen C. Welkom 1970
John T. Wells 1970
John F. Welzenbach, Jr. 1971
Tanya Wendling 1979
Ted Wendling 1977
Gretchen Wessinger 1932
Susana Wessling 1989
Candace Marie Weston 1973
Sally Weston 1983
Johanna Wetmore 2003
Robert W. Wheeler 1958,
   1962
Merrill D. Whitburn 1959,
   1960, 1962
Bradford G. White 1960
David Martin White 1974,
   1975
Edmund V. White 1961, 1962
Frederic R. White 1940

Mary Jo White 1977
Frank Whitehouse, Jr. 1947,
   2004
Edith Whitesell 1937
John D. Whitney 1964
Mary C. Wicker 1957
Krista A. Wicklund 1994
Kristen M. Wicklund 1998
Richard E. Widerkehr 1966,
   1967
Dallas Wiebe 1956
Mary G. Wiedenbeck 1969
William G. Wiegand 1946,
   1948, 1949, 1951
Sharon Kane Wieland 1990
Adam Lewis Wiener 1986
Karen Wigen 1977
Mary Catherine Wilds 1981,
   1982
Marvin Wildstein 1954
Peter Wiley 1994
Joseph H. Wilkinson 1965
Nancy M. Willard 1955, 1956,
   1957, 1958
Amy S. Williams 1986
Eric Williams 1992
Michael Williams 1968
Eugene L. Williamson 1954
Jean I. Willoughby 1959
James G. Wills 1953
Collin Margaret Wilsey 1932
Bethany L. Wilson 1938, 1939
Dorothy A. Wilson 1958
Elizabeth Wilson 1943
Glenn Wilson 1998
Helen Ann Finnegan Wilson
   1938
John M. Wilson 1948, 1950
Michael John Wilson 1994
Roy R. Wilson, Jr. 1950
T. C. Wilson 1934
Joyce Wiltsee 1939

Barton Lee Wimble 1962
Jeffrey J. Wine 1976, 1977
Lisa Wing 1988
Jennifer Beth Winograd 1993
Joyce M. Winslow 1968
Beth Winsten 1996
Nancy Winston 1956
Maggie Winter 2003
Richard B. Winters 1974
Suzanne Wise 1993
Florence Wiselogle 1958
Robert C. Wismer 1947
Thomas Wisniewski 2003,
   2005
Harold V. Witt 1947
Howard L. Witt 1978
Julie Wittes 1972
Howard R. Wolf 1967
Lucas Wolf 1984
Michael A. Wolf 1973
Maritta M. Wolff 1938, 1939,
   1940
Michael F. Wolff 1951
Lester Wolfson 1942
Bernard M. Wolpert 1938
Joseph D. Won 1988, 1991
Margaret L. Wong 1976
Anna C. Wood 1956
Eileen Wood 1940
Lee Mackie Woodruff, Jr.
   1947, 1949
Mary Joan Woods 1964
Douglas Woody Woodsum
   1994
Angus Woodward 1984
John Woodworth 1941
Sarah Elizabeth Worden
   2003
Joshua Worth 1991
Jennifer Wright 2005
Karen K. Wright 1967
Nathaniel Wright 2002

Shawn Forest Wright 1976
David F. Wrubel 1968
Charles Douglas Wunsch
   1976

Kim Yaged 1993, 1998
Charles Yager 1942
Seth Yalcin 1999
Kyle Yam 2002
Ben Yan 2000
Ellen Yang 2003, 2005
Farley E. Yang 1986, 1987
Barbara Yanowski 1956
Marilyn Yaquinto 1989
Donald A. Yates 1954
J. Michael Yates 1964
Linda Lung Teh Yen 1973
Brian Yetwin 2003
Daniel Yezbick 1995
John J. Yiannias 1956
Cynthia A. Yockey 1972
Brenda Yogus 1959
Marilyn Yolles 1957
Leo V. Young 1950
Mark J. Young 1956
Chang Sik Yun 1963

Phillip Lewis Zabawa 1950
Marc A. Zagoren 1960, 1961
Ernest Zaplitny 1959
Hyram M. Zeldis 1946
Simone Ellen Zelitch 1985
Paul N. Zietlow 1957
Michael Zilberman 1996
David Zinn 1987
Eric Zorn 1977, 1978, 1979,
   1980
Marcia A. Zoslaw 1972
Nabeel Zuberi 1989, 1990
Velma M. Zuliani 1966
Ellen Marcia Zweig 1975
Martha M. Zweig 1966

Hopwood Lecturers

The complete list of lecturers and their subjects follows:

1932.   Robert Morss Lovett. Literature and Animal Faith.
1933.   Max Eastman. Literature in the Age of Science.
1934.   Zona Gale. Writing as Design.
1935.   Henry Hazlitt. Literature Versus Opinion.
1937.   Christopher Morley. A Successor to Mark Twain.
1938.   Walter Prichard Eaton. American Drama Versus Literature.
1939.   Carl Van Doren. The First American Man of Letters.
1940.   Henry Seidel Canby. The American Tradition in Contemporary Literature.
1941.   Edward Weeks. On Counting Your Chickens Before They Hatch.
1942.   John Crowe Ransom. The Primitive Language of Poetry.
1943.   Mary Colum. Modern Mode in Literature.
1944.   Louise Bogan. Popular and Unpopular Poetry.
1945.   Struthers Burt. The Unreality of Realism.
1946.   Harlan Hatcher. Towards American Cultural Maturity.
1947.   Robert Penn Warren. The Themes of Robert Frost.
1948.   J. Donald Adams. The Writer's Responsibility.
1949.   F. O. Matthiessen. Responsibilities of the Critic.
1950.   Norman Cousins. In Defense of a Writing Career.
1951.   Mark Van Doren. The Possible Importance of Poetry.
1952.   Horace Gregory. Dramatic Art in Poetry.
1953.   Stephen Spender. The Young Writer, Present, Past, and Future.
1954.   John Gassner. Modern Playwriting at the Crossroads.
1955.   Archibald MacLeish. Why Can't They Say What They Mean?
1956.   Philip Rahv. Literary Criticism and the Imagination of Alternatives.
1957.   Malcolm Cowley. The Beginning Writer in the University.
1958.   John Ciardi. The Silences of the Poem.
1959.   Howard Nemerov. The Swaying Form: A Problem in Poetry.
1960.   Theodore Roethke. The Poetry of Louise Bogan.
1961.   Saul Bellow. Where Do We Go From Here? The Future of Fiction.
1962.   Mark Schorer. The Burdens of Biography.
1963.   Arthur Miller. On Recognition.
1964.   Alfred Kazin. Autobiography as Narrative.
1965.   Donald Davie. Sincerity and Poetry.
1966.   Peter Taylor. That Cloistered Jazz.
1967.   Robert Brustein. No More Masterpieces.
1968.   Denise Levertov. Origins of a Poem.
1969.   Peter De Vries. Exploring Inner Space.
1970.   Nadine Gordimer. Modern African Writing.

1971.   Theodore Solotaroff. The Practical Critic: A Personal View.

1972.   Caroline Gordon. The Shape of the River.

1973.   Robert W. Corrigan. The Changing of the Avant-Garde.

1974.   W. D. Snodgrass. Moonshine and Sunny Beams: A Rumination on A Midsummer Night's Dream.

1975.   Pauline Kael. On Movies.

1976.   John Simon. The Word on Film.

1977.   Walker Percy. The State of the Novel: Dying Art or New Science.

1978.   Tom Wolfe. Literary Technique in the Last Quarter of the Twentieth Century.

1979.   Joan Didion. Making Up Stories.

1980.   Al Alvarez. The Myth of the Artist.

1981.   Arthur Miller. The American Writer: The American Theatre.

1982.   Stephen Spender. The Obsession of Writers with the Act of Writing.

1983.   Maxine Hong Kingston. Imagined Life.

1984.   Norman Mailer. The Hazards and Sources of Writing.

1985.   E. L. Doctorow. The Beliefs of Writers.

1986.   Carolyn Kizer. Poetry of Social Concern Since World War II.

1987.   Joyce Carol Oates. Beginnings.

1988.   Donald Justice. The Prose Sublime.

1989.   Francine du Plessix Gray. Women and Russian Literature.

1990.   William Kennedy. Writers and Their Songs.

1991.   Robert Hass. Prisons and Families: Some Thoughts on Contemporary Poetry.

1992.   Richard Ford. What We Write About, and Why, and Who Cares.

1993.   Roger Rosenblatt. Nine Anti-Rules of Journalism.

1994.   Geoffrey Wolff. Writers and Their Characters.

1995.   Diane Johnson. The Writer as a Character.

1996.   Louise Glück. The Fear of Happiness.

1997.   Philip Levine. Two Journeys.

1998.   John Barth. Further Questions?

1999.   Lawrence Kasdan. POV.

2000.   Donald Hall. Starting and Keeping On.

2001.   Andrea Barrett. Four Voyages.

2002.   Edmund White. Writing Gay.

2003.   Richard Howard. The Fatality of Reading.

2004.   Mary Gordon. Flannery's Kiss.

2005.   Susan Orlean. Roads Taken (and not).

2006.   Charles Baxter. Losers.

Acknowledgments

Grateful acknowledgment is made to the following authors, publishers, and journals for the use of previously published materials.

Max Apple, "Bridging" from *Free Agents,* Harper and Row, 1984. Beth Bentley, "Choices" from *Little Fires,* Cune Press, 1998. Nelson Bentley, "The Lost Photograph" from *Collected Shorter Poems of Nelson Bentley,* Bellowing Ark Press, 1998. Michael Byers, "A Lovely Night" from *Northwest Review* 1, 2002. John Ciardi, "Aunt Mary," "The Catalpa," and "The Gift" from *Collected Poems of John Ciardi.* Reprinted by permission of the University of Arkansas Press. © 1997 by Ciardi. Thomas Clark, "Hazard Response" from *American Poetry Review,* Summer/Fall 2002. Thomas Clark, "November of the Plague Year" from *Divide,* Fall 1983. Cid Corman, "The Poppy" from *Stead: Poems of Cid Corman,* Elizabeth Press, 1966. Sharon Dilworth, "The Cousin in the Backyard." Reprinted by permission of the author. Mary Gaitskill, "Terra Form" appeared in slightly different form as "A Bestial Noise" in *Tin House* 7, 2001. Alyson Hagy, "Sharking" from *Graveyard of the Atlantic,* Graywolf Press, 2000. Kathleen Halme, "Diorama Notebook" from *Every Substance Clothed,* University of Georgia Press, 1995. Robert Hayden, "The Rabbi," "The Year of the Child (*for my Grandson*)," and "Aunt Jemima of the Ocean Waves" from *Collected Poems of Robert Hayden,* edited by Frederick Glayser. © 1985 by Emma Hayden. Used by permission of Liveright Publishing Corporation. Garrett Hongo, "On the Origin of Blind-Boy Lilikoi" from *Georgia Review,* summer 2004. Patricia Hooper, "In the Backyard" from *At the Corner of My Eye,* Michigan State University Press, 1987. Patricia Hooper, "Narcissus" from *Aristotle's Garden,* Blustem Press, 2004. Tung-Hui Hu, "Balance" from *Ontario Review* 58. Tung-Hui Hu, "A rock a fish" from *The Book of Motion,* University of Georgia Press, 2003. James Hynes, "Nelson in Nighttown." Reprinted by permission of the author. Lawrence Joseph, "Unyieldingly Present" from *Into It,* Farrar, Straus and Giroux, 2005. Laura Kasischke, "Black Dress" from *Gardening in the Dark,* Ausable Press, 2004. Laura Kasischke, "Clown" from the *Kenyon Review,* Spring 2000. X. J. Kennedy, "To Dorothy on Her Exclusion from the *Guinness Book of World Records*" and "Old Men Pitching Horseshoes" from *Cross Ties: Selected Poems,* University of Georgia Press, 1985. Reprinted by permission of the author. X. J. Kennedy, "At Paestum" from *Poetry,* August 2002. Reprinted by permission of the author. Jane Kenyon, "The Needle," "Happiness," and "Three Small Oranges" from *Otherwise: New and Selected Poems.* © 1996 by the Estate of Jane Kenyon. Reprinted by permission of Graywolf Press, Saint Paul, Minnesota. Rattawut Lapcharoensap, "Priscilla the Cambodian" from *Sightseeing,* Grove Press, 2005. Laurence Lieberman, "Carib's Leap" from *Dark Songs: Slave House and Synagogue.* Reprinted by permission of the University of Arkansas Press and Peepal Tree Press, Leeds, England, 2005. © 1996 by Laurence Lieberman. William Lychack, "The Old Woman and Her Thief" from *Ploughshares,* Spring 1998. Sarah Messer, "Starting with That Time" from *Bandit Letters,* New Issues Press, 2001. Howard Moss,

"Horror Movie" from *A Swimmer in the Air,* Scribner's, 1957. Marge Piercy, "Photograph of my mother sitting on the steps" and "Colors passing through us" from *Colors Passing Through Us,* Alfred A. Knopf, 2003. Frank O'Hara, "Animals," "A Byzantine Place," and "Poem" from *A Byzantine Place: 50 Poems and a Noh Play,* Collection of the Hopwood Room, University of Michigan, 1951. Matthew Rohrer, "The Evening Concert" from *A Hummock in the Malookas,* W. W. Norton, 1995. Matthew Rohrer, "My Government" from *Satellite,* Verve Press, 2001. Davy Rothbart, "Lie Big" from *The Lone Surfer of Montana, Kansas,* 21 Balloons Productions, 2002. Anne Stevenson, "Arioso Dolente" and "John Keats, 1821–1950" from *Granny Scarecrow,* Bloodaxe Books, 2000. Harvey Swados, "Where Does Your Music Come From?" from *Nights in the Garden of Brooklyn: The Collected Stories of Harvey Swados,* Viking Press, 1986. Larissa Szporluk, "Givers and Takers" from *Isolato,* University of Iowa Press, 2000. Melanie Rae Thon, "Punishment" from *Girls in the Grass,* Random House, 1992. Henry Van Dyke, "Summer Masquerades" from the *Antioch Review* 60, no. 4, Fall 2002. Ronald Wallace, "Redundancies" and "SmackDown!" from *Long for This World: New and Selected Poems.* © 2003 by Ronald Wallace. Reprinted by permission of the University of Pittsburgh Press. Keith Waldrop, "Transparent Like the Air" from *The House Seen from Nowhere,* Litmus Press, 2002. Rosmarie Waldrop, "Leonardo as Anatomist, Repeatedly" from *Blindsight,* New Directions, 2003. Nancy Willard, "The Ladybugs" and "Swimming Lessons" from *Swimming Lessons: New and Selected Poems,* Alfred A. Knopf, 1996.

Text design by Mary H. Sexton
Typesetting by Huron Valley Graphics, Ann Arbor, Michigan
Text font: Minion
Display font: Scala Sans

Designed by Robert Slimbach, the first version of Minion was
released in 1990. Inspired by classical, old style typefaces of the late
Renaissance, it is a versatile, highly readable typeface.
—Courtesy www.adobe.com

Scala Sans was designed by Martin Majoor in 1990 and published
by www.FontFont.com.
—Courtesy www.identifont.com